Billionaires and Stealth Politics

Billionaires and Stealth Politics

BENJAMIN I. PAGE
JASON SEAWRIGHT
MATTHEW J. LACOMBE

THE UNIVERSITY OF CHICAGO PRESS   CHICAGO AND LONDON

The University of Chicago Press, Chicago 60637
The University of Chicago Press, Ltd., London
© 2019 by The University of Chicago
All rights reserved. No part of this book may be used or reproduced in any manner
whatsoever without written permission, except in the case of brief quotations in critical
articles and reviews. For more information, contact the University of Chicago Press,
1427 E. 60th St., Chicago, IL 60637.
Published 2019
Printed in the United States of America

28 27 26 25 24 23 22 21 20 19   1 2 3 4 5

ISBN-13: 978-0-226-58609-0 (cloth)
ISBN-13: 978-0-226-58612-0 (paper)
ISBN-13: 978-0-226-58626-7 (e-book)
DOI: https://doi.org/10.7208/chicago/9780226586267.001.0001

Library of Congress Cataloging-in-Publication Data

Names: Page, Benjamin I., author. | Seawright, Jason, author. | Lacombe, Matthew J., author.
Title: Billionaires and stealth politics / Benjamin I. Page, Jason Seawright,
    Matthew J. Lacombe.
Description: Chicago ; London : The University of Chicago Press, 2019. |
    Includes bibliographical references and index.
Identifiers: LCCN 2018031838 | ISBN 9780226586090 (cloth : alk. paper) |
    ISBN 9780226586120 (pbk. : alk. paper) | ISBN 9780226586267 (e-book)
Subjects: LCSH: Billionaires—Political activity—United States. |
    Rich People—Political activity—United States. | Wealth—Political aspects. |
    United States—Politics and government—21st century.
Classification: LCC HC79.W4 .P34 2018 | DDC 320.973086/21—dc23
LC record available at https://lccn.loc.gov/2018031838

♾ This paper meets the requirements of ANSI/NISO Z39.48–1992 (Permanence of Paper).

Contents

Figure and Tables

Preface

This book grew out of a collaborative study of multimillionaires: the Survey of Economically Successful Americans and the Common Good, or SESA. A survey of the top one to two percent of wealth holders in the Chicago area, conducted by NORC at the University of Chicago, SESA was the first study of the political attitudes and actions of a representative sample of wealthy Americans. The findings—some of them noted in this book—seemed interesting. We hoped to build on them by conducting a definitive survey of a representative sample of multimillionaires across the United States as a whole.

For a good part of two years, we tried to assemble a consortium of foundations or wealthy individuals who would provide the millions of dollars required to select, contact, and conduct personal interviews with a truly representative, nationwide sample of multimillionaires. No luck. Meanwhile, however, one of us (Jason Seawright) was germinating a quite different idea. Why settle for multimillionaires, those notorious (perhaps unfairly notorious) "one-percenters," whose wealth was paltry compared to that of the very wealthiest Americans? Why not go for the wealthiest of all: billionaires? Billionaires would be impossible to interview, but perhaps publicly available information about them—if comprehensively gathered and carefully analyzed—could tell us a lot.

Accordingly, Seawright devised the systematic "web-scraping" technique for studying billionaires that is described in chapter 2 below. Benjamin Page signed on. Matthew Lacombe—then a graduate student at Northwestern University—was persuaded to combine his dissertation research on the NRA and gun control with major attention to the politics of billionaires. We obtained some generous—and, as it turned out, very patient—financial support. We hired a number of research assistants. We were off and running, though our initial sprint evolved into a marathon; the work ended up taking several years to complete.

For getting us started, we are particularly grateful to our collaborators on SESA, including Christopher Jencks, Larry Bartels, and Fay Lomax Cook, and to Eric Wanner and the Russell Sage Foundation, who funded SESA. For helping us try for a national survey of multimillionaires, and for then funding the billionaires project itself, we are very grateful to the John D. and Catherine T. MacArthur Foundation, especially Robert Gallucci, Julia Stasch, and Valerie Chang. They stuck with us for more years than anyone could reasonably expect. We also thank the Gordon Scott Fulcher research fund at Northwestern University and Northwestern's Department of Political Science, which has provided a stimulating and supportive environment for conducting multimethods research.

We benefited from careful and diligent work by several talented research assistants, including graduate students Jacob Rothschild and Laura Garcia and undergraduates Pauline Esman, Alexander Froy, Hane Kim, and Kenneth Hill.

We are grateful to Tom Ferguson and Paul Jorgensen, who generously shared their data on political contributions, and to a number of colleagues who have commented on various drafts of one or more sections of the book. They include Ed Gibson and Dan Galvin (particularly on the "boundary-control" strategy) and panelists and audience members at venues where we presented parts of our work: the Midwest Political Science Association (twice), the American Political Science Association, the University of Illinois at Chicago, Beijing Foreign Studies University, Cornell University, and the University of California at Santa Barbara.

We owe a great deal to Chuck Myers, our insightful and hard-working editor, and to four anonymous reviewers who pushed us hard and led us to make significant improvements in the book.

Most of all, we are grateful to our families and friends, who provided emotional support, put up with the travails of the writing process, and gave us some good ideas about billionaires too.

Introduction

In 2016, when millions of Americans voted for billionaire Donald J. Trump to be president of the United States, many of them hoped that Trump's personal wealth would free him from depending on wealthy donors and allow him to "drain the swamp" in Washington, DC. But then Trump appointed several billionaires and multimillionaires—including Betsy DeVos, Wilbur Ross, Linda McMahon, Steven Mnuchin, and Gary Cohn—to high government positions. And he pursued a number of policies that were perceived as billionaire-friendly: relaxing environmental and workplace regulations on businesses; proposing to cut corporate and high-end income taxes and to abolish the estate tax; and trying to reduce federal spending on health care and other social safety net programs.[1]

What was going on? Has the United States entered a new Gilded Age like that of the late nineteenth century, in which politicians of all sorts catered to the plutocrats of the time?

For several decades, the incomes and wealth of most working-class and middle-class Americans have stagnated, but the fortunes of those at the top have soared. The gap between the wealthiest and everyone else has become a chasm.[2] The few who hold one billion dollars or more in net worth have begun to play a more and more active part in politics, perhaps creating serious imbalances for democracy—imbalances that this book explores.

One billion dollars—$1,000,000,000, one thousand million dollars—is a lot of money. As of October 2017, according to *Forbes* magazine, 569 Americans enjoyed fortunes of $1 billion or more—in some cases, a great deal more. In autumn 2017, the ten wealthiest had a net worth of $89 billion, $81.5 billion, $78 billion, $71 billion, $59 billion, $48.5 billion, $48.5 billion, $46.8 billion, $44.6 billion, and $43.4 billion, respectively. The next ten did not lag far behind: number 20 was George Soros, with $23 billion.[3] Late in 2017 the grand total of wealth held by all 569 American billionaires taken together was $2.7 *trillion* ($2,700,000,000,000)—an astounding sum that exceeded the entire annual gross domestic product (GDP) of Italy (~$1.8 trillion) or France (~$2.5 trillion). In fact, the total wealth of US billionaires exceeded the total GDP of dozens of fairly populous countries added together.[4]

A bare *one* billion dollars is no longer enough to make the *Forbes* list of 400 wealthiest Americans, which closed out in 2017 at $2 billion. That left some 169 US billionaires off the prestigious *Forbes* roster.

To a billionaire, a mere *million* dollars here or there is basically pocket change. Billionaires have plenty of disposable wealth to spend on politics, if and when they choose to do so. Many do. Quite a few US billionaires regularly contribute hundreds of thousands—or millions—of dollars to political parties and candidates (most of the money goes to Republicans, but plenty of Democrats get it too).[5] Many also give to policy-oriented organizations and causes.

In the 2014 congressional elections, billionaires David and Charles Koch assembled nearly $300 million to help elect conservative Republicans. The Koch brothers laid plans (never fully carried out) to spend $889 million in 2016.[6] In that year Donald Trump got substantial financial help from billionaires Sheldon Adelson and Robert Mercer, among others. According to the Center for Responsive Politics, the top thirty US billionaires alone made over $180 million of reportable contributions in 2016.[7] This figure actually understates their total influence—perhaps understates it a great deal—by excluding secret "dark-money" contributions.

The vast sums invested by billionaires and multimillionaires in recent years have made up a big part of total political contributions in the United States, with money from the top 0.01 percent (1/10,000) of Americans making up an extraordinary 40 percent of total federal contributions as of 2012—again excluding dark money.[8]

Not only Donald Trump, but most other US billionaires, too, tend to favor wealthy-friendly public policies that diverge sharply from what majorities of Americans want. Many billionaires—including some who contribute to Democratic candidates—seek tax cuts for businesses and wealthy individuals. (A favorite aim is to abolish the estate tax.) Many billionaires favor completely free trade and investment across international borders, without providing much help to ordinary Americans whose wages are pressured downward by trade. Many billionaires want less government regulation of the economy. Many seek cuts in spending on social welfare programs like Social Security that are crucial to millions of middle-class and lower-income Americans.[9] Each of these policy ideas is far less popular among Americans with lower levels of wealth.

Recent research has shown that affluent Americans have a lot more influence on the making of public policy than average Americans do.[10] But the "affluent" people who have been studied constitute a large and diverse group; they include many members of the upper middle class, not just the exceptionally wealthy. We do not really know exactly *which* of the affluent have how much influence. If money tends to produce political influence, however, it makes sense that more money probably produces more influence: that multimillionaires have more political clout than merely affluent members of the upper middle class. And it makes sense that billionaires— who have about *one hundred times* as much wealth as the least wealthy members of the perhaps unfairly notorious "one percent"—can probably exert the most political clout of all.[11]

There has been at least one survey into the political attitudes and activities of a representative sample of multimillionaires.[12] But until now there has been very little systematic research into the politics of billionaires.

Darrell West has provided a thoughtful essay about US billionaires, putting them into a worldwide comparative context.[13] A few biographies of individual billionaires and their families include interesting political material. Jane Mayer has done important investigative reporting on several of the most politically active billionaires[14] of recent decades—Richard Mellon Scaife, John M. Olin, Lynde and Harry Bradley, and especially Charles and David Koch.[15] Theda Skocpol and her research group have examined the politics of the Koch brothers and their extensive network of wealthy conservative donors.[16] And Nancy MacLean has done remarkable archival research on the Koch-funded libertarian intellectual network centered at George Mason University.[17] But scholars have not been able to learn much about the politics of today's US billionaires *as a group*— the hundreds of very quiet billionaires, as well as the handful of noisy or visible ones.

The reason is simple: billionaires are hard to study. Most of them are very busy. They carefully protect their privacy. Most have no desire at all to reveal their private lives or their political views to outsiders. Most billionaires employ professional gatekeepers, whose jobs include fending off outsiders like journalists, social scientists, survey interviewers, and other snoops. Some wealthy people's gatekeepers themselves have gatekeepers.[18] To sit down and chat for an hour with even a single billionaire is a distant dream for most researchers. To systematically survey the political attitudes and behavior of a representative sample of billionaires would be utterly impossible.[19]

The best that can be done to get at the politics of most contemporary billionaires, then, is to gather and analyze *publicly available* information about them, including whatever letters and documents exist; official records of financial contributions to political candidates and causes; and reports of the billionaires' words and actions in print or electronic media.

In this book we examine the politics of the one hundred wealthiest US billionaires—the top tier of the *Forbes* 400-wealthiest list. We take what can be called a "web-scraping and public records" approach to studying these billionaires, analyzing two different types of publicly available data: Federal Election Commission (FEC) and state-level records of billionaires' financial contributions to political candidates and causes, and reports of billionaires' political words and actions that are available in electronic form on the World Wide Web.

Much can be learned from this material. A warning, however: none of the available evidence is sufficient for us—or for anyone else—to pin down the precise policy preferences, or all the political actions, of all billionaires.

Some scholars—notably including Adam Bonica, who has offered important insights into campaign contributors—have tried to use FEC contribution data to infer wealthy Americans' policy preferences.[20] Bonica's approach is to judge a contributor's policy preferences by the ideologies (as revealed in voting records) of the members of Congress that he or she contributes to. But this approach assumes that political contributions are purely ideologically oriented acts that reveal the contributor's personal policy preferences, as opposed to strategic acts that may have quite different motivations—such as gaining access to powerful incumbent officials whose ideologies may not resemble the donor's at all.

Bonica addresses the potential for strategic giving and presents some evidence that it does not create significant bias within his model on an aggregate level. However, billionaires—who have nearly limitless resources to contribute to candidates—may be unusually likely to engage in strategic contributing. The owners of firms based in a particular state, for example—or the owners of firms regulated by a Senate committee headed by a particular senator—may have good reasons to contribute to those key senators, regardless of whether the firm's owners like or loathe the senators' policy stands.

Efforts to estimate billionaires' policy preferences from their contributions, therefore, may make the billionaires look more "centrist" than they actually are, by averaging in billionaires' strategic contributions to politicians with whom they disagree along with heartfelt contributions to those with whom they agree.

Another problem is that the best current version of the contributions approach to inferring policy preferences (Bonica's) has imposed a one-dimensional, "liberal/conservative" issue space on donors' preferences. Except for party leaders and public officials,[21] however, Americans do not necessarily have preferences on both economic and social issues that fit neatly onto a single liberal/conservative dimension. Many people are liberal on one set of issues but conservative on another. Many billionaires, for example, are "libertarians": liberal on social matters but conservative on economics. To try to squeeze libertarians—including extreme libertarians—onto a single liberal/conservative dimension tends to make them look center-right on everything, rather than fairly liberal on social issues and extremely conservative on economics. Indeed, we will see that many libertarian billionaires contribute money to Republican candidates with whom they disagree markedly on social issues.

Political contributions by billionaires that are reported to the FEC or to state-level agencies are very important. They undoubtedly affect the outcomes of elections in ways that have real consequences for public policy and for people's lives. And they do provide some general indications about what the billionaires want from government (especially, we believe, on economics-related policies). We will certainly discuss them. But they are not sufficient for judging billionaires' *policy preferences,* which must be assessed in other ways. In fact, *officially reported* contributions cannot even give a full picture of billionaires' *political actions,* many of which are not reported to any official agency.

Reports to the FEC and other official agencies cover most contributions made directly to political candidates, to candidates' committees, or to the political parties. But there is no requirement to report contributions—including some extremely large ones—to certain kinds of "outside" or "independent" political groups and causes. (We have found that contributions to outside groups with policy-specific aims often constitute the best single indicator of billionaires' specific policy preferences.)[22] Contributions of dark money to influence elections go unreported. So do many other political activities, including holding fund-raisers, "bundling" others' contributions, and funding think tanks or unregistered lobbyists to influence policy making and the climate of opinion. To get at such actions requires something more than a purely "public records" approach.

We have been able to come up with some new information about billionaires' policy preferences by examining the billionaires' own media-reported *words*—what they have said about specific matters of public policy. And we have devised a new way to uncover many political *actions* by billionaires that go beyond the official data.

We have done this by means of a distinctive new research method: the systematic use of web-scraping techniques to identify virtually *all* publicly available words and actions—concerning certain specific issues of public policy—by the one hundred wealthiest billionaires, over a ten-year period. (Our techniques are described further in chapter 2.) We have sought to uncover what—if anything—the wealthiest billionaires have said in public about key political issues. We have also explored what sorts of candidates and causes they have given money to, and what else they have done politically—held fund-raisers; bundled contributions by others; given money to think tanks; formed, led, joined policy-focused organizations; or anything else.

The resulting new information has allowed us to investigate whether different sorts of words are spoken, or different kinds of actions are taken, by different types of billionaires—those who enjoy greater or lesser levels of wealth; inheritors versus entrepreneurs; billionaires whose businesses rely on direct interaction with consumers, versus those whose do not; or those whose fortunes were made in different industrial sectors, such as financial, high-tech, manufacturing, resource extraction, or retail.

More importantly, this new information has helped us achieve our ultimate aim: to assess how the wealthiest US billionaires fit into democratic politics. We want to know how politically active the billionaires are, in what ways; what political strategies they pursue; and whether they take advantage of their prominence to speak about politics, or whether they limit themselves to financial contributions or other lower-visibility actions. We want to know what kinds of public policies the billionaires seek, and how similar to or different those policies are from what majorities of Americans want.

We are especially concerned about billionaires' *political accountability.* When billionaires take political actions, how accountable or unaccountable are they to the citizenry as a whole? How easy or hard is it for others to tell what the billionaires are up to? Do billionaires take care to explain *why* they favor the particular public policies that they do? Do they try to persuade their fellow citizens to agree? Or do billionaires tend to skip the explanations and just act? Do some go so far as to try to *conceal* their actions, so that it is particularly hard for others to hold them accountable?

We will see that on several of the most important issues of the day—including taxation, Social Security, and immigration—many billionaires have tended to engage in what we call *stealth politics*. They try hard to influence public policy. They make large financial contributions to political parties, candidates, and policy-focused causes. They hold political fundraisers and bundle others' contributions. They establish, join, or lead policy-advocacy organizations. But despite these billionaires' prominence and their easy access to the media—which provides abundant opportunities to say just about anything they want to large audiences—they rarely talk openly about public policy.

Our exhaustive web searches indicate that most billionaires *have not spoken up publicly at all*—not even once, over an extended period of time—about the specifics of any of the major public policies we have studied. Our statistical analyses provide evidence that this silence is often designed to conceal billionaires' advocacy of policies that most Americans oppose. The unpopular policies that some billionaires quietly favor have frequently become official government policies with the force of law.

We see the strategy of stealth politics—along with the outsized, unequal political clout that billionaires likely wield—as presenting serious problems for democracy in the United States. Unequal influence itself undermines political equality, which may be considered central to the concept of democracy. But our main point in this book is a different one: that with stealth politics, billionaires' influence is often not only unequal but also largely *unaccountable* to and *unchallengeable* by the American citizenry. Stealth politics makes it hard for ordinary citizens to know what billionaires are doing or to mobilize against it.

Stealth politics is particularly likely to confuse ordinary Americans about the nature of billionaires' political actions because most of the handful of billionaires who *do* frequently speak out about public policy—billionaires with familiar names like Bloomberg, Buffett, Gates, or Soros, even (as presidential candidate) Donald Trump—have tended to voice more moderate (in a few cases even liberal) economic views than most of their fellow billionaires: views that are much closer to the opinions of average Americans.

If ordinary citizens try to judge the political leanings of US billionaires through media reports about Bloomberg, Buffett, and Gates, they are likely to get a very mistaken impression. They are likely to underestimate the extent to which billionaires' political activity may threaten the citizens' own values and interests. They may see the (now) highly visible actions of conservatives like the Koch brothers[23] as counterbalanced by the equally visible speech of liberal and moderate billionaires, without realizing that in the domain of financial contributions and quiet political actions there is no such balance.

Plan of the Book

Chapter 1 introduces our cast of characters: the one hundred wealthiest US billionaires, those who occupy the upper reaches of the *Forbes* 400 list of wealthiest Americans. We note the names, fortunes, and backgrounds of some billionaires near the very top of the list. We inquire where their money came from: inheritance? entrepreneurship? What sorts of businesses? We briefly explore issues of "fair compensation" involving merit and effort, help from others, and just plain luck. And we consider some political implications of vast concentrations of wealth.

Chapter 2 outlines the political actions that these billionaires have taken, especially their financial contributions. It describes our web-scraping research techniques. It then analyzes what the billionaires have done or said, over a ten-year period, about many specific policies related to taxes or Social Security. We report substantial evidence of stealth politics: a number of billionaires took powerful political action on behalf of policies opposed by most Americans, but were mostly or entirely silent in public about their stands.

Chapter 3 explores in more depth the tax-related and Social Security–related words and actions of four particular billionaires: Warren Buffett, John Menard Jr., Carl Icahn, and David Koch. These four were carefully selected to provide methodological leverage on issues of causal inference, causal mechanisms, and possible measurement errors, so that a closer look at them provides further confirmation of our stealth politics theory. But the cases are also of interest in themselves. They happen to represent nearly the full range of political philosophies that are embraced by US billionaires. Buffett occupies a center-left position on the liberal/conservative continuum, not far from the views of average Americans. Menard is a hard-line economic conservative; Koch a libertarian; and Icahn a sort of populist who served as an adviser to Donald Trump. Missing—not by accident—is any billionaire who can be called a thoroughgoing liberal on both social and economic issues. In the United States, economically liberal billionaires are very rare birds.

Chapter 4 applies the same web-scraping and public records techniques to billionaires' statements and actions concerning certain social, cultural, or moral issues. We find little evidence of stealth politics on the issues of abortion or same-sex marriage, where billionaires' policy preferences tend to be less divergent from those of the general public than they are on taxes or Social Security. When it comes to immigration policy, however— where some billionaires' taste for cheap imported labor clashes with many Americans' cultural or economic anxieties about foreign immigrants— stealth politics reappears. Many billionaires actively work in favor of high levels of immigration, especially for high-skill workers. But few say much about that in public.

Chapter 5 turns from national politics to the state and local level, where certain billionaires have made major financial investments in politics. It explores the "boundary-control" strategy, in which some billionaires work to restrict government spending and government regulation at the national level, while lobbying successfully at the state or local level to win lucrative government subsidies, tax breaks, and favorable regulatory treatment.

Chapter 6 relates our findings to general ideas about democracy. It mentions the damage to political equality that may result if the wealthiest Americans wield much more political influence than other citizens can muster. But it focuses on the special problems posed by stealth politics, which helps billionaires avoid being held accountable by their fellow citizens. The book closes by suggesting some possible remedies that citizens might want to pursue if they wish to make wealthy Americans more politically accountable. It also notes the broader types of reforms that would be needed if one wished to increase political equality and reinvigorate majoritarian democracy in America.

CHAPTER ONE

Who the Billionaires Are

We began our study of the one hundred wealthiest US billionaires in 2013. In that year, the total net worth of the *Forbes* 400 wealthiest Americans was $2.2 *trillion*—$2,200,000,000,000. As *Forbes* noted at the time, this was equal to the annual output of the entire economy of Russia.[1]

Topping the *Forbes* list was Bill Gates, with a net worth of $72 billion. Gates made his fortune by building the Microsoft software firm—which he founded in 1975, together with Paul Allen—and then diversifying his investments into such firms as tractor maker Deere & Co., Canadian National Railway, and Mexican Coke bottler Femsa. (By 2013, Microsoft stock represented less than one-fifth of Gates's fortune.) Despite giving away a lot of money to philanthropy—chiefly through the Bill & Melinda Gates Foundation—Gates had occupied the top perch among the wealthiest Americans continuously since 1994. In fact, Gates had led the list of wealthiest Americans during more than half of the thirty years that *Forbes* had been keeping track.[2]

Second on the 400-wealthiest list in 2013 came Gates's friend Warren Buffett, with $58.5 billion in net worth. The modest-living "sage of Omaha"—like Gates, a major philanthropist—acquired his fortune mainly by means of shrewd, highly diverse investments through holding company Berkshire Hathaway, which in 2013 had just acquired ketchup maker H. J. Heinz for $23.2 billion and Nevada's NV Energy firm for $5.6 billion in cash.[3]

In third place was Larry Ellison ($41 billion), founder of high-tech firm Oracle, which offers businesses and organizations a wide variety of hardware and software products, perhaps most notably for database management. Ellison built the company from an early relational database that he developed for the CIA. Although he had worked as an employee of Ampex Corporation while carrying out that project, he subsequently purchased the rights to it and became an entrepreneur.[4] Having started in 1977 with assets limited to $2,000 and database source code, Oracle is now the second-largest software company in the world in terms of revenue and is a foundational brand for internet and internal business operations worldwide.[5]

Ellison, an acerbic critic of Apple and Google, has lived more opulently than Gates or Buffett. In 2013 he owned several houses on Malibu's Carbon Beach, plus 98 percent of Hawaii's Lanai island, and had competed in the America's Cup sailing competition.[6] Ellison made headlines in 2008 when he challenged San Mateo County's tax assessment on his Woodside, California, estate—a replica of a sixteenth-century Japanese palace that cost Ellison $200 million to build. Despite that price tag, Ellison successfully contended that the property was worth only $64 million—$99 million less than the county's $163 million appraisal—due to the small market for sixteenth-century Japanese architecture and a lack of luxury amenities in the home. The break on property taxes Ellison received as a result of the adjusted appraisal cost local public schools alone an estimated $1.4 million.[7]

The brothers Charles and David Koch—highly active in libertarian and conservative Republican politics—came next on the 400-wealthiest list, with a net worth of $36 billion each. Their fortunes—which had enjoyed a big head start, thanks to their father, Fred Koch—were derived from the oil, natural gas, and chemical firm Koch Industries, which they rapidly expanded by reinvesting 90 percent of earnings and acquiring all or part of such diverse firms as electronics-component maker Molex, cellulose fiber producer Buckeye Technologies, and glassmaker Guardian Industries.[8]

Ranking sixth, seventh, eighth, and ninth on the 2013 *Forbes* 400-wealthiest list were four members of the Walton family—Christy, Jim, Alice, and S. Robson—with $33.3 to $35.4 billion each. Most of their money had been inherited from the Walmart fortune built by their father Sam Walton and their uncle James. Walmart, which started out in Bentonville, Arkansas, in 1962, grew into a huge retailing empire that (as of 2013) employed 2.2 million people in 11,000 stores worldwide.[9]

Tenth on the 400-wealthiest list in 2013 was Michael Bloomberg, whose fortune consisted mainly of his 88-percent ownership of the financial services firm Bloomberg LP, which he founded in 1982. By 2012, Bloomberg LP was producing annual revenue of $7.9 billion. Bloomberg—like the Koch brothers—has been very active politically; he served for twelve years as mayor of New York. In contrast to the Kochs, however, Bloomberg's policy views have been centrist to liberal, including strong advocacy of gun control.[10]

The next ten wealthiest Americans in 2013 included Sheldon Adelson, with $28.5 billion from resorts and casinos in Nevada, Macau, and Singapore—another very conservative political activist and donor—and Jeff Bezos ($27.2 billion), the founder and CEO of Amazon.com, who later (in 2017) added Whole Foods Markets to his portfolio. Then came Larry Page ($24.9 billion), cofounder and CEO of Google, an enthusiast of clean energy; Sergey Brin ($24.4 billion), cofounder of Google; and Forrest Jr., Jacqueline, and John Mars ($20.5 billion each), third-generation heirs to Mars, the world's largest candy maker—which then had some $33 billion in annual sales of such brands as 3 Musketeers, Juicy Fruit and Wrigley's gum, Twix, Skittles, Milky Way, Snickers, and M&M's. Next on the list were Carl Icahn ($20.3 billion), an activist investor and takeover artist; and George Soros ($20 billion from investments and currency speculation through his hedge fund firm), a major philanthropist in human rights, democratization, and education around the world, especially in his native Hungary—and one of the most politically active billionaires, donating to Democratic candidates. Number twenty on the list was Mark Zuckerberg ($19 billion), the then-twenty-nine-year-old founder of Facebook, whose stock had doubled in value in the past year. Zuckerberg was active in lobbying for immigration reform and technology education.[11]

The top wealth holders on the 2013 *Forbes* list continued with twenty billionaires who held between $10 billion and $18 billion each. In descending order: Steve Ballmer (Microsoft), Len Blavatnik (diverse investments in Russia and elsewhere), Abigail Johnson (third-generation executive at Fidelity Investments, the second-largest US mutual fund firm), Phil Knight (Nike athletic apparel and shoes), Michael Dell (Dell computers), Paul Allen (Microsoft and investments), Donald Bren (Irvine Co. real estate), Ronald Perelman (private equity investing), Anne Cox Chambers (inheritor of media conglomerate Cox Enterprises), Rupert Murdoch (21st Century Fox and News Corp media), Ray Dalio (Bridgewater Associates, the world's biggest hedge fund firm), Charles Ergen (Dish Network and EchoStar), Harold Hamm (Continental Oil), James Simons (Renaissance Technologies hedge fund, a wizard at mathematical models for trading), Laurene Powell Jobs and family (inheritors of stakes in Apple and Disney), John Paulson (Paulson & Co. hedge fund), Jack Taylor and family (Enterprise, Alamo, and National rental cars), Philip Anschutz (investments in oil, railroads, telecom, and sports), Richard Kinder (Kinder Morgan Energy Partners), George Kaiser (oil, banking), and Harold Simmons (buyout investor).[12]

The remaining sixty of our top one hundred billionaires from the 2013 *Forbes* list ran from Andrew Beal ($9.8 billion, banks and real estate) down to three brothers tied at #98: Daniel, Dirk, and Robert Ziff, each with $4.6 billion derived from their father's Ziff-Davis magazine empire plus subsequent investments.[13]

Conspicuously absent from our set of the one hundred wealthiest billionaires is Donald Trump, whose fortune in 2013 was estimated by *Forbes* at $3.5 billion. That fell below the cutoff for the top one hundred: only enough for Trump to make #134 on the list.[14] As a result, Trump has not been included in our systematic web scraping or statistical analyses. But we will have a word or two to say—here and in later chapters—about the United States' first billionaire president.

During the 2016 presidential election campaign, Trump claimed to have a net worth of $10 billion. Trump has notoriously offered highly divergent estimates of his net worth, however. During the mid-2000s, he mentioned figures that ranged from $1.7 billion to $9.5 billion. In a deposition for a lawsuit in which the billionaire alleged that a journalist had slandered him by publishing a low estimate of his net worth, Trump explained the variation: "My net worth fluctuates, and it goes up and down with markets and with attitudes and with feelings, even my own feelings. . . . Yes, even my own feelings, as to where the world is, where the world is going, and that can change rapidly from day to day. Then you have a September 11th, and you don't feel so good about yourself and you don't feel so good about the world and you don't feel so good about New York City. Then you have a year later, and the city is as hot as a pistol. Even months after that it was a different feeling. So yeah, even my own feelings affect my value to myself."[15] Still, even late in 2017, four years after Trump failed to make our top-100 cut, *Forbes* magazine—perhaps not privy to Trump's mood changes—estimated the value of his fortune to be just $3.1 billion, lower than it had been in 2013. That caused him to drop to #248 on the 2017 list.[16]

A complete list of our one hundred wealthiest billionaires—ranked in descending order of net worth as of 2013, and (for comparison purposes) including figures on their net worth in 2016 as well—is given in appendix 1. In 2016, most of the dollar figures were bigger—some much bigger—than three years before. Some reshuffling among the rankings is also evident. Most dramatic was the rapid rise of several computer- and internet-related fortunes. Amazon's Jeff Bezos leapt from #12 on the list (with $27.2 billion) in 2013 to #2 on the list (with $67 billion) in 2016. Facebook's Mark Zuckerberg jumped from #20 ($19 billion) in 2013 to #4 ($55.5 billion) in 2016. Google's founders also rose significantly: Larry Page from #13 to #9, and Sergey Brin from #14 to #10. (But Oracle's Larry Ellison slipped from #3 in 2013 to #5 in 2016.)[17] And, of course, a few of 2013's wealthiest billionaires dropped out of the top one hundred group or dropped off the *Forbes* 400 list altogether.[18] But most of the names stayed the same in both years, with all but nine of 2013's top one hundred remaining among the 400 wealthiest Americans three years later.

Rich, Old, White, Anglo Men

US billionaires as a group are much older (mostly in their sixties and seventies), much more often male, and much more frequently white and of Anglo-Saxon or other Western European origin than the very diverse American population as a whole. The average age of the one hundred wealthiest billionaires who were studied for this book is seventy years old, with sixty-nine individuals aged sixty-five or older. Of the one hundred, ninety-eight (a whopping 98 percent) are white, eighty-six are men, and eighty-five are white men.[19] Compare this to the general US population, which is approximately 77 percent white, half female, and only about 15 percent sixty-five years of age or older.[20] And of course, unlike the vast majority of Americans, all billionaires are—by almost anyone's definition—rich.

This need not mean that billionaires are generally prejudiced against— or insensitive to—women, minorities, the young, or the poor (although the possibility of such prejudices cannot be ruled out). But the billionaires' life experiences and their values and beliefs are often quite different from those of less-affluent Americans, most of whom are female, comparatively young, and/or members of minority groups. It may well be difficult for billionaires to understand or empathize with exactly what their fellow Americans are thinking, feeling, or needing—for example, what they want the government to do.

The largest and most self-evident gaps between billionaires and their fellow citizens involve money itself and related aspects of social and economic *class*. For most of their lives, most very wealthy Americans (even some we think of as having worked their way up from the bottom) have

enjoyed good nutrition, comfortable housing, nurturing parents, stimulating and helpful friends, and safe, pleasant neighborhoods to live in.
Their work has mostly focused on building up a business and accumulating capital, and their periods of economic hardship have mostly involved
entrepreneurial risk taking rather than a continuing day-to-day struggle
to pay rent and put food on the table. Once people attain great wealth,
their lives tend to be spent in well-protected bubbles—dwelling in expensive, well-guarded apartments or gated communities; working in comfortable top-floor offices; interacting chiefly with fellow elites rather than with
working-class or middle-class Americans.[21]

As a result, billionaires can easily lose touch with what most Americans are doing and thinking. Moreover, most billionaires have unique economic interests—in advancing their own particular businesses and in protecting wealth itself—that can conflict with the interests of most of their
fellow Americans.

If billionaires wield outsized political power, therefore, there is a dan-
ger that they may exercise that power in ways that (deliberately or not)
harm rather than help their fellow citizens. Billionaires' political actions
may fail to further the public good. They may become a serious threat to
democracy.

Age

It takes time to build a great fortune. Even just waiting to receive an inheritance can take up many years of a person's life. (Ask Prince Charles
of England.) Those who eventually become billionaires—who generally
enjoy supportive environments and top-notch medical care—tend to live
longer than most people do, so they usually stay on the most-wealthy lists
for quite a while. (David Rockefeller Sr. died at 101 years old in 2017.) For
all these reasons, billionaires tend to be much older than the rest of us.

Most billionaires are in their sixties or seventies, with quite a few in the
eighties or nineties. This is particularly true among the very wealthiest.
Among the top one hundred wealthiest Americans we identified in 2013,
for example, Bill Gates was a relatively youthful fifty-seven years old, but
Warren Buffett was eighty-three; Larry Ellison was sixty-nine; Charles
Koch seventy-seven; David Koch seventy-three; the four Waltons fifty-
eight, sixty-three, sixty-five, and sixty-nine; Michael Bloomberg seventy-
one; and Sheldon Adelson eighty. You had to reach down to #12, #13, and
#14 on the list to encounter Jeff Bezos (forty-nine years old), Larry Page

(forty) and Sergey Brin (forty). More seniors followed: the three Mars heirs (seventy-three, seventy-seven, and eighty-two); Carl Icahn (seventy-seven); and George Soros (eighty-three).[22]

Despite the recent rapid growth of young entrepreneurs' high-tech fortunes, under-forties are still relatively rare among US billionaires. In 2016, thirty-two-year-old Mark Zuckerberg, whose Facebook fortune had just leapt up to $55.5 billion, stood nearly alone as a relative youngster near the top, at #4 on the *Forbes* list. Only thirty-year-old heir Lukas Walton (#37 in 2016, with $11.2 billion) and Facebook's thirty-two-year-old Dustin Moskovitz (#44 in 2016, with $10.4 billion) came anywhere close. Just fourteen under-forties made the richest-400 list that year; they constituted only 3.5 percent of the list. Most of them were founders or owners of recent internet startups (e.g., Facebook, Airbnb, Snapchat), and most ranked toward the bottom of the wealthiest list.[23]

Even among the broader category of all billionaires, under-forties are rather scarce. In spring 2017, there were 565 US billionaires. The list included—besides several founders and co-owners of Facebook, Airbnb, and Snapchat—just a handful of young newcomers from Stripe, Instagram, Uber, Pinterest, and Dropbox.[24]

Gender

Most billionaires are men. In 2013, for example, just forty-eight (12 percent) of the wealthiest 400 Americans were women. Most of those had inherited their money; only seven (less than 2 percent of the whole list) were judged by *Forbes* to be "self-made" rather than inheritors. In fact, only three women got started without a husband's help.[25]

In these modern times, one might expect to find more and more women ascending to the peaks of corporate management, running startups, and amassing large fortunes. But there is little sign of it. In 2016, one had to go all the way down the *Forbes* 400-wealthiest list to #309 before reaching Meg Whitman, who made her $2.3 billion fortune leading auction website eBay and then serving as CEO of Hewlett Packard Enterprise.[26]

Race and Ethnicity

US billionaires—especially the wealthiest billionaires—are nearly all white. Scarcely any African Americans can be found among them, and none at all among the wealthiest one hundred we studied. Hardly any Latinos ap-

pear either. On the 2016 *Forbes* 400 list, the wealthiest Americans of His-
panic origin were Alejandro and Andres Santo Domingo at #111 and their
lower-ranking relative, Julio Mario Santo Domingo, at #290 (all heirs to
a Colombian beer magnate), along with Jorge Perez at #239 (Florida real
estate) and Arte Moreno at #335 (billboards and professional sports).[27]

There are considerably more Asian-origin names on that list, but not
a huge number, and none near the very top. The wealthiest Asian Americans included #47, Patrick Soon-Shiong (pharmaceuticals); #70, Shahid
Khan (auto parts); #90, John Tu and David Sun (computer hardware);
#190, Roger Wang (Los Angeles real estate); #214, Kieu Hoang (medical
equipment); #222, Romesh Wadhwani (software); #222, Do Won and Jin
Cook Sang (fashion retail); #232, Andrew and Peggy Cherng (fast-food
restaurants); #246, Min Kao and family (navigation equipment); #274,
Bharat Desai and Neerja Sethi (IT consulting and outsourcing); #321,
Rakesh Gangwal (airlines); #321, Jerry Yang (Yahoo!); #335, John Ka-
poor (pharmaceuticals); #361, Ram Shriram (tech); and #395, Jen-Hsun
Huang (semiconductors).[28]

In 2016, *Forbes* made a special point in its 400-wealthiest issue of
celebrating immigrants to the United States—including the magazine's
own 1917 founder, B. C. Forbes, and Andrew Carnegie, both from Scot-
land—as sources of innovation and as embodiments of the American
Dream. The number of immigrants making the 400-richest list has indeed
grown, doubling from just twenty in 1986 to forty-two (10.5 percent of the
list) in 2016. But those immigrants mostly came from relatively advanced
countries. *Forbes*'s favorite stories of overcoming poverty, disappoint-
ment, or oppression were those of Jan Koum (CEO of WhatsApp), born
in Ukraine; John Catsimatidis (owner of Gristedes, Manhattan's largest
supermarket chain), from Greece; Peter Thiel (founder of PayPal and
an early investor in Facebook), from Germany; and Thomas Peterffy, a
moneyless refugee from communist rule in Hungary who learned about
computers, founded a pioneering electronic-trading firm, and went on to
build the $14 billion Interactive Brokers Group. All these people are from
Europe.[29]

Spectacular examples of immigrant success also include Google's Sergey Brin, from Russia (#10 on the richest list, with $37.5 billion); hedge
funder George Soros, from Hungary (#19, with $24.9 billion); Len Bla-
vatnik, from Russia (#22, with $18.2 billion from diverse investments—
mostly in Russia); Elon Musk, from South Africa and Canada (#34, with
$11.6 billion derived from PayPal, Tesla, and SpaceX); Rupert Murdoch,

from the United Kingdom (#38, with $11.1 billion from media); and eBay's Pierre Omidyar, born of Iranian parents in France (#54, with $8.1 billion.) All immigrated to the United States from relatively advanced countries.[30]

Forbes's 2016 map and tally of immigrant origins made clear that few immigrants who have accumulated great wealth in the United States have come from the world's poorest countries. Most arrived from relatively wealthy places with strong educational systems and important elements of similarity to Anglo-American culture. True, among the forty-two immigrants on the 2016 400-wealthiest list, seven came to the United States from China or Taiwan, and five from India. But five came from Israel (highly developed, and with strong ties to the US and Western Europe), and a total of thirteen came from various European countries. Only one arrived from all of Latin America. And—setting aside two immigrants from affluent South Africa—only one came from the entire continent of Africa.[31]

Where They Live

The spring 2017 "world billionaires" edition of *Forbes* magazine included a map of metropolitan areas where all of the 565 US billionaires lived. Most of them—when at home—were to be found on the coasts: seventy-seven in New York; seventy in San Francisco/San Jose; forty-eight in Los Angeles; thirty-four in Miami/Palm Beach. A fair number of billionaires lived in Connecticut (sixteen) and in Boston; Westchester County; Long Island; New Jersey; Washington, DC; and out west in Seattle (ten or twelve each). Middle America is mostly empty of billionaires, except for several clusters in Texas (twenty-two in Dallas/Fort Worth, thirteen in Houston, seven in Austin, four in San Antonio) and a few in Chicago (sixteen), Atlanta (nine), Phoenix (nine), Las Vegas (eight), and Denver (seven).[32]

"Home," of course, can be a fuzzy concept for billionaires who own multiple dwellings in the United States or abroad. Some summer in the north and winter in the south. Some spend substantial time doing business in foreign countries or enjoying ski or beach vacations abroad.

Where the Money Comes From

At any given historical moment, most of a society's wealthiest people tend to reflect its well-established sources of wealth. For centuries in most of the world, that meant ownership of large tracts of land.[33] Then—with industrialization—a good many entrepreneurs and stockholders accumulated great wealth in manufacturing. At any moment the wealthiest may include some who have cashed in on new profit centers that have grown rapidly in the recent past.

In today's United States, the fastest-growing fortunes are those of founders, managers, or investors in *high-technology firms* that produce computer software (to a lesser extent hardware) or web-based applications for computers and mobile devices. An even larger—though no longer as fast-growing—group of billionaires consists of masters of *finance*: investors, traders, or managers of hedge funds or private equity firms.

But since it takes time to accumulate a fortune, and since our property and tax laws make it easy to pass wealth on to spouses and progeny, the current set of billionaires also reflects great wealth accumulations from the past. Sometimes from the distant past, as with fortunes made in oil, steel, and railroad businesses during the late nineteenth century—though most of that money is now widely dispersed among multiple heirs. More concentrated in a few hands are fairly recent fortunes like those made from Mars candies, Walmart retailing, and the Cox and Newhouse media empires.

Inheritance and "Self-Made" Wealth

Many big fortunes have been made by capitalizing on innovative business ideas: drilling for oil underground and burning it for energy; building transcontinental railroads; manufacturing and selling "horseless carriages" with internal combustion engines; producing telephones, radios, aircraft, and television sets; and, more recently, making and selling computers, software, mobile devices, and web-based applications and services. Many new billionaires are people who invented or (more often) seized upon great new ideas and figured out ways to make and sell appealing products—founding a new firm and holding onto substantial ownership as the firm's value soared. Some of the most successful billionaires, including Bill Gates, have shifted their wealth into other investments when their original firm's growth slowed.

Forbes magazine categorizes wealthy Americans' fortunes as "inherited," "self-made," or "inherited and growing." Steve Forbes and his staff are especially enthusiastic about "self-made" wealth. The proportion of the 400 largest fortunes that they have judged to be self-made has been increasing in recent years, reaching two-thirds (68 percent) of all

US billionaires' fortunes in 2017.[34] Based on historical experience, however, we may expect that the proportion of inheritors among the wealthiest Americans will rise once again after the finance and high-tech booms
crest and major fortunes derived from them are passed on to heirs. Economist Thomas Piketty has documented increasing flows of inheritances
and gifts in recent decades that may contribute to continued overall increases in the concentration of wealth.[35]

In any case, the concept of "self-made" wealth is complex, and the term
invites exaggeration. It is impossible to build a business without help from
partners or employees. No one is likely to have a shot at accumulating
great wealth without receiving a lot of help and support from parents,
peers, mentors, and indeed entire societies—and their governments. Governments often provide entrepreneurs' own schooling. Governments also
foster well-trained and disciplined work forces; fund basic research that
can yield profitable applications; facilitate or subsidize the financing of
startups; structure property rights in ways that encourage and protect the
acquisition of great fortunes; invest in infrastructure, law enforcement, and
other public goods necessary for the accumulation of wealth; and more.

Yes, many entrepreneurs come up with innovative ideas, work hard,
live thriftily, and play parts—sometimes, perhaps, irreplaceable parts—in
pushing those ideas to fruition. But their ability to do so depends heavily
upon what one might broadly call "luck"—being born in the right place,
at the right time, to the right parents.

Malcolm Gladwell points out that out of the seventy-five largest fortunes
in world history, a remarkable *fourteen* were accumulated by men who were
born in just one country (the United States) within nine years of each other
(around the mid-1830s): just in time to participate as young adults in the
big takeoff of US industrialization. Similarly, most of the world's first wave
of computer billionaires were born—again in the United States—around
1955, just in time to participate in the computer revolution that began
around 1975.[36] These titans were born in the right time and the right place.
Most made excellent choices of parents as well.

Industrial Sectors

The hottest US industrial sector today, in terms of producing new, top-
ranked US billionaires, is *technology*. But the largest single group of billionaires still comes from finance. In 2017, *Forbes* classified 142 US billionaires (25 percent of the total) as gaining their wealth from finance

and investments. Seventy-six billionaires (13 percent) were in technology. Fairly close runner-up sectors—but with far fewer billionaires ranking among the very wealthiest—were food and beverages (fifty-two billionaires); fashion and retail (fifty-one); and real estate (forty-three).[37]

We have already mentioned many of the high-tech billionaires who number among the wealthiest Americans: Bill Gates (Microsoft), Jeff Bezos (Amazon), Mark Zuckerberg (Facebook), Larry Ellison (Oracle), and Larry Page and Sergey Brin (Google). Others among the top twenty wealthiest Americans include Steve Ballmer (Microsoft), Michael Dell (Dell computers), and Paul Allen (Microsoft).

There is every reason to expect that the ranks of high-tech billionaires will keep growing, as more and more owners and managers of new internet startups command rapidly growing companies for long enough periods to amass great fortunes.

Finance is not exactly new, of course. More than a century ago, Marxists were already complaining about the emerging dominance of "finance capital," and the banker J. P. Morgan amassed one of the greatest fortunes of early-twentieth-century America. But in recent decades, onrushing economic globalization, which involves increasingly free international trade and increasingly mobile capital—together with new technology—have created many lucrative investment opportunities. The new, worldwide labor market that includes hundreds of millions of low-wage workers in poor countries may not be an unmixed blessing for workers in advanced countries (it tends to put downward pressure on their wages[38]), but it is definitely a boon for US businesses, wealthy individuals, and financiers. Investment opportunities abound in the United States and in fast-growing countries around the world—not just China and India, but also the "tigers" of Southeast Asia and various countries of Latin America and Africa.[39]

In both economic and political terms, capital has leapt ahead of labor. Investing in fast-growing industries at home and abroad—along with such variant branches of finance as currency speculation, computerized electronic trading, and the trading of derivative financial instruments—has become a royal road to riches.

Recently, for example, a startling number of hedge fund and private equity managers have actually each earned more than *one billion dollars in a single year.* Five did so in 2015, and two in 2016 (apparently a tough year for top hedge funders). This was not a fluke. Three hedge fund or private equity winners made more than one billion dollars each in 2014. Four did so in 2013. And three did it in 2012.[40]

It may tend to take longer to accumulate a really big fortune from a megasized annual income in finance than it does to pile up capital gains from ownership of a skyrocketing high-tech startup. And some hedge funds have not done very well since the 2008–9 financial crisis. Nonetheless, a good many stars from various parts of the financial services and investment sector have made it into the top ranks of wealthiest Americans. Eclectic investor Warren Buffett ranked #3 on the 2016 *Forbes* 400-wealthiest list. The wealth of #1-ranked Bill Gates should probably count as partly finance-based, because he greatly expanded his Microsoft fortune through diversified investments. George Soros (#19) is a clear case—a hedge fund manager who famously scored big by betting against the British pound.[41]

In the next tier of wealthiest billionaires, Paul Allen (#21), like Gates, leveraged his Microsoft winnings with diverse investments, particularly in Vulcan Aerospace. James Simons (#24), another hedge fund manager, has specialized in mathematical models to reap profits from trading inefficiencies. Ray Dalio, #25, founded the world's biggest hedge fund, Bridgewater Associates, which currently manages about $150 billion. Investor/takeover artist Carl Icahn was #26. Hedge fund magnate Steve Cohen had been penalized $1.8 billion and stripped of outside investors in an insider-trading scandal, but in 2016 he still presided over an $11 billion family fund and ranked #31 among the wealthiest Americans. Ronald Perelman, leveraged-buyout terror of the 1980s, was 2016's #33; David Tepper (Appaloosa hedge fund) was #35; Philip Anshutz (investments in oil, railroads, telecom, entertainment, and hospitality) was #39.[42]

Additional big finance-based fortunes include those of Stephen Schwarzman, #45 (Blackstone merger-and-acquisition advice, leveraged buyouts, asset management); Andrew Beal, #49 (banks, real estate); John Paulson, #52 (hedge funds); and Ken Griffin, #57 (Citadel hedge fund).[43]

The wealthiest Americans also include some people who occupy unique niches, like Michael Bloomberg (#6, Bloomberg LP business and financial news); Charles and David Koch (#7, oil, chemicals and petroleum); Sheldon Adelson (#14, casinos); Phil Knight and family (#18, Nike); and Donald Bren (#27, California real estate). And, as we have noted, quite a few inheritors of fortunes, including the Walton heirs (Walmart); the Mars candy family; Laurene Powell Jobs (widow of Apple founder Steve Jobs, and the biggest individual investor in Disney), the heirs to the Cox and Newhouse media fortunes, thirteen or fourteen heirs to grain giant Cargill, and more.

Fair Compensation?

Rather tangential to our main concerns—but perhaps worth asking now that we have introduced our billionaires—is the following question: Do America's billionaires deserve their riches?

One possible answer is: "Of course! They earned it." It may be useful to evaluate this claim in terms of economists' "marginal product theory" of wage determination, which asserts that—in a perfectly functioning, fully competitive labor market—each employee of a firm receives wages exactly equal to the market value of the products produced by the last equivalent employee hired by the firm, as the firm reaches its equilibrium level of profit-maximizing production.

A mouthful! But the essence is simple: under perfect market competition, an employee would get paid exactly what one particular equivalent employee (the last one hired) produces. When we turn to billionaires— most of whom are owners of capital, rather than wage or salary workers— the marginal product theory of wages is relevant only to provide a contrast or an analogy. And it says nothing at all about inherited wealth, a substantial part (roughly one-third) of all billionaires' wealth, which is rarely "earned" in the usual sense.[44] It is hard to come up with a compelling philosophical argument in favor of the inheritance of great wealth.[45]

The marginal product theory does not tell us much about billionaires who found, own, and/or invest in highly profitable and fast-growing businesses. Economists have a great deal to say about market-based returns to capital and the efficiency thereof, but little to say about whether current rewards to owners are fair or just.

Even Milton Friedman, one of the most eloquent enthusiasts for private enterprise and free markets, had to acknowledge that he found it "difficult to justify either accepting or rejecting" what he called "the capitalist ethic": "to each according to what he and the instruments he owns produces." Friedman noted that the value of what a worker produces depends heavily upon skills or endowments that he or she inherits from his or her parents, and that it is hard to find an ethical justification for rewarding such inheritance. More broadly, Friedman noted that "most differences of status or position or wealth can be regarded as the product of chance" at a far enough remove.[46]

Our point is certainly not that billionaires are worthless to society, or that all their wealth should be confiscated. Yet in thinking about billionaires' political strategies, it is important to bear in mind that no major voices in American society are calling for the wholesale confiscation of billionaires' wealth either. Rather, the political debates largely concern increases or decreases in their tax rates. In that context, it is useful to bear in mind that no compelling ethical or economic principle that we are aware of dictates that US billionaires have an inviolable right to every penny that currently passes into their hands, or that the highest marginal tax rates ought to be just 20 percent rather than 40 percent, 60 percent, or some other specific figure. Nor does any practical necessity seem to dictate tax cuts for billionaires, or prevent us from requiring them to share more of their gains with the wider society.[47]

In our view, the experiences of other times and places make clear that incentives other than ever-increasing wealth—such as exalted status, or a sense of self-fulfillment, or simply *relative* rather than absolute economic standing—can be sufficient to encourage extensive innovation, risk taking, and economic growth. It seems possible that society would be better off if billionaires were required to share more of their wealth. At minimum, this possibility should not be ruled out of bounds for vigorous, democratic debate.

But such a debate is not our main concern. We are chiefly interested in the *politics* of billionaires, not in matters of economics or moral philosophy. The following chapters analyze political talk and action by US billionaires, with an eye to what billionaires want from government, what they say and do about it, and what they get. In the course of these analyses we will encounter some normative questions of a different sort, concerning the role of *political accountability* in the workings or nonworkings of democracy.

CHAPTER TWO

Stealth Politics on Taxes and Social Security

B illionaires have formidable resources—economic assets, expertise, personal networks, high social standing—which, if they wish, they can deploy in attempts to influence public policy.[1] Such high-profile, politically engaged billionaires as Michael Bloomberg, Warren Buffett, Sheldon Adelson, the Koch brothers, George Soros, and Donald Trump may create the impression that US billionaires are highly active in politics, outspoken about the issues, and—perhaps most crucially—ideologically diverse and balanced. Are those billionaires typical or anomalous? What do the very wealthiest Americans as a group actually say and do about public policy?

As we describe and analyze the political words and deeds of billionaires over the next several chapters, we seek to answer a number of questions about the one hundred wealthiest US billionaires. Do most of them speak out frequently about public issues? Do they try to convince their fellow citizens that particular policies would be good or bad for the public interest? Do they make financial or organizational contributions to policy-related causes, or do they limit themselves to contributing to political parties and candidates? Is there harmony between their political speech and their financial efforts? Do their policy preferences vary widely, or do they tend to share the same—perhaps right-leaning—perspectives? Does their behavior vary according to the nature of the policies they favor? Their level of wealth? The source of their wealth (for example, inheritance or entrepreneurship, high or low exposure to consumers)?

For the most part, previous research has offered only fragmentary or anecdotal answers to these questions. Yet the questions are weighty. The answers have a bearing on democratic theory and practice. If billionaires in fact exert substantial influence on public policy, it seems possible that they might exert a kind of benevolent political leadership, leadership based on superior knowledge, expertise, and economic success. On the other hand—especially if they pursue narrowly self-interested policies that are opposed by most Americans—any special influence that billionaires wield might be seen as harmful, violating democratic norms of political equality.

We focus on a closely related issue: the *political accountability* of billionaires to the citizenry as a whole. Do politically active billionaires openly engage in public deliberation, so that members of the public can judge the reasoning behind their stands, accept persuasive arguments but reject unconvincing ones, and hold them responsible for their political actions? Or do some billionaires act quietly—even secretly—to push policy in directions opposed by most citizens without exposing themselves to judgment or debate?

In this chapter we examine billionaires' words and actions concerning federal government policies related to two of the most consequential and widely discussed economic issue areas in American politics: taxation and Social Security. We use web-scraping techniques and publicly available data on financial contributions to analyze everything that the one hundred wealthiest Americans—the top one-quarter of *Forbes*'s 400-wealthiest list—publicly said or did about various aspects of policies related to taxes or Social Security over a rather lengthy period: roughly ten years.[2]

We have found substantial evidence of *stealth politics*. On these issues, many billionaires have engaged in extensive political actions that aim to move public policy in directions that most Americans oppose. But they have rarely made serious political arguments in public or offered reasons for their actions. Most billionaires have said nothing at all about specific policies involving taxes or Social Security, particularly when their preferences are much more conservative than those of the general public. Many act, but very few explain why. They do not try to convince their fellow citizens to agree with them. They avoid accountability.

Taxes and Social Security

We began our analyses of billionaires' political words and actions with taxes and Social Security because of the great importance of those policy areas.

Taxes

Taxes provide most of the enormous amount of money (about $3.85 *trillion* in 2016 outlays) that the federal government spends on the whole array of domestic and foreign policies that it pursues.[3] The overall *level* of tax rates and the amount of revenue they yield have important effects on how much money is available to spend. That affects what the government can or cannot do: what we can or cannot "afford to do," as politicians like to say. The US government could do much more than it currently does if our tax revenues per person—below the Organisation for Economic Co-operation and Development (OECD) average and much lower than in most of the wealthiest countries[4]—were set significantly higher.[5] Tax cuts, on the other hand, generally reduce the amount of money that is available to spend on public goods and social programs.

The level of tax rates also affects "fiscal" policy—the balance or imbalance between revenue and spending (that is, the size of budget deficits or surpluses), which in turn leads to increases or decreases in the national debt and to possible effects on inflation and the rate of economic growth.

Choices *among taxes* as sources of government revenue, and decisions about exactly how each tax works, also have important effects. For example, reliance on different kinds of taxes or different rate structures can affect the extent of economic inequality in the country. When the federal *income tax* is made more progressive (i.e., when marginal tax rates on higher-income people are raised, or rates on lower-income people are lowered) or when average rates of a progressive income tax are raised so that that tax produces a larger share of federal government revenue, inequality in posttax incomes is reduced. On the other hand, when top-bracket income tax rates are *cut*, or the overall amount of revenue that comes from progressive income taxes is reduced—as was the case with large tax cuts made under Presidents Ronald Reagan, George W. Bush, and Donald Trump—economic inequality is increased. Relative to middle-income and lower-income Americans—and in absolute terms as well—the rich get richer.[6]

The federal *estate tax* has perhaps the most highly progressive structure of any US tax. It does not apply at all (as of 2017) to estates that are worth less than $5.49 million at the time of an individual's death. (In effect, the tax actually starts at double that level—$10.98 million—for couples.)[7] So the estates of the vast majority of Americans, about 99.8 percent of them, owe nothing at all at death.[8] For those who do pay the estate tax, official

rates look fairly high—40 percent on the portion of estates that exceeds
the starting threshold by more than $1 million. At relatively low levels of
wealth, however, the effective rates on whole estates are much lower. The
estimated effective estate tax rate for 2017 began at an average of just
8.8 percent for estates worth between $5 and $10 million and rose to an
average of 19.8 percent for estates worth more than $20 million, coming
out to an overall average of approximately 17 percent.[9]

For billionaires, though—at least for those who do not pursue tax avoidance schemes or who, unlike Warren Buffett or Bill Gates, do not give a
substantial part of their wealth to philanthropy—the effective rate is closer
to 40 percent. That can be a lot of money. The heirs to an estate worth $1 bil-
lion might have to pay nearly $400,000,000 in estate taxes. They might not
like that one bit. For society as a whole, on the other hand, such a levy would
produce a substantial amount of money to fund government programs and
might cause a meaningful reduction in wealth inequality. Any *increase* in estate tax rates—especially at the top—would further reduce inequality. On
the other hand, *cuts* in the estate tax—like those of 1997 and 2001—tend to
increase inequality of wealth and income. As we will see, a favorite policy
proposal of a number of billionaires is to abolish estate taxes entirely.

Very different is the *payroll tax* associated with Social Security. That
tax is very *regressive*.[10] A lower-income working person pays a rather high
proportion of his or her income in payroll taxes: a substantial 15.3 percent
of all wages.[11] That is a much higher rate than a more-affluent person
pays.[12] In fact, someone with $1.4 million dollars in wage and salary in-
come owes only about *one percent* of that amount in Social Security payroll
taxes.

How can that be? Mainly because the Social Security payroll tax is a
flat-rate tax but is applied only to relatively low amounts of income.

The Social Security payroll tax takes the same percentage—12.4 percent—of wages or salaries from most working people, which on the face
of it may seem fair. Moreover, half of the tax is essentially invisible, because it is nominally paid by employers and does not appear on workers'
pay slips. (Nearly all economists agree that the "employer's share" is actually paid by workers; it is subtracted from the wages they would otherwise
get.) So most Americans think of payroll taxes as "fair" taxes, and most
favor using such taxes—and similarly regressive sales taxes—as major
sources of revenue.[13]

But the apparent fairness of these taxes is largely illusory. The fair-at-
first-glance flat rate, and the (deliberate?) obscurity about the "employer's

share" do not tell the whole story. Especially important is the rather low "cap"—just $118,500 in 2016—on how much in wages and salaries is taxed at all. Any money earned above that $118,500 cap is not subject to the tax. So a person with anything up to $118,500 in wages or salary pays fully 12.4 percent of his or her income. But for someone who earns twice the cap amount, only half of his or her earnings are taxed, so that the tax rate on that person's total earnings is cut in half—to just 6.2 percent of earnings. A person who makes four times the amount of the cap pays just 3.1 percent of total earnings. And so on up the income scale. A billionaire with annual income of (say) $50 million would pay a mere 0.03 percent of it in Social Security payroll taxes. Hardly enough to notice.[14]

So Social Security payroll taxes are extremely regressive. Cuts in those taxes would increase the progressivity of the overall tax system. They would also tend to stimulate the economy, since lower-income people tend to spend rather than save the money from tax cuts. (Most have to spend the money on things like food, clothing, rent, and medical bills.) Temporary cuts in payroll taxes have sometimes been made, as in the 2009 stimulus that was designed to help the economy recover from the financial crash and Great Recession of 2008–2009. Historically, however, payroll taxes have more often been *raised,* making our tax system more regressive—particularly when progressive income taxes have been cut at the same time.

Social Security

Social Security—more precisely called Old Age, Survivors, and Disability Insurance (OASDI)—is the largest and arguably the most efficient and most effective domestic program of the US federal government. In 2016, spending for Social Security amounted to about $910 billion, 23 percent of total government outlays.[15] (Only Medicare and Medicaid health-care spending, taken together, come close in size.) Administrative costs of enrolling beneficiaries, calculating benefits, sending out checks, and dealing with problems are very low: roughly 1 percent of the money.

Social Security pays out retirement benefits to some fifty million seniors every month.[16] For about 61 percent of those people, Social Security provides at least half—and in many cases *all*—of their income.[17] For that reason, Social Security has had a major effect in lowering the once-high poverty rate among elderly Americans, from around 50 percent prior to its creation during the Great Depression, down to 35 percent in 1960, and to just 8.8 percent in 2015 as real Social Security spending per capita increased.[18] The program also provides important benefits for "survivors"—widows or widowers who have lost income formerly provided by a deceased spouse—and for disabled Americans.

Most Americans strongly support the Social Security program. Year after year, surveys regularly show that large pluralities favor expanding the program. A fair number of people are content keeping benefits as they are, but only tiny minorities favor cuts. Majorities of Americans oppose Social Security cuts of practically any sort, including reductions in annual cost-of-living adjustments or increases in the retirement age.[19]

But even though Social Security reduces overall inequality and is highly popular with most Americans, its very substantial budget makes it a tempting target for those who want to shrink the size of government or are looking for savings to offset large high-end tax cuts. This potential conflict makes Social Security—along with tax policy—an issue on which there may be a great deal of tension between billionaires' self-interest, on the one hand, and the needs and wishes of most ordinary Americans, on the other.

The Logic of Stealth Politics

Recent evidence indicates that affluent Americans have more influence on policy making than their less-affluent fellow citizens.[20] And their policy preferences tend to differ significantly from those of other citizens. Data from many national surveys, for example, reveal that the top one-fifth or so of US income earners—who can be called "the affluent"—tend to be less supportive than the nonaffluent of social welfare spending programs, progressive taxes, and economic regulation.[21]

The SESA study of a small but statistically representative sample of the top one to two percent of Chicago-area wealth holders ("multimillionaires") found similar—but considerably sharper—differences between the policy preferences of the truly wealthy and those of average citizens.[22] It seems reasonable to suspect that *billionaires*, too, have substantial political clout (perhaps more clout) and hold policy preferences that are quite different (perhaps even more different) from those of most Americans. Billionaires' wealth is far greater than that of mere one-percenters. It now takes only about $10 million in net worth to make it into the top one percent of US wealth holders.[23] The least wealthy billionaire, with just one billion (1,000 million) dollars, has about one hundred times the wealth of the least wealthy one-percenter.[24]

This likely combination of having substantial political influence and having policy preferences that diverge from those of the public suggests that many billionaires may prefer to take quiet rather than noisy political action. Why open oneself to criticism? Why arouse public opposition or counteraction?

A quiet political strategy might seem particularly appealing to billionaires who hold views clearly at odds with those of the average American. Those with more mainstream views, on the other hand, might tend to speak out more forthrightly. The beneficiaries of inherited wealth, too—some of whom may feel shy about their exalted (but in some people's view perhaps unmerited) positions in society, and who as a group are less open to new experience, less extroverted, and less risk acceptant than their more entrepreneurial peers[25]—may prefer to take political action without much fuss. Billionaires whose businesses are particularly vulnerable to consumer pressure—to public condemnation, whispering campaigns, even boycotts—may also prefer to keep any political activity that they engage in rather quiet.

This line of reasoning assumes that billionaires have a *choice*—that they can be quiet if they want to, or speak out on issues if they wish. Silence is not particularly problematic: if a person simply says nothing whatsoever about political issues, nothing much is likely to get into public print, video, or cyberspace. For billionaires, speaking out is also unlikely to be difficult. In every community (even Manhattan), local billionaires are likely to be major figures whose words and actions are of great interest. What journalist or blogger would turn down the chance to interview a billionaire? Any billionaire who wants to speak out on public issues, we believe, is very likely to be offered many bully pulpits from which to do so. Furthermore, if for some reason a billionaire were consistently shunned by the media, he or she could simply purchase an established media company. (Billionaire Amazon CEO Jeff Bezos—though hardly shunned—bought the *Washington Post* in 2013 for a sum equivalent to less than one percent of his net worth.)[26] Or a billionaire could found a new media company to serve as a mouthpiece.

All in all, if a billionaire does not speak out in public about an important issue, his or her silence can reasonably be treated as reflecting a deliberate decision.

When we began our research, we expected that unwillingness to offend others would motivate many or most billionaires to *not* to speak out frequently in public about policy issues, even on very important issues that they likely care a great deal about, such as taxes and Social Security. But we also expected that—in line with the well-documented tendency of affluent and wealthy citizens to participate in politics at particularly high levels[27]—many billionaires *would* take political action directly related to these policy issues: that, for example, they would give money to policy-oriented causes and would hold fund-raisers and bundle contributions by others.

We did expect to find systematic variations among billionaires, however. The level of wealth that people enjoy tends to affect their policy preferences. For example, more-affluent people tend to be more conservative on various economic issues. One possibility is that the monotonic association of greater affluence with greater economic conservatism continues right to the top, even among billionaires who hold smaller or larger fortunes. A different possibility is that as billionaires' wealth rises, their policy preferences may at some point actually begin to move in the opposite direction. Some very high level of wealth may be felt to be "enough." Or, more precisely, if the subjective marginal value of wealth declines as wealth increases, while considerations related to altruism, social pressure, or the provision of public goods remain fixed or grow, then at some point the perceived net marginal costs of high taxes and high social welfare spending may begin to tip over into perceived net benefits.

Given the likelihood that policy preferences vary with wealth even within this superwealthy group, we expected to find political silence more common at wealth levels where billionaires' views are most at odds with the views of the general public. We also expected that—controlling for wealth level—the inheritors of great wealth and billionaires who are most directly exposed to consumers would be least likely to speak out on the issues.

Studying the Political Words and Actions of Billionaires

Our study concerns the very wealthiest one hundred Americans, the top one hundred denizens of the *Forbes* 400 list as of October 2013: from Bill Gates at the top (with $72 billion in net worth), to Daniel and Dirk Ziff at the bottom (with just $4.6 billion each).[28] All one hundred billionaires taken together had a combined net worth of about $1,291 billion (that is, about one and one-quarter *trillion* dollars—more than the entire annual

GDP of Mexico or the Netherlands, and only slightly less than that of Australia or South Korea).[29] All one hundred are listed in appendix 3, along with their net worth and their scores on some of our dependent variables.

It is not possible to ascertain billionaires' policy preferences by surveying a representative sample of them.[30] Even the Survey of Consumer Finances by the National Opinion Research Center (NORC)—the only existing survey that regularly interviews a representative sample of wealthy Americans, which is conducted for the Federal Reserve Board and is known for the high level of cooperation it elicits—does not attempt to contact *Forbes* 400 billionaires.[31] They are simply too busy and too protective of their privacy to survey. Nor do we believe that one can reliably infer billionaires' policy preferences from their contributions to political candidates and parties,[32] since donations made to moderate or opposite-party officials for nonideological reasons like cultivating access may make the donors look more "moderate" than they actually are.

It is relatively straightforward, however, to ascertain the *publicly stated* issue stands of billionaires or of any other prominent individuals. In these days of ubiquitous electronic media, careful online searches can reveal virtually every utterance that they make in public. Formal speeches or videos, op-ed columns, letters to the editor, journalistic interviews—even offhand or overheard comments—can generally be dredged up.

For this chapter, we focus on what the one hundred wealthiest billionaires have said, over a roughly ten-year period, about specific policies related to taxes and Social Security. On tax policy, we scrutinized everything they said about capital gains rates; corporate tax rates; the estate tax; the earned income tax credit; carbon taxes; the charitable tax deduction; the so-called Buffett Rule; flat tax proposals; a financial transaction tax; and, more generally, tax revenue expansion or wealth redistribution. On Social Security, we examined everything the billionaires said about payroll tax rates; the payroll tax cap; Social Security privatization; means testing; the retirement age; and, more generally, Social Security reform and benefit reductions.[33]

Web Scraping and Search Terms

Separately for each of the one hundred wealthiest billionaires, we carried out a systematic internet-based search for all statements that could be found concerning specific policies related to taxation or Social Security policy.

A crucial aspect of this research involved the careful development of a refined set of policy-related search terms: terms that would capture all statements that are relevant to our policy issues but not produce such an overwhelming number of irrelevant hits that the wheat gets lost in chaff. In theoretical terms, the objective is to map the "semantic field"[34] associated with each policy domain: that is, the family of terms actually used by billionaires and others to refer to that domain as a whole or to specific parts of it. The semantic field includes language employed by social scientists, but also the sometimes quite different terminology employed by diverse supporters or opponents of various alternatives in a given policy domain.

It is helpful to imagine the semantic field as a network, in which a concept in a domain is linked with another term in that domain if they are often used together. For example, the terms "estate tax" and "death tax" should be linked, because they are both likely to occur in a number of written or spoken texts concerning taxes that are applied to the property of wealthy individuals at the time of their death. However, terms that relate to the same policy domain but have quite different ideological connotations may not be directly connected; they may instead have one or more steps of separation. For example, not many texts are likely to refer to Social Security using both the language of the "social safety net" and references to "generational theft." Thus, these terms would lack a direct link in the conceptual network. Nonetheless, they would be indirectly linked at one step of separation because both co-occur regularly (but not always) with the phrase "Social Security."

Our search procedure started with the most obvious and visible term for each policy domain (e.g., "tax[es]" or "tax[ation]" and "Social Security").[35] Using that term as a keyword, we carried out Google News/general web and LexisNexis searches not restricted to the words of billionaires or any other particular individuals. We read the top several hits on each search and noted the alternative terms that were used in US public discourse (as exemplified by those texts) to refer to the relevant policy domain. We then repeated the process iteratively, using each prominent search term that was uncovered in the previous search. Because we followed each term connected with the initial term for at least five search steps, rather than predetermining a target number of terms to characterize each domain, the process is more similar to a series of random walks than to a traditional snowball sample. As a result, it is reasonable to expect that our sample of search keywords replicates the topological properties of the original network—and, of greater substantive interest for this project, captures the most-connected nodes.[36] Hence there is good reason to believe that our process has captured a considerable proportion of the actually existing political terminology connected with each policy domain.

Some results of this iterative procedure were predictable. For example, in addition to searching for statements made about the "estate tax," we were also led to search for statements about the "death tax." In addition to searches related to support or opposition to "tax increases," we also searched for positions on "revenue enhancement." We ultimately settled on twenty-four keywords related to taxation and ten keywords related to Social Security (see appendix 2).

After developing this comprehensive list of keywords, we turned to the web to begin searching.[37] We originally used two main resources: Google News/general web search and LexisNexis Academic search. Google and LexisNexis provide complementary resources. Google produces a very large number of potentially relevant web pages and, helpfully, includes links to videos of interviews with our subjects. Google's search results, however, are sometimes noisy and include numerous websites of dubious authority or pronounced ideological predispositions.[38] LexisNexis produces a smaller number of results and does not include video links, but it draws exclusively from mainstream journalistic and academic sources. After collecting data for approximately one-quarter of the sample, however, we discovered that LexisNexis searches did not uncover *any* relevant political statements missed by Google searches. After this discovery, we decided to use Google exclusively.

Once we began conducting web searches, we quickly realized that some of the *Forbes* billionaires who are widely believed to be very active politically are nonetheless rather tight-lipped when it comes to discussing politics. The Koch brothers (David and Charles) are a leading, although an imperfect (and now, ironically, a *celebrated*), example of this. While they have occasionally spoken in public about their political views, and while—in recent years, with help from investigative journalists—most politically informed Americans have become aware of the general thrust of their political stands, the brothers nonetheless speak publicly a great deal less often than they make large financial contributions to political causes. And when they do speak out, they tend not to take specific policy stands. Sometimes they even deliberately misrepresent the main thrust of their preferred policies, as when Charles Koch insisted that he "agree[d]" with Bernie Sanders on several matters.[39] This combination is suggestive of what we call "stealth politics."

Of course the most famous examples of stealth politics, like the Kochs, are far from the best examples. As we will see, many other billionaires have been just as quiet but much more successful at stealth politics. They remain obscure even to citizens who pay a lot of attention to politics.

Political Actions

In order to study actions as well as words, and to further explore our hypotheses about stealth politics, we also included in our search *highly specific, issue-oriented* actions, including financial contributions to *issue-specific* organizations. The Center for Responsive Politics, which runs the Open-Secrets.org website, is a very helpful resource on these matters. Our research included a search for each of the *Forbes* billionaires in OpenSecrets' online database of reported contributions to candidates and political action committees (PACs). Though some existing PACs are candidate-rather than policy-specific, many are narrowly and explicitly focused on a small set of specific issues. Donations to these sorts of PACs are included in our raw data on political actions because their specific policy content is easy to measure. We also took note of board and advisory positions at policy-specific organizations.[40]

We did *not* include contributions to candidates, parties, or candidate-specific PACs as policy-specific actions. For the reasons noted above, and because parties and candidates typically take stands across a range of unrelated issues, we are not convinced that they can be reliably used to measure the goals of billionaires' political activity. We did, however, gather Federal Election Commission (FEC) data on the billionaires' total party and candidate contributions, which are reported below. We also separately searched for media reports of instances in which the billionaires served as bundlers of political contributions or hosted political fund-raisers.

Our pursuit of policy-oriented actions as well as words was complicated by the exemption of various types of 501(c) organizations from the mandatory reporting of financial contributions to which explicitly political organizations are ordinarily subjected. As a result, our search had to rely to some extent on investigative efforts by journalists and open-government organizations to uncover dark-money contributions. Again, the Center for Responsive Politics, particularly in its collaboration with the *Washington Post*, proved to be a helpful resource. Our search inevitably missed many dark-money contributions that were funneled through certain types of 501(c) organizations—no surprise, since one point of dark-money contributions can be to hide them—but by this procedure we were nonetheless able to identify some additional policy-specific political actions. To the extent that certain particularly secretive contributions were missed, any findings of stealth politics are likely to be *under*stated, not overstated.

Although our web scraping followed a carefully defined process and was as methodical as possible, it inevitably required some exercises of judgment. Sometimes journalists' accounts of speeches and interviews alluded to policy positions without including direct quotations. In such cases, we had to search for transcripts or videos, or settle for paraphrases of stands that were confirmed by other journalists' reports. Other times, search results included links to discussions of interviews and speeches on blogs or news aggregation sites. These sites typically drew from accounts by traditional journalists, which we had to track down before we could search for transcripts or videos. This search process was often arduous.[41]

Since we are interested in silence as well as voices, we were careful to use numerous different keywords related to each policy topic to search several outlets, even when we had reason to believe that a particular billionaire had *not* taken any public political positions. The payoff for scrupulously careful searching is that, when we failed to find political statements, we could be reasonably confident that no such statements were made.

Coding

After compiling all tax- and Social Security–related words and actions for each of our one hundred billionaires, we produced measures on three sets of dependent variables: (1) a simple count of the number of public *statements* made by each billionaire on each policy subissue and on tax and Social Security policy as a whole (together with a dichotomous variable indicating presence or absence of at least one statement on the issue or subissue); (2) a dichotomous variable indicating presence or absence of political *action* on each issue or subissue (both overall, and separating personal issue-oriented financial contributions or memberships from bundling or raising contributions from others); and (3) measures of the liberal-conservative *directionality* of each billionaire's statements and of his or her political actions on each subissue (and on all tax and all Social Security issues taken together).

The measures for each billionaire were aggregated in various ways to produce frequency distributions and to test our expectations about variation by wealth level and source of wealth.

The Silence of the Lions

One of the most important findings from our web scraping concerns the extent to which the wealthiest American billionaires have spoken out in public concerning taxes or Social Security. They have very seldom done so.

On tax policy, only twenty-six of the one hundred wealthiest billionaires—that is, only about one-quarter of them—made any public statement at all concerning whether any specific tax—or taxes in general—should be raised, lowered, abolished, or kept the same. Despite the fact that tax policy is highly important and had been vigorously debated in public on numerous occasions, nearly three-quarters of the billionaires were entirely silent, or made only vague statements (for example, that a policy domain is "important") that completely lacked a liberal, conservative, or centrist policy direction.

This is not for lack of opportunity. The billionaires had plenty of time to speak; our searches reached back at least ten years.[42] They had plenty of opportunity to speak. (Again, many journalists would be delighted to interview billionaires.) But most chose silence. (See table 2.1 and appendix 3.)

Our figure of about one-quarter (26 percent) of the billionaires speaking out on taxes may actually tend to give an inflated impression of the extent to which they took stands, because it is aggregated over all the different types or subissues of tax policy that we examined. Taking specific subissues one by one, only 19 percent of the billionaires said anything at all about personal income tax rates; only 13 percent about corporate tax rates; just 8 percent about the estate tax; a mere 6 percent about carbon taxes; and a similarly meager 5 percent about capital gains taxes.

Moreover, most of those who spoke out did so very infrequently. Most of the tax-related statements we found were made by just four highly prominent, publicly engaged, centrist, or liberal-leaning billionaires: Michael Bloomberg (twenty-three comments or statements); Warren Buffett (nineteen); Bill Gates (fourteen); and George Soros (nine).[43] Most of the other billionaires who spoke out at all did so only once or twice over the roughly ten-year search period. They usually spoke only very briefly, and often quite vaguely.[44] (See appendix 3.)

Our findings concerning Social Security are even more striking. Only *three* (3 percent) of the one hundred billionaires made even a single comment about Social Security policy. Warren Buffett made seven comments;

TABLE 2.1 **Frequencies of Statements on Taxes and Social Security**

	Issue Type						
Direction of Stance	Taxes (Any Issue)	Personal/ Income Taxes	Corporate/ Business Taxes	Carbon Taxes	Capital Gains Taxes	Estate Taxes	Social Security
More	14	10	4	6	4	5	2
Less	14	7	9	0	1	3	1
Same	2	2	0	0	0	0	0
Contentless	3	1	2	1	0	0	1
Completely Silent	71	80	85	93	95	92	96
Silent or Nondirectional	74	83	87	94	95	92	97

Note: Each entry is the number of the one hundred wealthiest billionaires who, over a ten-year period, made one or more specific statements about a given type of policy.

Michael Bloomberg made four; and George Soros made just one.[45] No others took any publicly visible stand at all on Social Security (see table 2.1 and appendix 3).

We find this to be extraordinary. Social Security, after all, is by far the largest item in the federal government's budget. It makes payments to many millions of retired or disabled Americans, and many millions more count on future Social Security payments to be their main source of retirement income. Social Security has been very prominent in the news and in public debates. For at least four decades, there have been vigorous controversies over whether or not Social Security is "going broke" and, if so, what to do about it. There has been an intense, well-funded campaign to "privatize" the system: to end guaranteed payments and substitute individual retirement accounts.[46] Yet large majorities of the public oppose practically any kind of cut in guaranteed benefits.[47] Surely the wealthiest Americans were not unaware of these controversies.

Our search for comments was comprehensive. We looked for any Social Security references related to payroll taxes, benefit reductions, privatization, "reform" generally, or retirement age. Is it possible that only 3 percent of the wealthiest US billionaires held any views at all on any of these matters? We doubt it. We believe that the pervasive silence represents a series of conscious decisions not to speak, rather than an absence of opinions.

There are limits to what we can know about the policy preferences of people who say nothing at all concerning an issue. But we suspect that

TABLE 2.2 **Regression Predicting Number of Statements about Taxes**

	B (SE)	t-Value	Pr(>|t|)
(Intercept)	0.0290 (0.5489)	0.05	0.9579
Wealth	0.1531 (0.0252)****	6.09	0.0000
Consumer Facing	−0.8686 (0.6129)	−1.42	0.1596
Heir	−1.0187 (0.6379)	−1.60	0.1136

****$p < .001$.

Note: The dependent variable is the total number of statements made by each billionaire concerning any aspect of tax policy. Residual standard error: 2.889 on 96 DF; multiple R-squared: 0.3197; adjusted R-squared: 0.2984; F-statistic: 15.04 on 3 and 96 DF; p-value: 4.25e−08.

for some billionaires, one factor entering into the decision not to speak may have been a reluctance to expose unpopular positions to public view. The SESA survey of multimillionaires found that most of them were extremely worried about budget deficits. They were much more open than the general public to cutting Social Security. They were also less enthusiastic than most Americans about progressive taxation.[48] If billionaires, like those multimillionaires, tend to favor unpopular policies related to taxes and Social Security, that would help account for their silence.

Our suspicions are not allayed by the fact that among the rather few billionaires who *did* speak out, the same number (fourteen) advocated more taxes as advocated less taxes,[49] nor by the fact that the very few Social Security comments were narrowly divided (two for the expansion of Social Security, one for its reduction). This pattern is perfectly consistent with the possibility that those with more popular opinions (on these issues, that means more moderate or liberal opinions) were more likely to speak out.

We explored this idea further by analyzing what factors predict the number and the directionality of tax-related statements by different billionaires. Table 2.2 displays the results of an ordinary least squares regression[50] predicting the total number of tax-related statements that each billionaire made by the level of wealth (in $ billions) of that billionaire, whether or not his or her fortune was largely inherited,[51] and whether or not he or she was substantially exposed to consumers.[52]

It turns out that the level of a billionaire's wealth is a strong and highly significant predictor of the number of statements he or she makes about tax policy. The regression coefficient for wealth predicts, in fact, that a billionaire at the very top of our wealth range (at $72 billion in net worth) would make fully *ten* (10.2) more tax-related statements than a billionaire at the bottom ($4.6 billion). This result fits nicely with the high frequency of statements by Gates, Buffett, and Bloomberg, and with the very low frequency among the least wealthy. But it is not overly dependent on any particular observation.[53] The relationship is rather strongly linear. The regression as a whole accounts for nearly one-third of the variance, and the bulk of that is accounted for by wealth level.[54]

The same regression analysis also suggests—though it does not conclusively demonstrate—that our expectations concerning consumer exposure and inherited wealth may be correct. Controlling for wealth level, being an heir or being exposed to consumers tends to have a small negative impact on the number of tax-related statements made, though these coefficients do not quite meet standard levels of statistical significance.

We learned still more about wealth effects by examining predictors of the *directionality* of tax policy stands among those who made at least one relevant statement, using a simple additive index that combined advocacy of raising or lowering taxes on any of five specific tax issues: personal income, corporate, estate, capital gains, and carbon taxes.[55]

Wealth level turns out to be a fairly strong predictor of the directionality as well as the frequency of tax-related statements, as table 2.3 indicates. Wealthier billionaires tend to favor getting more revenue from each of several kinds of taxes in order to fund government programs. This is consistent with the idea that wealth may have declining marginal utility, and that at some high level of wealth some billionaires may begin to see the benefits of government spending as exceeding any losses to them personally as a result of higher taxes. It fits the fact that Gates, Buffett, and Soros each advocated increased revenue from all or nearly all of the five types of taxes mentioned, and that the lower-wealth billionaires tended to favor cutting taxes.

TABLE 2.3. **Regression Predicting Directionality of Statements about Taxes**

	B (SE)	t-Value	Pr(>|t|)
(Intercept)	−0.7137 (0.5370)	−1.33	0.1958
Wealth	0.0688 (0.0205)***	3.35	0.0025
Consumer Facing	−0.2685 (0.6516)	−0.41	0.6838
Heir	−0.8060 (1.2581)	−0.64	0.5276

***$p < .01$.

Note: Directionality is coded −5 to +5 to reflect the number of types of taxes each billionaire favors: increasing (+) or decreasing (−). Residual standard error: 1.697 on 25 DF; multiple R-squared: 0.335; adjusted R-squared: 0.2552; F-statistic: 4.198 on 3 and 25 DF; p-value: .01551.

Once again, the relationship was rather strongly linear, and about one-quarter of the variance was accounted for.[56] This analysis also indicated that—controlling for wealth level—being an heir or being exposed to consumers had no detectable influence on the directionality of tax stands; the coefficients came nowhere close to statistical significance. This suggests that billionaires may behave strategically in deciding whether or not to speak out publicly, but that they do not tend to modulate the *substance* of any message they deliver—or falsify their preferences—in anticipation of how the public might respond.

Putting together the above results, we can see that a billionaire's level of wealth is statistically entangled with his or her policy stands. One reasonable interpretation, which fits well with other findings, is that the effect of wealth level on frequency of statements about taxes represents—in part—a tendency for fewer statements about taxes to be made by billionaires who are more conservative on tax policy (less in harmony with prevailing public views) and who are also relatively less wealthy than some of the famously liberal-to-moderate billionaires at the top of the distribution. This tendency is broadly consistent with half (the silence half) of the idea of stealth politics. What about the other half, which involves quiet political action?

Political Action

Despite their general silence about tax and Social Security policies, US billionaires tend to be very active politically, just as resource theories of political engagement would predict.[57]

Our searches revealed that a remarkable *one-third* (actually a bit more: 36 percent) of the one hundred wealthiest billionaires hosted political fund-raisers and/or bundled others' contributions to political causes. Bundling is an extremely high-level form of political activity, associated with membership in elite fund-raising groups (dubbed "Pioneers," "Rangers," and the like) that offer easy access to top-ranking public officials.[58] Within the US population as a whole, bundling is an extremely rare activity, engaged in by well under 1 percent of Americans. (Bundling is rarely asked about in nationally representative surveys, since it would be a waste of time to do so.) In the SESA survey of multimillionaires, one of the most highly trumpeted findings was that one-fifth (21 percent) of the top 1 percent or so of wealth holders reported bundling others' contributions.[59] Billionaires bundle even more often.

TABLE 2.4 **General Political Activity by the One Hundred Wealthiest Billionaires**

Type of Contribution	Percentage (of Billionaires)	Average Annual Contribution Size
Bundled others' contributions or hosted one or more fund-raisers	36%	N/A
Made reportable contributions to state or federal political parties or candidates, outside groups, or ballot initiative efforts	92%	$509,248
Among major-party contributors:		
Contributed primarily or exclusively to Republicans	64%	$384,121
Contributed primarily or exclusively to Democrats	36%	$110,821

Note: Entries are the number (identical to the percentage) of the 100 wealthiest Americans who engaged in bundling or fund-raising sometime during a ten-year period (according to our web searches) or who made the indicated type of political contributions from 2001 to 2012 (according to contribution data gleaned from the *Follow the Money* database of the National Institute on Money in State Politics.

Billionaires also tend to give a lot of money to political causes, as indicated in table 2.4. In the twelve years from the beginning of 2001 to the end of 2012, for example, fully 92 percent of the wealthiest billionaires made a reportable federal or state political contribution of some kind. Ninety percent made a contribution to a candidate, 70 percent to a party, 40 percent to a ballot initiative, and 38 percent to an outside group.[60] Money giving is much less common in the general population (only 18 percent of Americans reported making campaign contributions in a 2008 survey[61]), and of course ordinary citizens generally give much less money.

The figure of 92 percent of billionaires contributing also exceeds the 60 percent of SESA multimillionaires who reported making a political contribution in the previous three or four years. The billionaires who made contributions invested an average *annual* total of $509,248—an amount that dwarfs the average of $4,633 that SESA multimillionaires reported giving in the twelve months prior to that survey.[62] It is also useful to remember that our figures for billionaires deal only with *reportable* contributions, not unreported dark money, so that their total political contributions may well have been substantially higher.

As one might expect of very wealthy people, most billionaires (64 percent of those who made partisan or ideological contributions) contributed primarily or exclusively to Republicans or conservative groups, and the

TABLE 2.5 **Frequency of Billionaires' Policy-Related Actions on Taxes and Social Security**

	Issue Type						
Direction of Stance	Taxes (Any Issue)	Personal/ Income Taxes	Corporate/ Business Taxes	Carbon Taxes	Capital Gains Taxes	Estate Taxes	Social Security
More	0	0	0	0	0	0	3
Less	13	3	5	3	4	12	4

Note: Each entry is the number of the wealthiest one hundred billionaires who took one or more policy-related actions, over a ten-year period, on a given type of policy.

bulk of their money (averaging $384,121 annually) went to Republicans or conservative groups rather than to Democrats or liberal groups ($110,821) (see table 2.4).[63]

When we move away from contributions to political parties or candidates, and focus on issue-specific, policy-oriented contributions to political causes, contributions, of course, are less frequent and smaller. Yet, as table 2.5 indicates, a solid 12 percent of the billionaires made a contribution to an organization with a narrow mission that took a clear stand on estate taxes—in every case seeking to cut or eliminate estate taxes. (These individuals were clustered toward the top of the wealth distribution.) Smaller but still noticeable proportions of billionaires acted in relation to corporate taxes (5 percent, all seeking lower taxes), capital gains taxes (4 percent, all wanting them lower), personal income taxes (3 percent), and carbon taxes (3 percent)—all working for lower taxes.

A similar-sized 7 percent of our billionaires acted on Social Security by contributing to policy-focused groups, with 3 percent favoring more in Social Security benefits and 4 percent favoring less. (These relatively evenly balanced actions, of course, exclude the billionaires' many contributions to economically conservative Republican candidates, who quietly supported the Paul Ryan agenda of reducing guaranteed Social Security benefits.)

These findings about actions hint at stealth politics, in that they disclose the existence of a fair number of billionaires who acted in ways opposed to the policy preferences of the average citizen. In the general public, the proportion of people favoring "more" spending on Social Security has always overwhelmingly outweighed the proportion favoring "less." Most members of the general public favor increasing rather than cutting corporate income taxes. Most favor progressivity (and ending "loopholes" for the wealthy) in the personal income tax, and most oppose total repeal of the estate tax on the largest estates.[64]

Additional clues come from a regression analysis predicting the ideological direction of political action (on either or both taxes and Social Security) that is reported in table 2.6.[65] This prediction interacts all the independent variables from earlier models with a variable that measures whether or not billionaires made at least one relevant public statement. This set of interactions allows us to look for further evidence of stealth politics; it tests whether patterns of political action are different among those who talk than among those who do not.

In interpreting this interaction, it is important not to think of speech as causally prior to action; rather, the interactions allow us to split between silent and vocal billionaires to see which kinds of spending strategies *go with* each approach to political speech. Once again, the level of wealth proves to be important: among those who did *not* speak, higher wealth led to *more conservative overall patterns* of political action related to taxes or Social Security. That is, among those who did not engage in political discourse, the wealthiest were more likely to engage in conservative-leaning political action, just as the stealth politics idea would suggest. By contrast, among those who did speak publicly, there is no significant relationship in the data between wealth and the ideological direction of political action. (As one would expect—since these actions are not very public—neither being an heir nor being exposed to consumers made an appreciable difference.)

TABLE 2.6 **Regression Predicting Directionality of Nonstatement Actions on Taxes and Social Security**

	B (SE)	t-Value	Pr(>|t|)
(Intercept)	0.1814 (0.2474)	0.73	0.4652
Makes at Least One Relevant Statement	−0.4500 (0.4108)	−1.10	0.2762
Consumer Facing	0.0556 (0.2673)	0.21	0.8356
Heir	0.1567 (0.2591)	0.60	0.5468
Wealth	−0.0499 (0.0139)****	−3.58	0.0006
At Least One Statement × Consumer Facing	0.4579 (0.4794)	0.96	0.3420
At Least One Statement × Heir	−0.0083 (0.8109)	−0.01	0.9919
At Least One Statement × Wealth	0.0355 (0.0188)*	1.90	0.0612

*$p < .1$.
****$p < .001$.
Note: Directionality is coded −5 to +5 to reflect the number of types of taxes each billionaire favors increasing (+) or decreasing (−). Residual standard error: 1.036 on 92 DF; multiple R-squared: 0.1496; adjusted R-squared: 0.08494; F-statistic: 2.313 on 7 and 92 DF; *p*-value: .03223.

TABLE 2.7. **Regression Predicting Bundling or Hosting at Least One Fund-Raiser**

	B (SE)	t-Value	Pr(>|t|)
(Intercept)	0.3923 (0.0979)	4.01	0.0001
Makes at Least One Relevant Statement	0.3539 (0.1626)**	2.18	0.0321
Consumer Facing	−0.1405 (0.1058)	−1.33	0.1874
Heir	−0.2819 (0.1026)***	−2.75	0.0072
Wealth	0.0048 (0.0055)	0.86	0.3905
At Least One Statement × Consumer Facing	−0.3667 (0.1898)*	−1.93	0.0564
At Least One Statement × Heir	0.2710 (0.3210)	0.84	0.4007
At Least One Statement × Wealth	−0.0028 (0.0074)	−0.38	0.7041

*$p < .1$.
**$p < .05$.
***$p < .01$.
Note: The dependent variable is dichotomously coded based on whether a billionaire bundled campaign funds or hosted one or more political fundraiser. Residual standard error: 0.4101 on 92 DF; multiple R-squared: 0.3001; adjusted R-squared: 0.2469; F-statistic: 5.636 on 7 and 92 DF; *p*-value: 1.97e−05.

Less clarity emerges regarding bundling and fund-raising, as indicated by the regression reported in table 2.7. Wealth level had no significant effect, perhaps because the ideological directionality of this activity is not easy to measure—and hence the left- and right-leaning dynamics separated out in earlier analyses are here mixed together. However, being an heir or exposed to consumers did tend to dampen fund-raising activity—perhaps because fund-raising is a more public activity than belonging to an organizational board or giving money, and therefore more subject to public objections and pressures. This is consistent with the positive association we found between fund-raising/bundling and making a public statement.

Several major funders of American political campaigns appear to fit the stealth politics pattern: at least they have *tried* to be stealthy, though a few have been outed by investigative reporters. For example, the Center for Responsive Politics (CRP) and the *Washington Post* uncovered massive political spending (much of it not subject to reporting requirements) by Charles and David Koch—who reportedly intended to spend about $900 million on Republican candidates during the 2016 election campaigns, before the nomination of Donald Trump led them to scale back spending and direct most of it to nonpresidential candidates. CRP and the *Post* also discovered heavy spending by Sheldon Adelson—who is estimated to have spent more than $100 million during the 2012 election cycle.[66] But we have found that—over a ten-year period during which they were intensely active behind the scenes—the Kochs and Adelson generally made few policy-related comments in public, and most of those were quite vague. On taxation and Social Security, Charles Koch had nothing whatsoever to say. David Koch made only one statement, as did Adelson.

The Koch brothers, who have extensive oil and gas interests and who devote major resources to advancing specific, generally very conservative economic policies with respect to environmental and other government regulations, typically say little or nothing in public except to advocate "economic freedom" in very generalized terms. Adelson sometimes makes emotionally charged but substantively vague rhetorical statements, like this attack on the Obama administration (from a *Forbes* interview): "What scares me is the continuation of the socialist-style economy we've been experiencing for almost four years. That scares me because the redistribution of wealth is the path to more socialism, and to more of the government controlling people's lives. What scares me is the lack of accountability that people would prefer to experience, just let the government take care of everything and I'll go fish or I won't work, etc."[67]

While this quote clearly leans in a conservative ideological direction, it seems hopeless to infer specific stances on taxation, Social Security, or any other specific policy domain from these general considerations about redistribution, socialism, and accountability. As best we can tell, neither Charles or David Koch nor Sheldon Adelson has ever laid out for public scrutiny an account of specific policy positions he favors or reasoned arguments to support them, except during David Koch's long-forgotten 1980 run as the Libertarian Party candidate for vice president of the United States. Koch's disappointing showing in that race—winning just 1 percent of the vote nationwide, after campaigning on a platform that advocated hard-line libertarian positions (abolish Medicare, Medicaid, and Social Security; end all individual and corporate income taxes; abolish the Security and Exchange Commission, the Environmental Protection Agency, and even the FBI and CIA)—may have helped convince the Koch brothers that stealth politics would be more effective.[68]

It is interesting to contrast a typical, specific policy statement made by Warren Buffett, who has taken a number of stands that could be characterized as moderately liberal or center-left and are probably closer to the views of average Americans: "I would leave rates for 99.7 percent of taxpayers unchanged and continue the [then] current two-percentage-point reduction in the employee contribution to the payroll tax. This cut helps the poor and the middle class, who need every break they can get."[69] Similarly, Bill Gates—architect and champion of the Giving Pledge, by

which billionaires promise to donate at least half their wealth to philanthropic causes—has made a number of fairly specific policy statements
like the following: "A bigger estate tax is a good way to collect money
when the government is going to have to raise more taxes. . . . Very rich
estates that have benefitted from the rules and stability of this country,
if you had a choice to be born here or be born somewhere else knowing
that you had to pay an estate tax you would still pick the benefits that our
system provides. Warren [Buffett] and I are great examples of what the
system can do for us."[70] Again, Michael Bloomberg, a moderate Republican, has frequently taken specific positions like this one: "In addition, demand for revenue will necessitate bringing back the estate tax—because
it makes too much sense. It will both raise revenue and encourage more
wealthy Americans to donate to charity. Government should incentivize
the maxim I plan to follow: The ultimate in financial planning is to bounce
the check to the undertaker."[71]

Our data indicate, however, that the centrist positions—and the frequent, open making of specific policy statements—by Gates, Buffett, and
Bloomberg are quite atypical of the one hundred wealthiest US billionaires. The Koch brothers and Sheldon Adelson, while unusual in the enormous magnitude of their political spending, are much more typical than
Gates, Buffett, or Bloomberg in not speaking out about public policy but
quietly engaging in extensive political activity, most of which supports
conservative causes and candidates.

A citizen who judged the policy stands of US billionaires as a group by
their media-reported public statements could be badly misled. On the estate tax, for example, the billionaires' few public statements tended to support *increasing* the tax (five statements to three), but their policy-focused
financial contributions and other actions strongly *opposed* the estate tax
(twelve to zero).

Taxes, Social Security, and Stealthy Billionaires

Since we cannot see into the hearts or minds of US billionaires, we cannot
be sure exactly how many deliberately pursue the strategy we are calling "stealth politics"—attempting to influence public policy in directions
not favored by average Americans while avoiding public statements about
policy. But the patterns in our data indicate that many of them do behave
in that way.

Our intensive web searches revealed surprisingly few specific statements by the one hundred wealthiest US billionaires concerning Social Security or taxation policies. These are important issues, concerning which nearly all Americans—presumably including billionaires—have definite opinions. Our searches covered a period of more than ten years, so the billionaires had abundant time to speak out if they wished to do so. We believe that they also had plenty of opportunity to speak: many print and electronic journalists are eager to report whatever billionaires have to say. But most of the billionaires chose silence.

Only a small handful of the wealthiest billionaires—particularly Michael Bloomberg, Warren Buffett, Bill Gates, and George Soros—made a notable number of specific policy statements concerning one or more issues related to taxation or Social Security. Most (71 percent) of the one hundred wealthiest billionaires said nothing whatsoever in public about any aspect of these issues. Nothing about income taxes, the estate tax, business taxes, a carbon tax, capital gains taxes, payroll taxes, Social Security privatization, the retirement age, Social Security benefit reductions, or anything else.

Yet *a large majority* of the billionaires engaged in political activity, some of them quite extensively. Nearly all (92 percent) made a reportable federal or state political contribution of some kind between the beginning of 2001 and the end of 2012. A remarkably high portion (36 percent) bundled contributions from others and/or hosted political fund-raisers. Quite a few engaged in actions directly related to the issues of taxes or Social Security, including contributing money to groups dedicated to specific policy aims concerning taxes or Social Security. Where we can measure ideological orientation, most of these actions (in contrast to the billionaires' limited public rhetoric) were aimed in a conservative direction—overwhelmingly, for example, toward repealing the estate tax, reducing capital gains and personal and corporate income taxes, and opposing carbon taxes.

There was a systematic tendency for the *wealthiest* billionaires to speak out more often—and in a more centrist or even liberal direction—than the least wealthy. This pattern is consistent with (though it cannot prove) the proposition that many of the less wealthy billionaires avoid speaking out precisely because they favor policies that would be unpopular or controversial with average Americans, including their business customers. (We found some indications that those billionaires whose businesses are most directly exposed to consumers—along with inheritors of wealth, who may be self-conscious about their fortunes—tend to speak out some-what less than others.)

As we have noted, our data very likely *underestimate* the extent of stealth politics by billionaires. We were able to trace dark money only in cases where investigative journalists or others had uncovered and publicized it. But—enabled by the tax code and probably encouraged by Supreme Court decisions[72]—dark (unreported) money represents an increasingly big factor in US electoral politics.[73] Nor do our data permit us to tell whether many billionaires use stealthy tactics in the lobbying and legislative realms, like the tactic that Darrell West has dubbed "get a senator": persuading a single senator to prevent repeal of a special benefit (a tax exemption, for example) by threatening to filibuster any effort to do so.[74] The essence of stealth politics is to try to engage in *secret* action. The nature of our data permits us to identify only semisecret actions: actions that are obscure or unknown to most ordinary citizens but have leaked into the public record.[75]

Billionaires' Impact on Public Policy

Given their abundant resources and their high levels of political activity, it appears likely that the wealthiest US billionaires, as a group, exert significant influence on the shape of US public policy. If so, one might well be concerned about whether their influence violates norms of democratic political equality. The fundamental principle of "one person, one vote" would be seriously undermined if actual US politics began to resemble a system of "one dollar, one vote." Billionaires and other wealthy Americans have been spending a lot of dollars on politics.

How much success do billionaires actually have in their efforts to influence public policy? Do they win more often in some policy areas than others? For example, are billionaires and multimillionaires especially successful at shaping policy concerning core economic interests that they nearly all share, such as keeping their own taxes as low as possible? And (relatedly) do they succeed at restricting government spending on big programs like Social Security, which require a lot of tax revenue? It does seem likely that the overall policy impact of billionaires is greatest when there is a high level of consensus among them so that nearly all billionaires are working together for the same sorts of policies.

Unfortunately, however, it is impossible—at least at present—to come up with precise answers to these questions. There is no way to obtain reliable, comprehensive data on what sorts of policies each billionaire favors or opposes. A systematic survey of billionaires is not feasible. So we cannot be sure how much consensus or disagreement there is among them on any particular issue.

Nor can we conduct a systematic quantitative study of billionaires' influence along the lines of the studies that have revealed substantial influence on policy by a much broader group of "affluent" Americans (the top 20 percent or so of income earners). Martin Gilens's data on the survey-measured policy preferences of average Americans and (separately) affluent Americans over a broad range of 1,779 proposed policy changes, together with his measures of interest group alignments on those issues, can be used to analyze whose preferences tend to have how much effect on actual policy decisions.[76] No comparable data exist for billionaires.

But of course multimillionaires and billionaires are *included* among Gilens's affluent citizens.[77] Indeed, it is quite possible that a large part of the influence that affluent Americans as a group exert is actually wielded by a few of the wealthiest people among them. If more money tends to produce more political influence, it seems reasonable to infer that those with the most money have the most influence.

So the findings from Gilens's data bolster the idea that billionaires probably wield substantial influence on policy. Moreover, Gilens's data indicate that the policy preferences of individual affluent Americans have been almost entirely unrelated to (statistically uncorrelated with) the lineups of major corporations and business groups over a wide range of issues.[78] Affluent Americans (including billionaires) often have personal ideologies and personal policy preferences that differ from the profit-making aims of the corporations they partly or wholly own. Affluent individuals and organized business groups both have substantial, independent influence on policy making.[79] So the wealthiest Americans appear to be major political actors—a distinct conceptual category of actor—who have important, independent impacts on policy making.

In order to say more than that—to make judgments about exactly which public policies billionaires have or have not influenced, and to what extent they have done so—we would need to consider historical and journalistic evidence concerning specific policy decisions in which billionaires may have played a part. We make some efforts to do this in chapter 5 and in our concluding chapter. For now, we simply note that there exists some evidence that billionaires have played important roles in policy making concerning taxes and Social Security.

Despite the strong support among most Americans for protecting and expanding Social Security benefits, for example, the intense, decades-long campaign to cut or privatize Social Security that was led by billionaire Pete Peterson and his wealthy allies appears to have played a part in thwarting any possibility of expanding Social Security benefits. Instead, the United States has repeatedly come close (even under Democratic Presidents Clinton and Obama) to actually *cutting* benefits as part of a bipartisan "grand bargain" concerning the federal budget. [80]

Working through the Republican Party (in which a number of billionaires play major roles), the wealthiest Americans also appear to have played a significant part in enacting tax cuts that have benefited the wealthy. This is most evident with the estate tax—which, as we have seen, is a particular obsession for a number of the wealthiest billionaires.[81] The minimum size of estates subject to the tax has gradually been raised, so that fewer and fewer estates have been subject to the tax at all. (At present, only about 0.2 percent of all estates—estates of $5.49 million and above for the unmarried and double that amount for the married— are subject to the tax.) And the estate tax rate on the biggest estates has been cut from 70 percent in the late 1970s, to 55 percent at the turn of this century, to its current level of 40 percent.[82] Similarly, the wealthiest Americans very likely played an important part in the 1981, 2001, and 2017 legislation that sharply cut marginal income tax rates on the highest-income Americans and—in effect—shifted more and more of the burden of federal taxes onto regressive payroll taxes.[83]

The Accountability Problem

Quite aside from the troubling question of whether people with large amounts of money should be permitted to have outsized political influence, we believe that political influence without *political accountability* can create special problems for democratic politics.

Billionaires' political activity is only rarely accompanied by explicit public discussion of what sorts of policies they favor and why. This means that ordinary citizens have no way to judge whether or not the billionaires— extremely successful people, often very intelligent and knowledgeable— have something useful and convincing to say about public policy. Their silence may detract from the quality of political debates and deprive citizens of a possible source of political leadership.

By the same token, however, if billionaires are mistaken about what sorts of policies would best serve the public interest—or, worse, if they deliberately pursue narrowly self-interested policies that would be detrimental to the average American—their silence may help shield them from political accountability. It is difficult to argue against, judge, or counteract someone whose political views and actions are concealed.

We believe that stealth politics is not good for democracy.

CHAPTER THREE

Four Billionaires Up Close

S tatistical patterns can be illuminated, confirmed, called into question, or elaborated upon by looking closely at specific cases. In this chapter, we grapple with what stealth politics looks like in real life by examining more closely the cases of four of our one hundred wealthiest billionaires: Warren Buffett, John Menard Jr., Carl Icahn, and David Koch.

These case studies serve several purposes. One is simply to illustrate in concrete terms how stealth politics works. These four billionaires exemplify different types of resources, self-interests, and political philosophies that tend to translate—as the stealth politics theory predicts—into different patterns of political speech and action.

As we have noted, Warren Buffett is quite unusual among billionaires in holding centrist-to-liberal views about various economic and social welfare policies. Just as the theory predicts, Buffett—unlike the more conservative billionaires—frequently speaks out about his opinions in public. David Koch is much more typical of US billionaires in his libertarian views (economically very conservative, socially somewhat liberal) and—again as the theory predicts—he is generally silent about policy issues. Koch is atypical, though, in combining extreme conservatism with an extremely high level of wealth, and in investing enormous amounts of money in politics. The much less well-known John Menard Jr.—like Koch and many other billionaires—is highly conservative on economic issues (he is an especially fierce opponent of labor unions) and quite active politically while keeping very quiet in public. Carl Icahn is unusual: he is something of a Donald Trump–style right-wing "populist," espousing economic nationalism and expressing certain concerns about the well-being of American workers. Icahn's case, which fits less well with the theory, has led us to reflect about how the theory could be modified to account for Icahn or any other populist billionaires who might emerge in the Trump or post-Trump period of American politics.

Taken together, then, three of these cases (Buffett, Koch, and Menard) rather neatly illustrate the patterns of stealth politics. But our aim is not just to illustrate.

Indeed, we selected and analyzed these cases largely for methodological purposes, in order to further test and (if necessary) to elaborate on or modify the stealth politics theory. By examining both extreme cases and outliers, for example, we can find indications of whether we missed any relevant information: whether any policy-related statements or political actions were not unearthed by our systematic web searches. We can judge whether and why our theory may have gone wrong. We can provide more fine-grained evidence of how processes work in specific billionaires' real lives. We can explore the origins of billionaires' wealth and consider ways in which that may have influenced their political philosophies and political behavior. We can also scrutinize the causal mechanisms by which stealth politics works.

In short, multimethod research that combines quantitative analyses with carefully selected and carefully conducted case studies can often illuminate political processes in ways that neither type of method can do alone.[1]

In this chapter we provide some background material on how each billionaire became wealthy, in order to help understand the individuals while also highlighting how their personal financial interests may relate to certain areas of public policy. We explore more closely the statements on economic policy by these billionaires that we found through our earlier web searches, and also examine any new statements we could unearth using broader search terms and watching out for less visible venues.[2] In the new searches, we examined the contents of any major publications and looked for even vaguely political statements that did not show up in our main data collection, in order to test the assumption that our systematic searches already found virtually everything these billionaires had said about taxation, social programs, and economic policy more generally. Finally, this chapter describes the precise nature of each billionaire's political activities, so as to give qualitative substance to billionaires' activities and illuminate some forms of political action that are less well known than financial contributions, bundling, or forming PACs. Our examination of the Koch and Menard cases, in fact, revealed some novel kinds of political action that we had previously been unaware of.

Selecting Cases for Close Study

Case studies can most effectively complement and strengthen quantitative studies if they are selected according to clear principles. The cases discussed in this chapter were systematically selected to detect measurement error in our variables or possible misspecification of our models. Warren Buffett— who frequently discusses politics—and John Menard Jr., who has never, according to our systematic searches, publicly discussed taxes or Social Security, were selected among extreme cases in terms of the frequency or infrequency with which they spoke in public about taxes or Social Security. While Buffett stands alone as the single most politically vocal billionaire, Menard is only one of many silent billionaires at the opposite extreme. Of the seventy-one billionaires who (according to our data) made no statements at all about economic policy, Menard was selected randomly.[3] Icahn and Koch were selected as deviant cases because they had the biggest residuals in regression analyses predicting the directionality of policy-related actions. In our data, Icahn appeared to take much less conservative action than the model predicted—in fact we found no action at all; and Koch seemed to take much *more* conservative action than predicted.

Examination of cases that are deviant or take extreme values on key variables provides the best opportunity to identify sources of measurement error or omitted variables that can distort the findings from quantitative analyses. In other words, if there are distortions in our quantitative data regarding stealth politics, these four cases should be unusually likely to reveal such problems.[4] That makes them a useful focus for intensive qualitative inquiry.

Measurement errors in the context of stealth politics could take various forms. First, there might be simple coding errors: instances in which statements or actions by billionaires were incorrectly categorized. Second, there could be deeper problems in the measurement process. For example, some billionaires might have made policy-relevant public statements that were not recorded by Google or that were not detected by our search procedure. Errors of this sort might lead to incorrect inferences that a particular billionaire was engaged in stealth politics when in fact the billionaire in question had publicly discussed that issue in a venue or format that we simply missed. Or third, there may be missing information about contributions or fund-raising actions on the part of billionaires. This category of error could lead to underestimates of the proportion of billionaires who engage in stealth politics.

Case studies cannot definitively rule out any of these three types of measurement error, but they do provide a way to test for their prevalence. In the following cases, we search for these types of error by comparing the data collected via our web-scraping procedures with the results of additional open-ended web inquiries and of other forms of research. Beyond carrying out this correspondence test between the systematic, quantitative indicators and a broader but less systematic pool of qualitative evidence, we believe that our case studies help shed substantive light on why billionaires do what they do and on precisely how American billionaires attempt to exercise political power.

Warren Buffett

Modest-living Warren Buffett, known as the "Oracle of Omaha" for his successful investments and his insightful utterances, was—at the time our study began—the second- wealthiest among all Americans, with a fortune of $58,500,000,000. This despite giving away $2 billion in the previous year to the Gates Foundation, which brought his total philanthropic contributions close to $20 billion. Even after that hefty gift, Buffett's fortune had risen by $12.5 billion in the course of the previous year, largely because of a 34 percent rise in the value of his stock in Berkshire Hathaway after Buffett engineered Berkshire's acquisition of iconic ketchup maker and food giant H. J. Heinz.[5] By autumn 2016 Buffett had dropped to #3 among wealthiest Americans, behind fast-rising Jeff Bezos of Amazon, but Buffett was still worth a respectable $65,500,000,000.[6]

Warren Buffett was born in 1930 to a solidly middle-class Omaha family. His father worked first as a journalist and then as a stockbroker and found success even through the depths of the Great Depression. Buffett began his involvement with investments as a young child, reading about them and involving himself in his father's brokerage business. He began investing for himself and his sister, Doris, by the time he was twelve years old—purchasing three shares of one of his father's favorite stocks, Cities Service preferred, which he sold (much too soon) for a small profit. Between such investments and a series of small-time jobs, Buffett accumulated personal wealth of a then-remarkable $1,000 by the age of 14.[7]

As Buffett worked his way through college and young adulthood, he was employed in a series of jobs related to newspaper circulation and sales. He also pursued stock investments. In the process, Buffett accumulated personal savings of nearly $20,000 by the age of twenty-one. At that point he moved into investing and stockbroking as a full-time career, taking out a $5,000 bank loan to help fund his personal investments and signing on to work for his father's brokerage firm. Later, Buffett went to work for the Graham-Newman firm. At the age of twenty-six he left Graham-Newman with savings of $174,000 and formed his own hedge fund, with family and friends as the only partners in the enterprise.[8] From that point forward, Buffett's investing success gradually and consistently snowballed to his present level of extraordinary wealth.[9]

Buffett is now the chairman and CEO of Berkshire Hathaway, a multinational conglomerate that holds stakes in a wide range of industries including energy, manufacturing, retail, transportation, and financial services. The company is the sole proprietor of many large and well-known companies, including GEICO (one of Buffett's earliest favorites), Fruit of the Loom, and BNSF Railway.[10] Berkshire Hathaway is also the largest current shareholder in United Airlines and Delta, and holds major positions in Kraft Heinz Company, American Express, the Coca Cola Company, Southwest and American Airlines, and many more.[11] Buffett's wealth thus entails a measure of control over a significant portion of the American economy.

We selected Buffett for study as the single billionaire who scored highest on our speech variable. As we saw in the previous chapter, Buffett has been one of the most talkative billionaires when it comes to taxation and Social Security. The same applies to government economic policy in general.

Buffett has spoken to numerous media outlets about politics, and has even penned his own political op-eds. In particular, Buffett has been a very vocal supporter of redistributive economic policies. He is one of the most visible advocates of progressive taxation (tax rates that increase substantially as a function of income) in contemporary American discourse. In the 1993 Berkshire Hathaway letter to shareholders, captured both in our original systematic search and in the case-study process, Buffett wrote, "Charlie [Munger, Buffett's business partner] and I have absolutely no complaints about these taxes. We work in a market-based economy that rewards our efforts far more bountifully than it does the efforts of others whose output is of equal or greater benefit to society. Taxation should, and does, partially redress this inequality."[12]

Buffett has frequently advocated higher taxes on the wealthy. For years he has highlighted the ways by which wealthy Americans manage to minimize their tax bills. In an October 30, 2007, interview with *NBC Nightly*

News, Buffett said, "I'll bet a million dollars against any member of the *Forbes* 400 who challenges me that the average [tax rate] for the *Forbes* 400 will be less than the average of their receptionists."[13] Similarly, in a July 7, 2011, conversation with CNBC, Buffett complained, "My cleaning lady is being charged a payroll tax. Her payroll tax, counting the portion her employer pays, is higher than my capital gains tax. . . . I mean, I am treated like I am the bald eagle or something—that I have to be protected at all costs."[14]

In more recent years, Buffett has called specifically for a minimum tax rate of 30 to 35 percent for the wealthy. On November 14, 2011, Buffett told CNBC, "You change the Social Security rule somewhat and millions of people will feel it, they'll really feel it. You change the Medicare rules and millions of people will feel it. You get a minimum tax of 30 or 35 percent on incomes of a million or ten million or over, the truth is, those people won't even feel it. But at least the American people, as a whole, will feel somehow that the ultrarich have been asked to participate to a small degree in this overall sacrifice that we're all going to be asked to participate in."[15]

Taken together, these and similar statements point toward what has come to be known as the "Buffett rule," defined in a National Economic Council report to be "the basic principle that no household making over $1 million annually should pay a smaller share of their income in taxes than middle-class families pay."[16] While this precise formulation was not offered by Buffett himself, it serves as a useful summary of the views he has often expressed about taxation and economic inequality. The fact that this attention-catching idea came to have Buffett's name attached to it in a high-profile official report illustrates Buffett's distinctive role as perhaps the most prominent advocate in contemporary American political discourse for increased personal income tax rates on the wealthy.

Buffett has also made a public case for higher corporate tax rates and capital gains rates. One reason he has advanced for this view is his argument that it is a "myth" that American companies are paying 35 percent corporate income tax rates.[17] In the 2003 Berkshire Hathaway report, Buffett wrote, "If class warfare is being waged in America, my class is clearly winning. Today, many large corporations . . . pay nothing close to the stated federal tax rate of 35 percent. . . . We hope our taxes continue to rise in the future—it will mean we are prospering—but we also hope that the rest of Corporate America antes up along with us."[18]

Buffett is likewise an outspoken advocate of the estate tax. He has argued: "Dynastic wealth, the enemy of a meritocracy, is on the rise. Equality of opportunity has been on the decline. . . . A progressive and meaningful estate tax is needed to curb the movement of a democracy toward plutocracy. . . . In a country that prides itself on equality of opportunity, it's becoming anything but that as the gap between the super-rich and the middle class is widening."[19]

While Buffett has argued extensively in favor of taxation—in the context of a political culture in which few visible actors make similar arguments—he does not indiscriminately favor increasing government revenue. Rather—as evidenced by several of the quotes above—Buffett's interest in increasing taxes on corporations and the wealthy is motivated in part by concerns about economic efficiency and in part by concerns about inequality. In connection with inequality, he has criticized the Social Security payroll tax for disproportionately falling on lower- and middle-income workers, and he supports raising the cap on income subject to it so that those with high incomes pay more.[20]

All these statements—including statements from cable news programs and corporate shareholder reports not located by our original searches—fit comfortably with the subset of Buffett's statements that were detected and recorded through our systematic web search procedure. Our closer examination of the case did reveal two domains of public expression in which Buffett's statements had not always been captured by that procedure: cable news interviews and Berkshire Hathaway annual statements. Yet these omissions are not particularly troubling. Some statements made in those venues were in fact found in the systematic news searches. Furthermore, what Buffett said in the statements we missed was highly consistent with what he said in the statements found earlier. Thus we somewhat underestimated the already high *frequency* with which Buffett spoke out, but we did not miss any important substantive positions that he took. All in all, the evidence from the Buffett case study fits with the hypothesis that there was no important, systematic measurement error in our analysis of public statements.

Turning to political action, there is evidence that Buffett has been actively engaged in funding politics—although less so than some other billionaires, and with a distinct avoidance of dark money or other low-visibility strategies. Buffett has hosted fund-raisers for Democratic candidates, both during and after the period of our data collection (including for Hillary Clinton during the 2016 election cycle). Although he has made direct contributions to numerous candidates—almost entirely Democrats—his political spending is relatively modest for a billionaire. No available source, for example, shows Buffett as having written a six-figure political check.

Indeed, Buffett has said publicly that he will not write large checks to candidates or their super PACs because he does not "believe that the elections should be decided by the super-rich."[21] Furthermore, Buffett has expressed public opposition to super PACs and unlimited campaign spending. The available evidence suggests that he has generally followed these principles in his own behavior. The one time he is known to have donated to a super PAC, he claims to have done so in ignorance.[22] There is no evidence from investigative reporters or others of Buffett making non-FEC-reported dark-money contributions.

Buffett fits the stealth politics theory well. His expressed policy preferences on taxes and Social Security align well with the views of the general public, and he speaks out about politics much more frequently than the average billionaire. This fits the theory because we expect billionaires with positions similar to those of the general public to feel little reluctance about speech. Buffett's outspokenness is also consistent with the theory's predictions regarding inherited wealth (which is predicted to be associated with less speech), since Buffett's fortune is mostly self-made.

Furthermore, while many of the firms that Buffett indirectly owns are consumer facing, there is sharp branding separation between Berkshire Hathaway and the (often long-established) businesses in which it invests. It seems unlikely that most Americans realize they are supporting Buffett when they purchase a soda, car insurance, or an airplane ticket. Hence, Buffett may face less pressure from the public not to speak politically than most consumer-facing billionaires do. That said, Buffett's companies have occasionally faced politically motivated boycott efforts. The most successful was a 2002–2003 boycott organized by Life Decisions International and other members of the pro-life movement. This boycott was motivated by Buffett Foundation donations to Planned Parenthood that were funded through a Berkshire Hathaway charitable-contributions program. In response, Life Decisions International encouraged a boycott of The Pampered Chef, a recently-acquired Berkshire Hathaway company.[23] Notably, this boycott targeted only one readily-identifiable brand. Other efforts at boycotting Buffett have been hampered by the difficulty of parsing out enterprises partly or substantially owned by Berkshire Hathaway. For example, in a 2016 online conversation reacting angrily to Buffett's public stance on prices for home-generated solar electricity in Nevada, a commenter named Philip Andrew wrote, "This is evil! Shame on Warren Buffett. Where's a list of all his companies so that we can #boycott #warrenbuffett."[24] No commenter provided such a list, and the outraged commentary moved away from the idea of a boycott.

Buffett's willingness to speak out on politics fits well with the contention of the stealth politics theory that the very richest billionaires tend to hold relatively pro-redistribution views and (for that reason) are more likely both to speak out and to take relatively egalitarian stands than those further down the list of wealthiest Americans.

John Menard Jr.

While Warren Buffett is an iconic American billionaire and has been the subject of innumerable articles and several books, much less has been written about the life of John Menard Jr. Midwestern readers may well have shopped at Menards, the chain of stores that Menard founded and owns, but it is likely that even they know little or nothing about the man himself.

This relative obscurity notwithstanding, in the autumn of 2013 (when we began our study) John Menard Jr. was #57 among the wealthiest Americans, with a net worth of $7,500,000,000.[25] By fall 2016, he had risen to #46 and had a net worth of $9,400,000,000.[26] Menard's wealth has flowed from a business that he built from scratch. He is the founder, president, and CEO of Menards, a retail home-improvement store chain that operates at nearly 300 locations spread across twelve states in the Midwest and Great Plains. Menards ranks a distant third in size among home-improvement firms nationally (after Home Depot and Lowe's), but John Menard Jr. is much richer than the founders of those bigger chains because Menard kept his firm private and retained ownership and control firmly in his own hands.[27]

Menard was born in 1940, in Eau Claire, Wisconsin. His father was a math professor, and his mother taught in a Catholic grade school. They left these jobs during Menard's adolescence to become large-scale dairy farmers. The Menards chain is an outgrowth of John Jr.'s experience working as a contractor to pay his way through college. He learned that he could make a great deal of money by selling building supplies at retail prices on Sundays, when lumberyards were closed. Based on that insight, Menard founded his first store and gradually grew the business to the point where it made him one of the wealthiest people in America.[28]

While the media have not reported on Menard as frequently as many other billionaires—and our data indicate that he has generally been silent about politics—there has been some press coverage of scandals related to his personal life. An as-yet-unresolved lawsuit alleged that Menard threatened economic consequences on the wife of his business partner if she did not engage in sexual relations with Menard and his wife. Another lawsuit that is apparently still in litigation alleged that Menard fired attorney Lisa Trudeau to punish the abovementioned business partner and in retaliation for Trudeau's rejection of Menard's sexual advances. Beyond their prurient details, these lawsuits suggested that Menard may have forced associates out of business deals in retaliation for personal conflicts.[29]

We selected Menard randomly from among our billionaires who had extremely low scores on the speech variable—that is, from among those who our data indicated did not speak publicly about taxes or Social Security *at all.* Our main job in reexamining his case was to look harder and ferret out anything he actually said that we had missed. When we looked harder we did not find any omitted statements at all—a reassuring sign of absence of measurement error. As it turned out, however, our new searches did turn up some interesting new evidence about Menard's political *actions.*

Despite his silence about political issues, Menard has been highly active politically in a variety of ways—including traditional political fundraising, but also going well beyond that. Our initial web search located news reports that revealed $1,500,000 worth of undisclosed, dark-money contributions Menard made between 2011 and 2012 to Scott Walker, during Walker's successful Republican gubernatorial campaign in Wisconsin. Those contributions were funneled through the Wisconsin Club for Growth, an outside group that spent large sums on Walker's behalf during the subsequent recall election, in which opponents tried to oust Walker. Menard's contributions to Wisconsin Club for Growth became known only as a result of a legal investigation into whether the group had illegally coordinated with the Walker campaign.[30]

In addition to his donations to the Wisconsin Club for Growth, Menard has also given substantially to help fund the Koch brothers' political endeavors. In 2011, *Mother Jones* magazine published a transcript of a leaked recording from a Koch brothers' donor conference in June of that year. In one speech, Charles Koch read a list of donors who had given a million dollars or more, and Menard was included on the list.[31] We cannot tell exactly how big Menard's donations were or what they aimed at, since the recorded speech offered no elaboration. However, it appears that most of Menard's donations to the Wisconsin Club for Growth came after June 2011, suggesting that his inclusion on the Koch brothers' list reflects other unknown spending in promotion of right-wing libertarian ideals.

Although the Walker-related Wisconsin Club for Growth donation is Menard's only dark-money contribution about which any meaningful details are known, the size of that contribution, as well as the suggestive evidence from the Koch seminar, support an inference that this particular foray into secret political money may not have been unusual for him. Furthermore, Menard's political activities have not been limited to semisecret contributions. Menard has also made numerous legally disclosed contributions to candidates and parties—almost all of which went to Republicans.[32]

Beyond giving money to political candidates and groups, Menard has also shaped policies within his own business that have significant political consequences. Managers of Menards home-improvement stores used to be required to sign an employment contract that included a clause cutting their salary by a punishing 60 percent if their branch of the store ever unionized.[33] While this clause was ruled illegal and has been discontinued by Menards, the National Labor Relations Board has fined the company for other anti-union policies. For example, Menards was found to have instituted a policy banning merit pay increases to employees who engage in union activity.[34]

These anti-union actions no doubt partly represent economically self-interested behavior by Menard and his company, since labor unions that conduct pay negotiations between employees and a company tend to raise wages and thereby increase labor costs. But such company policies also have broader political consequences. Labor unions have historically been a major voice for working- and middle-class citizens in American politics.[35] So restraining union activity not only forestalls potential cost increases to the Menards home-improvement stores; it also closes off an important avenue of political participation and representation to employees of the company.

Menard has not confined his politicized business policies to simply closing off modes of political engagement for his employees. He has also taken the unusual step of providing and incentivizing extensive ideological training for his employees as part of their careers. Menards offers employees access to a program called "in-home training," which consists of internet coursework. The curriculum includes the expected sorts of vocational materials related to career advancement within the company but also extensive discussions of American politics and history from a conservative ideological position. For example, in a training unit on "American Job Security," employees read that "A government dedicated to individual liberties is one that understands that private property is to be protected, not taken or taxed." The materials are not ideological just in spots, but rather contain thoroughgoing treatments of conservative positions about government debt, regulation, wages, environmental policy, inequality, and so forth.[36] Employees and store managers are given career and financial incentives to support participation in this training program. Thus the in-home training becomes an important mode of political activism for Menard.

Overall, Menard's behavior constitutes a paradigmatic example of stealth politics in action. A somewhat clearer example, in fact, than that of the much more immediately recognizable Koch brothers. Although the Koch brothers have rarely expressed specific political views in public settings, the broad outlines of their highly conservative opinions and actions have— presumably against their wishes, and after a long period of successful stealthiness—recently been uncovered and widely reported in the media. The Kochs have occasionally even spoken to the press (though generally in vague terms). By contrast, our initial web search results found John Menard Jr. to have been completely silent in public about policies related to Social Security and taxes. Our subsequent closer look confirmed that point and extended it. We found no public utterances whatsoever by Menard about any policy issues, or even about politics in general. In light of the fact that Menard is a sufficiently public figure that one can uncover important details about his political contributions, his politically charged corporate policies, and even his personal and sexual life, our inability to locate a single politically meaningful statement by him must surely reflect a deliberate political silence.

In harmony with the stealth politics theory, Menard's silence clearly does not reflect an apolitical attitude or an avoidance of political commitments. Menard has been highly active politically. His financial support of Scott Walker and numerous other conservative candidates, as well as his contributions to the Koch network, strongly suggest that his preferences on taxes, Social Security, government regulation, and related issues are well to the right of the preferences of average Americans. Furthermore, Menard has leveraged his wealth for political purposes in idiosyncratic ways that go far beyond political contributions.

On a more methodological note, it is important to emphasize that our deeper examination of Menard's political talk and actions did not identify any coding errors. Our exhaustive follow-up inquiries into Menard did not reveal any relevant public statements that had escaped our web-scraping procedure. Instead, this follow-up confirmed that he was completely silent, politically, in public. Our case-study search for additional evidence confirmed that Menard actively deploys his wealth for political purposes, and indeed it revealed that Menard engages in some atypical and quite interesting forms of political action that turn internal policies of his company into political instruments. This case suggests that in other cases as well, billionaires who engage in standard political spending that is discoverable by systematic web searches may also carry out additional, unknown types of political activity. Measurement error is seen not to be an issue in this case.

Carl Icahn

In the autumn of 2013, Carl Icahn held the #18 position on the *Forbes* list of wealthiest Americans, with a net worth of $20,300,000,000.[37] Three years later—after one of the worst investment stretches of his career, due in large part to sagging values in the energy sector[38]—Icahn had dropped to #26. But he still had a net worth of $15,700,000,000, no mean sum.[39]

Icahn was raised in a basically middle-class home in a modest neighborhood in Queens, New York. Much like Warren Buffett, Icahn built his wealth through investment. After working as a stockbroker for seven years, he founded the business that would become Icahn Enterprises, a conglomerate that now holds investments in a wide range of industries including energy, retail, transportation, casinos, and manufacturing. Icahn gained notoriety in the 1980s as what some called an "activist investor" but others called "corporate raider" or "buccaneer." He executed hostile takeovers of several prominent publicly traded corporations. His dramatic takeover of Trans World Airlines (TWA) in 1985 was one of his earliest and most notable successes.[40] Since then, Icahn has waged proxy battles over several companies, including a persistent but unsuccessful effort in the 1980s and 1990s to take over USX (the holding company for United States Steel),[41] and, more recently, a high-stakes, high-visibility—but also unsuccessful—2013 battle with fellow billionaire Michael Dell over control of Dell's eponymous computer company.[42]

We selected Icahn for close study because he deviated more sharply than any other billionaire we studied from the pattern found in our chapter 2 regression analysis predicting the direction of policy-related actions on taxes and Social Security. Based on his scores on the independent variables predicting the directionality of actions, the model predicted that Icahn would engage in fairly substantial right-leaning political action. But our data showed no policy-focused political action at all by Icahn, in either a liberal or a conservative direction, and a bit of speech that actually took a liberal stand. Icahn has had a substantial public persona, frequently appearing on television—especially on CNBC. But our web-scraping procedure revealed only one public statement on taxes or Social Security policy, in which Icahn supported increasing income taxes for the wealthy. We found no policy-related actions at all.

Our reanalysis of his public appearances confirmed that Icahn generally did not speak about politics in specific terms before about 2015. Thus he was correctly scored for the time period covered by our systematic data-collection process. As to his actions: while our original searches had revealed that Icahn hosted a few candidate or party political fund-raisers during the earlier period, he was scored as much less active than most billionaires at his level of wealth. Closer inspection confirmed that Icahn was indeed much less politically active before 2015 than the statistical analysis predicted. But he has recently ramped up his political activity a great deal, largely in the rightward direction that the model predicts.

Icahn emerged in our original data as essentially silent and mostly politically inactive. Our subsequent deeper investigation transformed this impression, with respect to his behavior *after* the period of our main study. Beginning in 2015, Icahn became a vociferous participant in politics, making a number of specific policy statements and publicly stating his support for Donald Trump—with whom he had had a decades-long relationship that was centered on his involvement with the Trump Taj Mahal casino in Atlantic City.[43] In 2015 Icahn announced plans to launch a $150,000,000 super PAC dedicated to fiscally conservative policy causes including corporate tax "reform" (i.e., mainly rate cutting).[44] In late 2016, after Trump's election as president, Icahn accepted an advisory role on business regulation with the Trump administration—a position that immediately raised ethical red flags, given Icahn's wide-ranging investments.[45] Icahn's involvement with the Trump administration turned out to be brief; he resigned from his position as a special adviser on regulations in mid-2017 amid revelations that he was attempting a regulatory rollback that would save him personally millions of dollars.[46]

The fact that Icahn was (in earlier times) mostly silent about politics certainly does not mean that he was altogether silent on other topics. Icahn has long been highly vocal about issues of corporate governance, and he has consistently cast these issues in quasi-political terms. For example, as of June 2017 his blog was headed by a self-quote from a 1988 Texaco shareholders meeting: "A lot of people die fighting tyranny. The least I can do is vote against it."[47] While this quote seems to have a strongly political flavor, in context it represents advocacy for shareholder power within corporate governance institutions, and the tyranny in question involves the power of boards and CEOs over shareholders.[48]

Icahn shifted toward public engagement on more traditional political matters in early September 2015, when he announced his support for Donald Trump. Icahn explained that Trump would help the country by cutting the regulatory burden on business.[49] He then went on to formally endorse Trump's presidential candidacy during a September 30 interview on CNBC:

> I'm sort of being an activist in the country now. I think it's sort of a no-brainer. You can't keep it going the way it is. We're dysfunctional. . . . You don't have limited government today. You've got an extremely strong Federal Reserve, so on the one hand you're saying, oh, we've got to watch the deficit, and all these Tea Party guys, oh, we can't spend money, and they don't look around, right next door, at the Fed in the last few years has gone out and printed up four trillion dollars. . . . You need a guy in there that understands business and understands that kind of thing, and understands the . . . risks in what the Fed is doing now. . . .
>
> [Donald Trump] is sending a message to the middle class, and literally how screwed they are getting . . . How do you justify a mediocre CEO getting $42 million a year and the guy who's working for him out there, really doing the work, is getting $50 thousand a year. I mean, there's no justification for it in a free society where you can just vote.[50]

Icahn's views in this statement are somewhat mixed in terms of classic liberal-conservative economic distinctions—they lean toward Trump-style populism—but they are unambiguously political.

Later in the fall of 2015, Icahn escalated his intervention into politics. He announced the creation of a super PAC and committed $150,000,000 of his own money. It is not clear whether this actually happened, but Icahn did write a letter to Congress discussing his motivation. In that letter he strongly opposed corporate tax "inversions," in which US companies relocate and reconstitute themselves as entities headquartered in another country. He saw this trend as harming the US economy and argued that it can be ended through "international tax reform" that dramatically reduces the taxes US companies pay when they bring cash into the domestic economy from foreign subsidiaries.[51]

While this letter took a clear stance in favor of lowering one particular kind of tax on businesses, Icahn mentioned no additional policies in the letter. He subsequently published an op-ed in the *New York Times* in which he again argued against tax inversions, without taking a stand on any other policies.[52] This rather specialized tax activism represents the bulk of Icahn's specific policy statements, but he has also made some general comments with policy relevance. For example, in the context of a dispute with Bernie Sanders regarding union contracts in an Atlantic City casino, Icahn wrote, "The income gap in this country is a major problem and I agree (with certain exceptions) that those that manage capital, as well as many CEOs, are ridiculously overpaid. If this problem is not addressed, there may well be disastrous consequences for the country."[53]

On balance—and taking into account events subsequent to our statistical analyses—Icahn presents a very unusual profile as a political actor. He has recently become heavily committed to speech and action on one relatively narrow issue related to the taxation of multinational businesses. In addition, he has expressed a blend of fiscally conservative concerns about the Federal Reserve, populist concerns about the fate of the middle class, and liberal or progressive concerns about inequality. This profile makes Icahn a fascinating political figure, one who (like campaigner Trump) has combined a definite lack of adherence to the orthodoxies of either major political party with a high level of wealth and fame that enables him to command attention for his views when he wants to command it. Icahn's early political silence and inactivity may reflect the fact that, before Trump, there was no major political figure—Republican or Democratic—who shared Icahn's more-or-less populist mixture of views and could win Icahn's verbal and financial support.

In terms of measurement concerns, Icahn presents no particular problems for our account of stealth politics. We have found no evidence of coding errors or missed political speeches or actions during the period covered by our quantitative analyses. More substantively, Icahn's significant media footprint during the period covered by our searches—together with his subsequent vociferous (and unconventional) speech and action—tend to confirm our general points that billionaires have easy access to the media, and that billionaires who hold less unpopular opinions tend to speak out more. At the same time, Icahn's case reminds us that actors can and do change their profiles of political speech and participation, in reaction to shifts in the national political context, their personal situations, or for other reasons.

From a broader analytic point of view, Icahn may actually have little to do with the stealth politics theory one way or the other. The theory may simply not apply. Icahn's somewhat populist policy views—while representing an increasingly important ideological strand in American and Western European politics—do not fit neatly along the economic liberal-conservative political continuum around which some of the theory's predictions are built.[54] Icahn's fit with the stealth politics framework is also complicated by the related fact that several of Icahn's stands were less unpopular with the general public than the extreme economic conservatism of most billionaires. When Icahn has taken on potentially unpopular positions, such as his most apparently *self-interested* stand (in favor of cutting taxes on corporations when they repatriate profits, which would add to the value of his companies with big overseas cash reserves), he has been somewhat shielded from consumer or political punishment by his distance from the companies he had invested in. Hence, Icahn's early silence was probably not motivated by the fear of popular disapproval that provides the main motivation for stealth politics. Instead, as we have suggested, Icahn may have been silent and inactive because the world of American politics did not then resonate with his populist worldview. But when Donald Trump appeared on the political scene, Icahn suddenly found a major ally and a motive for acting and speaking out vigorously.

This suggests that if Trump, Steve Bannon, or others should manage to reshape American politics around support or opposition to right-wing populism, or if many other populist billionaires emerged, our theory might need to be modified accordingly. But in the predominantly economically liberal versus economically conservative political world that existed at the time of our study (and persists at the time we are writing), the stealth politics theory accounts well for the behavior of most billionaires—who, on economic issues, generally range along a continuum from extreme conservative to left-centrist. The theory simply does not apply to an individual like Icahn who holds quirky or populist views. If one wanted to modify the theory to apply to Icahn, one might conceptualize the holding of populist views as an omitted variable that—in an economically liberal versus conservative world—should be included as a predictor of political silence and inactivity.

David Koch

David Koch and his brother Charles were tied at the #4 position on the *Forbes* list of wealthiest Americans in fall 2013. Each had a net worth of $36,000,000,000.[55] As of fall 2016, David's net worth had risen to $42,000,000,000, and it jumped to $48,500,000,000 by the autumn of 2017, although—as high-tech billionaires' fortunes climbed even faster—Charles and David Koch then stood at just #6 on the *Forbes* list, below Gates, Bezos, Buffett, Zuckerberg, and Ellison.[56]

David Koch is the executive vice president and a principal owner of Koch Industries, a privately held conglomerate founded by his father, Fred, that has holdings in a wide range of industries, including energy, manufacturing, agriculture, and financial services. Koch Industries has grown substantially—both before and after Fred's sons took it over. It is now the second-largest privately held company in the United States, bringing in over $100 billion in revenue annually.[57] As a privately held company, Koch Industries does not have to disclose much detailed information about its operations, and the Kochs have tended to be as secretive about their businesses as they are about their political activities. Koch Industries appears to value growth above all. (We earlier mentioned that it regularly reinvests some 90 percent of its earnings.) Koch Industries has been described as a "giant private equity fund . . . looking to invest wherever it sees potential for long-term profits."[58] It expanded into electronics in late 2013, through a $7.2 billion acquisition of Molex, which makes parts for a range of consumer electronics products. More quietly (through Koch Membrane Services) it has made substantial investments in water bottling and supply—a play that has been described as laying the "foundation of a privatized water industry."[59] Despite its closely guarded secrets, it is clear that Koch's business interests are wide ranging.

We selected David Koch for close study because he was the most deviant case in our regression predicting the ideological direction of policy-related actions in the opposite direction from Carl Icahn. That is, David Koch's policy-specific actions related to taxes and Social Security were farther to the political *right* than predicted by the model. Unlike several other of the very wealthiest billionaires, Koch is definitely not center-left on economic issues. He is a hard-line economic conservative.

David Koch is now well known for his involvement in politics. Decades ago, David and (more actively) his brother Charles began quietly funding a libertarian intellectual network built around conservative economist James Buchanan and (eventually) centered at the Cato Institute and in various institutes at George Mason University in Virginia. That network became highly influential in promoting a libertarian variant of "public choice" theory. It contributed to changing college curricula and public discourse, and very likely succeeded at reshaping how a good many Americans think about the desirability of minimizing the size and activity of government.[60]

More recently, the Koch brothers have organized and funded literally dozens of political organizations and think tanks focused on public policy, the most prominent of which is Americans for Prosperity (AFP). As discussed further in chapter 5, AFP and related groups have pumped hundreds of millions of dollars into politics each election cycle (they announced plans to spend just under $900 million on the 2016 elections).[61] And the Kochs do not just make campaign contributions: their organizations run very sophisticated operations that actually rival the functions of political parties.[62] Koch groups almost exclusively support conservative Republican candidates and ideologically conservative causes.

Koch mainly contributes dark money that is not reported to the FEC. This makes his political activities difficult to follow. However, owing to energetic efforts by investigative journalists and scholars—most notably by journalist Jane Mayer, a team at the *Washington Post*, and Theda Skocpol and her research group—much more is now known about the extent of Koch's political activities, including his dark-money contributions, than is known about the political activities of most billionaires.[63]

For example, the political network coordinated by David Koch and his brother (again: Charles is actually the more active one[64]) is known to have contributed about $412,000,000 in the 2012 electoral cycle, approximately as much as the combined contributions of the entire US labor union movement.[65] The Kochs' core organization, AFP, provided much of the initial logistical, organizational, and financial support for the Tea Party movement during the early years of the Obama administration.[66] The overall strength of the Koch network has been described as rivaling the strength of the Republican Party.[67]

The Kochs have also supported many different conservatively oriented political actions, including efforts to roll back unionization in Wisconsin and Michigan and to prevent federal taxes and regulations aimed at combating climate change.[68] Taxes or regulations designed to cut greenhouse gas emissions or other forms of pollution would raise costs for Koch Industries' core businesses in oil extraction and refining, chemicals, and paper. The Kochs and Koch Industries have engaged in a number of tussles with the Environmental Protection Agency and other regulators over their emissions of toxic waste, oil spills, and the like.[69]

Despite his heavy involvement in political action, David Koch is relatively quiet in public about politics and is very vague about his policy preferences when he does speak. Our original web-scraping procedure identified only one statement in which Koch revealed a specific policy preference related to taxes or Social Security. Our subsequent closer look—not restricted to the focused keywords of our systematic web searches—did reveal that David Koch and his brother Charles have often spoken in general terms about politics, offering support to the generally center-right concepts of "economic freedom" and a "free society," as well as voicing libertarian opposition to "crony capitalism." Charles speaks out more frequently than David does, but even in Charles's statements it is generally difficult to identify specific policy stances.

Nonetheless, David Koch did in fact—long ago—actually take highly visible positions on public policy. Back in 1979 Koch offered himself as a candidate for the vice presidency under the Libertarian Party label. (The party happily accepted, since Koch also offered to pour his own money into the 1980 Libertarian campaign.[70]) As part of his campaign announcement to party members, Koch stated that the legal regime imposing restrictions on campaign contributions (from which, with respect to his own campaign, he was exempt) "makes my blood boil." After receiving the nomination, Koch ran on a hard-line, economically conservative party platform that advocated the repeal of many taxes and the abolition of many government agencies. He gave a major policy speech in which he denounced the Carter administration's energy policies, including taxes on oil imports.[71] Yet these statements were made more than three decades ago. In all the years since then, David Koch has rarely made even remotely explicit policy arguments. Hence our web-scraping search process, which found no relevant statements for David Koch, accurately reflected the political posture he adopted during our study period and over a period of at least three decades.

Given the extent of Koch's behind-the-scenes political involvement—on behalf of candidates whose positions on taxes and Social Security are far more conservative than those of average citizens—and his lack of public discussions of policy, Koch's recent behavior constitutes a prominent *attempt at* stealth politics. (Success is another matter. In recent years, many of Koch's political activities have been widely publicized.)

The public statements that Koch and his brother do make appear to be intentionally designed to obscure their political aims. Their language is usually unspecific, vaguely appealing, and very difficult to oppose. Who, after all, does not want a "free society"? A striking example of Koch rhetoric appeared in a 2016 *Washington Post* op-ed by Charles Koch.[72]

Referring to Bernie Sanders, Koch wrote: "The senator is upset with a political and economic system that is often rigged to help the privileged few
at the expense of everyone else, particularly the least advantaged. He believes that we have a two-tiered society that increasingly dooms millions
of our fellow citizens to lives of poverty and hopelessness. He thinks many
corporations seek and benefit from corporate welfare while ordinary citizens are denied opportunities and a level playing field. I agree with him."

Koch went out of his way to highlight his "agreement" with a political
figure whose liberal policy positions were polar opposites from the extremely conservative positions taken by Koch-led organizations and by the
candidates who receive Koch money. Later in that op-ed Koch wrote that
he disagreed with Sanders's "desire to expand the federal government's
control over people's lives," but he did not specify any particular implications of that disagreement for taxes or Social Security or any other policies (except, oddly, prison reform)—despite the great importance of taxes
and Social Security to redistributive policies.

A reexamination of Koch's statements collected through our systematic web-scraping procedure did not reveal any coding errors. Additional
open-ended searches, and an examination of Koch's statements subsequent to our quantitative analysis, did not reveal any measurement errors
either. Although David Koch—and, more often, his brother—sometimes
talks about politics in public, our web-scraping procedure did not miss
relevant political statements in which Koch took a clear policy stance on
taxes or Social Security.

Stealth Politics Confirmed

Our closer examination of a handful of billionaires has provided a useful
check on the systematic quantitative analyses discussed in other chapters
of this book. Fortunately, on the measurement front, the four individual
billionaires we looked at in depth yielded no evidence that we had missed
significant instances of public position taking in our earlier, systematic
process of web scraping. Our further look at Warren Buffett suggests that
billionaires who were coded as quite vocal may actually have spoken out
even a bit more often than we initially thought, but on the same issues and
with the same ideological orientation as in our systematic data collection.
Perhaps more important, the Menard, Koch, and Icahn cases indicate that
billionaires we coded as silent were indeed silent during the period covered by our searches.

For John Menard Jr., David Koch, and Carl Icahn, our additional open-ended searches and close qualitative scrutiny of statements provided no evidence of any policy-relevant public speech that had been missed earlier. Icahn and Koch did take policy stands before or after the period for which the quantitative data were gathered. But we found no evidence that these billionaires, whom we had coded as silent, actually spoke up during the studied period. If they did so, they did it very quietly indeed.

In terms of financial contributions and other forms of direct, policy-focused political action related to taxes and Social Security, the case studies again confirmed the overall accuracy of measurements in our quantitative data. Billionaires did indeed spend money and support policy-oriented organizations in the ways that our systematic data indicated.

Beyond measurement issues, the case of Carl Icahn led us to reflect more deeply about the assumptions underlying the stealth politics theory. Why did the theory not apply well to a billionaire like Icahn with quirky or populist views? How might the theory be modified to account for Icahn?

In a nutshell: we suspect that both Icahn's early political silence and his anomalous political inactivity may have reflected a lack of motivation to participate, given the disharmony between the structure of his views and the basic dimensions of competition among other economic and political elites, until the ascendance of Donald Trump encouraged Icahn to burst forth into vociferous speech and action. We also suspect that if the political world were to change, or if many billionaires emerged holding views that did not fit on the usual economic liberal-to-conservative continuum, the theory of stealth politics might require serious alteration. To date we have seen no signs of such a transformation,[73] but the Icahn case offers a reminder that political and social theories are often dependent on historical context. When social or political reality changes, theories may need to change too.

Our case studies provided some interesting new information about political action by billionaires. Our studies of David Koch and John Menard Jr. revealed that some billionaires engage in forms of political activism that go far beyond financial contributions to campaigns or PACs. Billionaires can also deploy their business firms as political tools, as we saw in Menard's use of employment contracts and employee vocational training to fight unionization and try to inculcate conservative ideology. (Some billionaires may also direct corporations they own to lobby Washington for policies that fit the billionaires' personal priorities, rather than for the more usual corporate profit-maximizing purposes.[74] But we have no evidence one way or the other about this.) As the Koch case spectacularly illustrates, billionaires can also fund politically oriented foundations and think tanks, provide infrastructure and logistical support for social movements, build coalitions from the ground up, and indeed rival the power of major political parties.[75]

Billionaires, then, can try to leverage their economic assets to influence politics through methods that go far beyond campaign contributions. This suggests that the problem of billionaires' often stealthy attempts at political influence cannot be reduced solely to concerns about the *Citizens United* Supreme Court decision,[76] or to advocacy of campaign finance reform. Perhaps, as Anthony Downs once argued, economic inequality inevitably produces political inequality.[77] Perhaps, short of a drastic transformation of American society that would radically curtail citizens' ability to amass large fortunes—or would severely restrict their freedom to use those fortunes politically—it may be impossible to do anything to limit the political influence of billionaires. But we are not so sure.

In the final chapter of this book, we mention some reform proposals that would make it harder for billionaires to act stealthily, and other proposals that we believe could—if one wished to do so—markedly reduce the effectiveness of billionaires' political actions.

CHAPTER FOUR

Keeping Quiet on Social Issues

E conomic issues like taxation and Social Security greatly affect peoples' material well-being. But social, cultural, and religious issues like *abortion* and *same-sex marriage* often cut more deeply into peoples' most fundamental beliefs and identities. Some Americans see access to clinical abortions as crucial to sexual privacy, reproductive rights, and women's control over their own bodies, while others consider abortion to be a violation of God's will, a mortal sin. Some consider the right to marry a loved one of the same sex as following from the fundamental freedom to form a family and to express one's personal identity, while doing no harm to anyone else. Others see such marriage as indecent, immoral, and sinful.[1]

On such issues, emotions tend to run high. Since the political upheavals of the 1960s, public policies related to abortion and same-sex relationships have come to play central parts in American politics. Conflicts over "freedom to choose," "the right to life," "gay rights," and "traditional families" have sharply divided Americans from different geographic regions, different life circumstances, and different religious traditions. The prevailing American ideologies of "liberalism" and "conservatism" were once primarily economic, focusing on views concerning government economic regulation and social welfare programs. But liberal and conservative ideologies have gradually been redefined—within our two-party system, which tends to squeeze all issues onto a single dimension—to include many policies that touch on social, cultural, and religious values.[2]

When it comes to social issues like same-sex marriage or abortion, the politics of billionaires differ from their political behavior on economic issues like Social Security and taxes. To be sure, there are some similarities. On social issues, too, billionaires mostly stay very quiet in public. Few speak out about their policy preferences. Again, many billionaires are very active politically in ways that directly or indirectly affect public policy, so that similar questions about elusiveness and lack of political accountability arise. On social as well as economic issues, billionaires' hefty political influence is somewhat insulated from scrutiny or control by ordinary citizens.

But some of the *reasons* for billionaires' silence—and some of the normative implications of that silence—are different when it comes to abortion and same-sex marriage. One general motivation for avoiding political stands applies especially strongly to these very divisive issues: if billionaires spoke out loudly about them they would very likely offend many people on one side or another, provoking criticism and attacks that would make them uncomfortable and perhaps hurt business. On the other hand, on these social issues, billionaires—some with libertarian political philosophies— tend to be less distant from most Americans (a majority of whom favor rights to abortion under at least some circumstances,[3] and a majority of whom have moved in recent years toward accepting same-sex marriage[4]) than they are with their very conservative views on economic issues like taxes and Social Security. Moreover, on social issues, the billionaires are much less vulnerable to charges of pursuing their own narrow economic self-interests.

As a result, when we turn to abortion and same-sex marriage, we find different patterns concerning which billionaires speak out and which do not. On balance, billionaires may have somewhat less reason to conceal their stands.

Of course, consumer-facing businesses can face higher costs on these issues. This is indicated by our chapter 3 account of a boycott against one of Warren Buffett's businesses over its donations to Planned Parenthood, and by the widely discussed liberal effort to boycott Chick-Fil-A because of its donations to groups opposed to same-sex marriage.[5] Yet these two examples also suggest something about limits to public pressure concerning these kinds of social issues. The Buffett boycott was resolved by accounting changes such that the donations were given by Buffett personally rather than by his corporation, Berkshire Hathaway, so the boycott ended without any significant change in the targeted political behavior. The Chick-Fil-A boycott was counterbalanced by a movement of social conservatives supporting the restaurant chain. There may be inherent limits to the intensity of social pressures that billionaires face in this realm, because of the deep divisions within the general American citizenry on these issues. By contrast, for a billionaire to openly advocate sharp cuts in Social Security benefits would provoke nearly universal public condemnation.

As one might expect, based on reduced prospects of social or economic pressure on billionaires in the social realm, here they display less disjunction between speech and action. With respect to abortion and same-sex marriage—as opposed to taxes and Social Security—billionaires less often engage in stealth politics. We find no evidence that many billionaires work for policies opposed by large majorities of Americans and deliberately conceal their policy preferences for that reason.

The story is somewhat different when it comes to what billionaires say and do about *immigration policy*, which combines both social and economic elements. The immigration policy case helps illuminate under what circumstances and why billionaires do or do not pursue stealth politics.

Most billionaires *do* disagree markedly with majorities of Americans about immigration policy. Socially, few billionaires share the cultural anxieties of those middle-class and working-class Americans who fear or resent "foreigners" in their midst. Billionaires generally live in separate, affluent neighborhoods and send their children to separate private schools. Few billionaires fear job or wage competition from immigrants. In fact, many billionaires benefit from immigration by hiring immigrants as low-wage workers. So, many billionaires have reasons to work actively for pro-immigration policies but to conceal what they are doing. Stealthy—or at least *semistealthy*—politics returns.

Studying Billionaires' Words and Actions on Social Issues

Since it is not feasible to interview a representative sample of the very wealthiest Americans on social issues (or anything else[6]), we once again turned to the same systematic, internet-based web-scraping techniques described in chapter 2. Once again we sought to uncover all publicly recorded words and actions by the one hundred wealthiest US billionaires—in this case, all their words and actions related to the social issues of abortion and same-sex marriage and the mixed issue of immigration.

As with taxes and Social Security, we focused on words or actions related to *specific policies* within these broad policy domains. On abortion, for example, we wanted to find out what the billionaires said or did about legal prohibitions of "partial birth" abortions, or about parental consent requirements, or about any other type of law or regulation designed to limit or to protect abortion rights. On same-sex marriage, we looked for billionaires' words and actions concerning any policies that would affect civil unions, domestic partnerships, or legal marriages by same-sex couples. On immigration, we sought to discover what the billionaires said or did about specific policies related to levels of legal or illegal immigration; immigration "reform" proposals, such as those concerning paths to citizenship for undocumented workers; measures for border protection; deportation rules and procedures; work visas for highly skilled immigrants; naturalization rules; the DREAM Act for those brought to the United States as children; and any others. We designed our web searches to unearth any general references to one of the broad issue areas as well as any references to specific policies within each issue area.

If a billionaire said or did anything relevant, we wanted to find it. Every publicly reported utterance—whether a formal speech, a video, an op-ed, a letter to the editor, a journalistic interview, even an offhand or overheard comment—was fair game.

After conducting the same kind of semantic-field-based search process described in chapter 2, we ultimately settled on twelve keywords related to abortion, eleven related to same-sex marriage, and fifteen related to immigration. (For a full list of keywords used, see appendix 5.)

After developing this comprehensive list of keywords, we turned to the web and used Google News/General Web[7] to begin searching. Billionaire by billionaire, we searched for all relevant statements concerning each of our three types of social issues by each one of the one hundred wealthiest Americans.[8] We also employed the same strategies as used in chapter 2 to discover issue-specific political *actions*.

Active, Quiet, but Less Stealthy Billionaires

As we have seen, the wealthiest US billionaires are extremely active in a general political way, making many large contributions to political parties and candidates (mostly Republicans), and often acting as campaign fund-raisers.

In our research for this chapter, we found that a fair number of billionaires also engage in *policy-specific actions* on abortion, same-sex marriage, and immigration, mostly on the "liberal"[9] or libertarian side. They have much more often taken actions favorable than unfavorable toward same-sex marriage and immigration (especially immigration of high-skilled workers), though on abortion their actions have been evenly divided between pro-choice and pro-life.

As far as publicly reported *speech* goes, the wealthiest billionaires are rather quiet about specific social issues, just as we earlier found to be true of tax and Social Security policies. Very few billionaires have made multiple public statements. Most have said nothing at all. But when they have spoken out, an overwhelming majority of them have taken a liberal or libertarian position: pro-choice, supportive of same-sex marriage, or favorable toward immigration, particularly of skilled workers.

On these social issues, billionaires' actions have thus generally been in harmony with their publicly reported words. They have generally taken liberal or libertarian stands in both speech and action. This suggests that they are not acting in the "stealthy" fashion that we found for tax and Social Security policies, where moderate words by a very few prominent, relatively liberal billionaires have provided a misleading picture of all billionaires' preferences—given the unpopular, highly conservative (but generally hidden) actions on economic policies that others have taken.

Our statistical analyses tend to confirm the absence of stealthiness on social issues. Yet billionaires' behavior concerning immigration has been somewhat different, perhaps semistealthy. And, as we will argue below, silence about important issues of public policy by major political actors can have unfortunate consequences whether it is deliberately stealthy in our sense or not.

A Great Deal of General Political Activity

Just as resource theories of political engagement would predict[10] (and as we reported in chapter 2), billionaires tend to be very active politically, especially in making financial contributions and soliciting contributions from others.

Remarkably, for example, our earlier searches revealed that *more than one-third* (36 percent) of the one hundred wealthiest billionaires hosted political fund-raisers and/or bundled others' contributions to political causes. Bundling is a high-level form of political activity that often wins a bundler direct access to top-ranking public officials. Within the US population as a whole, bundling is extremely rare. Even among the top 1 or 2 percent of US wealth holders, only about one-fifth have reported bundling.[11] Billionaires stand at the very pinnacle of activity in American politics.

Billionaires have a lot of money to give to political causes. As we noted in chapter 2, fully 92 percent of the one hundred wealthiest billionaires made at least one FEC-reportable federal or state political contribution between 2001 and 2012 (recall table 2.4). Money giving is much less common in the general population or even among multimillionaires,[12] and of course the billionaires' average annual total of $509,248 per person in reportable contributions between 2001 and 2012 dwarfed what ordinary Americans could hope to give. It is also important to remember that our figures deal only with *reportable* contributions, not unreported dark money, so that billionaires' total political contributions have undoubtedly been substantially higher.[13]

As one would expect of very wealthy people, most billionaires (64 percent of those who made partisan or ideological contributions) contributed primarily or exclusively to Republicans. The bulk of their money (an average of $384,121 annually) went to Republicans or conservative groups, as opposed to the $110,820 that went to Democratic or liberal groups, parties, or candidates. There is good reason to believe that billionaires' general political contributions have helped bring about victories by Republicans in state, local, and federal races around the country. By the same token, billionaires' contributions to the Republican Party and Republican candidates have almost certainly facilitated conservative-leaning policy decisions on the issues of abortion and same-sex marriage—even though rather few billionaires may have intended to have those particular effects.

Substantial Actions Focused on Specific Social Issues

As compared to general contributions to political parties or candidates, highly issue-specific, policy-oriented contributions to particular political causes tend to be smaller and less frequent. Yet, as table 4.1 indicates, a fair number of the one hundred wealthiest billionaires have made a contribution to (or otherwise supported) an organization with a narrow mission that took a clear stand on each of our three social issues. Sixteen of them (16 percent) acted on same-sex marriage; 11 percent acted on immigration; and 8 percent took one or more policy-related actions on abortion. More than one-quarter of the billionaires—27 percent of them—acted on one or more of the three social issues.

A striking feature of table 4.1 is the indication of substantial *libertarian* or socially liberal action among billionaires. Those who engaged in policy-related action were evenly divided (4 to 4) on abortion. But their actions tilted heavily (12 to 4) toward favoring same-sex marriage. Some, like Amazon's Jeff Bezos, took *big* action: Bezos donated $2.5 million in support of Washington State's same-sex marriage referendum. Similarly,

TABLE 4.1 **Frequencies of Policy-Related Actions on Social Issues**

	Issue		
Direction of Stance	Abortion	Same-Sex Marriage	Immigration
Pro	4	12	11
Con	4	4	0

Note: Entries are the number of billionaires who took one or more policy-related actions of a given type.

billionaires' actions overwhelmingly (11 to 0) went toward supporting current or increased levels of immigration. Again some—like Facebook's Mark Zuckerberg—took major action: Zuckerberg created the immigration-reform-centric lobbying group FWD.us. This fits well with scholars' findings that more-affluent Americans tend to be more socially liberal. It also fits with our impression that many or most billionaires are libertarians—liberal on social issues but conservative on economic issues.

Few Public Statements about Social Issues

As we have noted, it is easy for billionaires to speak out about public policy if and when they want to. Many journalists and bloggers would be happy to publicize their remarks. It would probably be good for society if they did speak out: as highly respected, knowledgeable figures, many billionaires probably have a great deal that they could contribute to collective deliberation. Furthermore, given their high levels of political activity and (presumably) their substantial political influence, democratic norms of political accountability would seem to dictate that billionaires should make known what they are trying to get the government to do. We believe that billionaires should feel a duty—and perhaps should be obliged, as big-money givers and important political actors—to open their views to public challenge and debate.

On the other hand, we have noted reasons why billionaires might prefer silence. Social issues, though less entangled with self-interest than economic issues, are often highly controversial. Controversy can be unpleasant. Although we have suggested that there may be limits to dangers from one-sided pressures concerning social issues, there might be money at stake. Taking a political position might lead to a loss of support from angry customers, shareholders, or business associates. Silence might be safer.

TABLE 4.2 **Frequencies of Statements on Social Issues**

Number of Statements (Across Issues)	Number of Billionaires
23	1
8	1
7	1
6	3
5	1
4	2
3	0
2	6
1	14
0	71

It turns out that on social issues—just as on economic and social welfare policies—silence generally prevails. Our exhaustive web searches revealed that, over a roughly ten-year period,[14] fully 71 percent—nearly three-quarters—of the one hundred wealthiest Americans *said nothing whatsoever* in public about specific policies related to any of the three social issues we studied: abortion, same-sex marriage, or immigration.

This is definitely not a reflection of indifference to these issues throughout American society. Policies related to abortion, same-sex marriage, and immigration were widely and intensely debated during the years we covered. A Google News search using the keyword "abortion," for example, returned over 6.6 million results, while "immigration" generated 24.2 million, and a cluster of three search terms related to same- sex marriage produced over 10 million.[15] By way of comparison, "taxes" produced 24 million results, while "Social Security" generated 13 million. Thus there is plenty of evidence of sustained public discourse on each of these issues— and evidence that the discussion on social issues has been of roughly the same magnitude as that on economic themes. But fewer than one-third— just 29 percent—of the billionaires took any part whatsoever in those public debates (see table 4.2).

Moreover, with a single exception (Michael Bloomberg), those billionaires who spoke at all about our social issues said very little about them. Bloomberg, a political candidate and then mayor of New York—where he was no doubt expected to voice his views on these issues as a matter of course—was our champion talker, with a total of twenty-three remarks, statements, or writings that touched upon the three social issues.

Bloomberg was also the only billionaire who took policy-related actions on all three issues.

Hardly any other billionaires said much at all. Mark Zuckerberg made eight statements; Rupert Murdoch made seven; Bill Gates, Warren Buffett, and Sheldon Adelson made six statements each; Steve Ballmer made five; and David Koch and Laurene Powell Jobs each made four statements. No billionaires other than these nine made more than two statements—over a ten-year period—concerning all three social issues taken together. Another twenty billionaires made just a skimpy one or two statements each. Finally, as noted earlier, seventy-one of our one hundred billionaires said nothing at all (see table 4.2 and appendix 4).

It seems accurate to say, then, that the wealthiest billionaires have generally been *very quiet* about these important, hotly debated social issues.

When the billionaires have spoken out about social issues, they have overwhelmingly taken a socially liberal or libertarian side. On abortion, they made pro-choice rather than pro-life statements by a ratio of six to two[16] (see table 4.3). Supporters of same-sex marriage far outnumbered opponents, by thirteen to two. On immigration, quite a few speakers made a distinction that we will discuss further below: seven of the sixteen who spoke out favored maintaining or increasing immigration only for *skilled* workers. (Another two strongly emphasized increasing immigration for skilled workers, but also voiced support for a pathway to citizenship for unskilled undocumented immigrants.) But nearly as many (seven) advocated increasing immigration generally. Not a single one of the sixteen billionaires

TABLE 4.3 **Frequencies of Statements on Abortion, Same-Sex Marriage, and Immigration**

Abortion		Same-Sex Marriage		Immigration	
Direction of Stance	Count	Direction of Stance	Count	Direction of Stance	Count
Pro-choice	6	Support same-sex marriage	13	Increase immigration	7
Pro-life with exceptions	0	Support civil unions	0	Increase only for skilled workers + path to citizenship	2
State issue	1	State issue	0	Support only for skilled workers	7
Pro-life	1	Oppose same-sex marriage	2	Decrease immigration	0

Note: Statements about at least one issue were made by 29 billionaires out of the 100 billionaires we studied. Entries are the number of billionaires who made one or more statements of a given type.

who spoke out about immigration advocated the position—highly popular among the American public—that immigration should be *decreased*.[17]

Some examples of what the billionaires had to say: On same-sex marriage, Warren Buffett declared, "Certainly, our managers know how I feel. I am 100 percent for full rights, in every respect, for gays and lesbians."[18] Similarly, eBay cofounder Pierre Omidyar strongly criticized California gubernatorial candidate Meg Whitman's support for the anti–same-sex marriage Proposition 8.[19] Mark Zuckerberg reacted to the Supreme Court's decision to legalize same-sex marriage nationwide by stating, "Our country was founded on the promise that all people are created equal, and today we took another step towards achieving that promise."[20] On abortion, Michael Bloomberg said, "I happen to be very much pro-choice. I'm not in favor of abortion, but I do think it's totally up to the woman's right to choose."[21]

Interestingly, some notable billionaires who—on economic issues— are strongly *conservative*, espoused pro-choice views and/or pro–same-sex marriage views but also implied that such views are not particularly important to them. David Koch, for example, acknowledged to Barbara Walters that he supports both abortion rights and same-sex marriage, but indicated that those issues do not factor into his decisions to support candidates. Walters asked, "You support gay rights. You support a woman's right to choose. But conservative candidates you support, many of them, do not have those views." Koch replied by agreeing with Walters but immediately shifting to economic issues, saying, "That's their problem. I do have those views. What I want these candidates to do is to support a balanced budget. I'm very worried that if the budget is not balanced that inflation could occur and the economy of our country could suffer terribly."[22] Somewhat similarly, Sheldon Adelson said to the *Wall Street Journal* that, on abortion, "We're [he and his wife] pro-abortion rights" but indicated that he continues to support the GOP, because of its anti-union policies, which are apparently much more important to him.[23]

On immigration, billionaires who spoke out often did so from a business-oriented perspective. For example, former Microsoft CEO and current NBA basketball team owner Steve Ballmer said, "It does get complicated in the US because of broader immigration issues, particularly immigration from Mexico. The two—visas for skilled workers and illegal immigrants— have nothing to do with each other, but politically, they probably need to be addressed together. We are certainly prepared to participate in a discussion for a broader immigration reform, which allows us to bring in high-tech talent."[24] Similarly, Leonard Lauder of cosmetics giant Estée Lauder wrote in a *Wall Street Journal* op-ed, "Our visa system makes it extremely difficult for anyone with a great business idea to come here and stay. Our universities are teaching many more brilliant young foreigners, yet our immigration system often prevents them from remaining here after graduating. We should be creating incentives and opportunities for foreign students to remain in the United States—especially those in critical fields like science, engineering, and technology."

Even most of the billionaires who support increased immigration more broadly (that is, beyond just programs like the H-1B visa that targets specialty occupations) spoke about immigration in economic terms. For example, Bloomberg, an immigration proponent, framed his support for the DREAM Act and his opposition to deportations by saying, "Ending deportations of innocent young people who have the potential to drive tomorrow's economy is long overdue, as are many common-sense reforms needed to center our immigration policy around our economic needs."[25]

Considering all three social issues, billionaires' statements, as well as their policy-specific actions, generally accord with evidence from various sources that affluent Americans—though mostly economically conservative—tend to be socially liberal.[26] That is, combining the evidence here of billionaires' social liberalism with the evidence in chapter 2 of their widespread economic conservatism, many billionaires appear to be *libertarians*.

Of course that does not mean that the billionaires treat social and economic issues as equally important. Billionaires' record of heavy contributions to Republican candidates (most of whom have, in recent years, been conservative on social as well as economic issues) suggests that many billionaires may adopt David Koch's position: they may swallow Republicans' social conservatism for the sake of the economic conservatism that they consider more vital.

A complete listing of our one hundred billionaires, together with the number and direction of statements and actions (if any) by each billionaire concerning each social issue, is given in appendix 4.

Harmony between Talk and Action

In chapter 2 we described a rather sharp contrast between the public statements made by a few of the wealthiest billionaires about taxes and Social Security (which tended to be moderate or liberal) and the policy-related actions of other billionaires, which were overwhelmingly conservative.

This played an important part in our conclusion that many billionaires engage in *stealth politics*: they quietly work for policies that are quite un-popular with the general public, while deliberately saying little or nothing in public about the specifics of those policies.

Not so with social issues. On policies concerning abortion, same-sex marriage and immigration, both the statements and (except for abortion) the policy-related actions of billionaires tilted strongly in the same direc-tion: a liberal or libertarian direction. This consistency largely carries through to the individual level. Many of the same billionaires who spoke out on these issues also took actions related to them, and their talk and action generally went in the same direction. Of the seven billionaires who both talked and acted on same-sex marriage, for example, six consistently expressed support, and one consistently expressed opposition. All seven billionaires who both talked and acted on immigration consistently fa-vored increasing immigration levels, either for skilled workers only or in general. Only two billionaires—David Koch and Harold Simmons—were inconsistent, in both cases concerning abortion. (Both were pro-choice in rhetoric but antiabortion in action; see appendix 4.)

This is one key reason why we judge the wealthiest one hundred bil-lionaires to be less stealthy on social issues than on taxes and Social Se-curity. Another reason is that their policy-related actions (with the excep-tion of immigration, to be discussed below) do not appear to be badly out of harmony with the views of majorities of the American public. Still another reason is that on the tax and Social Security issues, regression analyses concerning the direction of policy-related actions (with interac-tion terms for speech or silence) indicated that *non*speakers—as opposed to speakers—took distinctly more conservative, more unpopular actions, which they had incentives to conceal.[27] When we conducted parallel re-gression analyses for social issues, we found no such evidence.

Which Billionaires Speak and Act on Social Issues?

Wealth and Prominence

Even a cursory glance at appendix 4, which arrays our billionaires in de-scending order of their net worth, reveals that publicly reported statements and actions related to social issues tended to be most common among the very wealthiest billionaires. To put this more precisely: the simple correla-tion between number of statements a billionaire made (summed across all

TABLE 4.4 **Correlations of Wealth and Visibility with Statements and Actions on Social Issues**

	Wealth	Visibility
Statements		
Total	0.37	0.49
Abortion	0.19	0.20
Same-Sex Marriage	0.27	0.34
Immigration	0.39	0.55
Actions		
Total Action Index	0.32	0.56
Abortion	0.29	0.19
Same-Sex Marriage	0.17	0.38
Immigration	0.21	0.52

three sets of issues) and the magnitude of his or her wealth (the log of the total amount) is a substantial and highly significant 0.37. Similarly, the correlation between the number of social issues on which a billionaire took a policy-related *action* and the magnitude of that billionaire's wealth is a solid 0.32 (see table 4.4).

This may not seem at all surprising: the very wealthiest billionaires also tend to be the most prominent, the most reported on. No doubt they are pestered most insistently for quotes and scrutinized most closely for actions, since they are most likely to be of interest to broad audiences.

In order to check whether prominence rather than wealth is in fact the key factor, we devised a simple measure of visibility: we recorded the number of hits in Google News for a search of a billionaire's name plus the name of the main business from which his or her wealth was derived. We believe this to be a generally reliable (though rather blunt) instrument for measuring public visibility. We then used the logarithm of this variable (a measure of the *magnitude* of visibility) to estimate statistical relationships. By that measure, prominence or visibility is related even more closely than wealth to the number of statements made and actions taken concerning social issues. For total statements and total actions across all three issues, the correlation coefficients are a robust 0.49 and 0.56, respectively (see table 4.4).

The best test involves multivariate analysis. In regression analyses predicting the total number of statements and the total number of policy-focused actions that each billionaire took, by (at the same time) both the billionaire's wealth and his or her visibility, the visibility coefficients were highly significant (at the $p < .001$ level), but the wealth coefficients were nonsignificant even at the $p < .05$ level.[28] This indicates that celebrity, in the sense of prominence or visibility (affected, of course, by wealth)—more than wealth per se—directly affects how many statements and actions each billionaire takes on social issues.

We now turn to other factors that may affect the number and direction of statements and policy-related actions for each one of our three sets of issues: abortion, same-sex marriage, and—of particular interest—immigration, which in important respects differs from the others.

Talking and Acting on Abortion

As we have seen, only eight billionaires made public statements about abortion. (As table 4.4 indicates, there was a tendency—though not as strong a tendency as on other issues—for wealthier billionaires to make those statements.) We also saw in table 4.3 that most of these statements were pro-choice. The small number of statements, and the meager variation in direction, meant that it was impossible to sort out statistically the impact of various hypothesized factors on either the number or the direction of abortion statements. Numerous regression analyses failed to produce any statistically significant coefficients. For abortion statements, we were simply unable to test our expectation that (controlling for wealth or visibility), concerning heirs[29] and consumer-facing business, people[30] are less likely to speak out.

Much the same thing is true of abortion policy-related *actions*, which were taken by only eight billionaires. Here at least there was more variation in direction, with four billionaires taking pro-life actions and four taking pro-choice actions. But our one apparently productive regression analysis was almost certainly an artifact.[31] We cannot say anything with confidence except that the most highly visible billionaires are somewhat more likely to make statements and take actions related to abortion policy.

Same-Sex Marriage

We can say somewhat more about who spoke out or took action on same-sex marriage, where more billionaires made statements (fifteen did so) and/or took policy-specific actions (sixteen did so—see tables 4.1 and 4.3). Again the wealthiest billionaires spoke out most: the number of statements made tended to rise with level of wealth and especially with level of visibility. When both variables were included in the same regression, the coefficient

TABLE 4.5 **Regression Predicting Number of Same-Sex Marriage Statements**

	B (SE)	t-Value	Pr(>|t|)
(Intercept)	−0.7304 (0.3998)*	−1.83	0.0708
Wealth	0.0099 (0.0116)**	0.85	0.0370
Consumer Facing	−0.4212 (0.2572)	−1.64	0.1049
Heir	0.1144 (0.2844)	0.40	0.6883
Log(Visibility)	0.1590 (0.0591)***	2.69	0.0084

*$p < .1$.
**$p < .05$.
***$p < .01$.
Note: Residual standard error: 1.14 on 95 DF; multiple R-squared: 0.1509; adjusted R-squared: 0.1151; F-statistic: 4.22 on 4 and 95 DF; p-value: .003455.

for wealth dropped to less than half the value it had had by itself, though it remained barely statistically significant at the $p < .05$ level (see table 4.5).[32] Here we were able to test our expectation that heirs and billionaires with consumer-facing businesses tend (other factors being equal) to make fewer public statements. The coefficient for consumer-facing did not quite reach statistical significance according to standard criteria, but it was substantial and in the expected direction, indicating that being in a consumer-facing business may indeed tend to lead billionaires to be quieter in public about controversial policy issues. There was no sign at all in this regression that inheritors of wealth are more reluctant to speak out about public policy (a tiny coefficient with the "wrong" sign). But of course one might argue that the effects of being an heir work *through* a general aversion to visibility, which is accounted for here.[33] There is indeed evidence that some inheritors of great wealth, like the Mars candy family, work hard to avoid publicity of almost any kind. (Most members of the Mars family refuse to even be photographed, and the company's headquarters are located in an unmarked brick building.)[34]

We also analyzed same-sex-marriage-related *actions*. As table 4.6 shows, billionaires who spoke about same-sex marriage were moderately but significantly more likely to act in a pro–same-sex-marriage direction. This is evidence against the applicability of stealth politics; in contrast to economic issues, billionaires who speak on this key social issue are also likely to act—and are likely to act in ways consistent with their speech.

Furthermore, wealthier billionaires are more likely to have contributed money in support of same-sex marriage. In contrast to some other results in this chapter, auxiliary regression analysis showed that the effects of wealth are not replaced by visibility on the issue of same-sex marriage.

TABLE 4.6 **Regression Predicting Direction of Nonstatement Actions on Same-Sex Marriage**

	B (SE)	t-Value	Pr(>|t|)
(Intercept)	0.0857 (0.0754)	1.14	0.2586
Makes at Least One Relevant Statement	−0.6683 (0.2617)**	−2.55	0.0123
Consumer Facing	−0.0463 (0.0874)	−0.53	0.5978
Heir	0.0232 (0.0875)	0.27	0.7914
Wealth	−0.0089 (0.0038)**	−2.32	0.0225
At Least One Statement × Consumer Facing	0.2983 (0.2436)	1.23	0.2238
At Least One Statement × Heir	0.2728 (0.3139)	0.87	0.3871
At Least One Statement × Wealth	0.0121 (0.0085)	1.42	0.1591

**$p < .05$.
Note: Residual standard error: 0.3747 on 92 DF; multiple R-squared: 0.1589; adjusted R-squared: 0.09493; F-statistic: 2.483 on 7 and 92 DF; p-value: .02214.

Thus, the resource effect here is not merely a proxy for celebrity. Perhaps billionaires at all wealth levels support same-sex marriage at roughly the same levels, but the wealthiest billionaires have the most money to contribute to that cause.

Semistealthy Billionaires on Immigration

Policy issues related to immigration offer us a good opportunity to illuminate the different politics of social and economic issues and the conditions under which billionaires do or do not engage in stealth politics. Immigration combines a social dimension (cultural acceptance or rejection of foreigners, particularly from Mexico) with an economic dimension (enthusiasm for or dislike of immigration of workers from abroad, which may lower wages for competing domestic workers but which, by the same token, tends to lower labor costs for employers). On both dimensions, billionaires tend to hold quite different views from the average American.

For decades, most Americans have strongly opposed *illegal* immigration into the United States. Many have been upset about *legal* immigration as well.[35] As figure 4.1 demonstrates, national surveys by the Chicago Council on Global Affairs (CCGA) have regularly found—since they first started asking about it in 1994—that majorities of Americans have said "controlling and reducing illegal immigration" should be a "very important" goal of US foreign policy. Very large majorities have said it is at least "somewhat important."[36] Prior to 2012, CCGA surveys even regularly found majorities (but gradually declining majorities) of Americans saying that "large

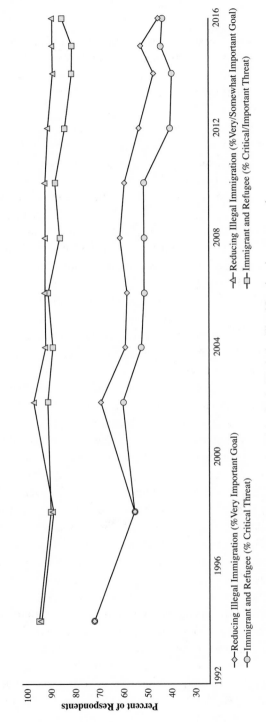

FIGURE 4.1 Perceived Threat of Immigration and Importance of the Goal of Reducing Illegal Immigration, 1994–2016

SOURCE: Chicago Council on Global Affairs, 2016 US Public Opinion Topline Report

—◇— Reducing Illegal Immigration (%Very Important Goal)
—○— Immigrant and Refugee (% Critical Threat)

—△— Reducing Illegal Immigration (%Very/Somewhat Important Goal)
—□— Immigrant and Refugee (% Critical/Important Threat)

Percent of Respondents

numbers of immigrants and refugees coming into the United States" constitute a "critical threat" to the "vital interest" of the United States. In 2002, for example, 60 percent said so. Rather remarkably, in that year a higher proportion of Americans felt that immigration was a "critical threat" than perceived a such a threat from China becoming a world power, or from global economic competition, or from global warming.[37]

Donald Trump's successful 2016 campaign for the presidency was fueled to an important extent by his strident opposition to immigration from Mexico (Trump repeatedly promised to build a "beautiful wall" to keep out rapists and other criminals) or from predominantly Muslim countries (he promised a "Muslim ban" that would shut out possible terrorists).[38] Trump's success in defeating both Republican and Democratic opponents in 2016 may have resulted in part from his noisy repudiation of both parties' long-standing pro-immigration and pro-free-trade stands.[39]

Among ordinary Americans, worries about immigration are based on at least three different types of reasons: security-related, economic, and cultural. One set of reasons involves fears that terrorists may slip into the United States undetected, perhaps among refugees from war-torn countries in the Middle East. Another concern is that economic competition from low-wage immigrants may take jobs away from native-born Americans or undercut their wages. A third set of worries involves cultural anxieties—stresses felt about interacting with people who speak a foreign language, engage in unfamiliar customs and behavior, or are just plain disliked for racist or other reasons. Analysts have found that cultural, economic, and security-related concerns each have substantial independent effects on attitudes about immigration.[40]

Billionaires are different. For one thing, they probably worry less about terrorist acts by immigrants. Billionaires are likely to be aware that no immigrants committed terrorist acts in the United States over the course of a decade, and that stringent security measures are taken at our borders (e.g., international cooperation in scrutinizing airline flights for passengers on terrorist watch lists). And billionaires often have their own protected homes and workplaces, with private security arrangements that cannot totally negate terrorist threats but probably reduce anxiety. Billionaires also have much less reason than other Americans to feel cultural anxieties about immigration from Mexico or elsewhere, since they can choose their own neighborhoods (often segregated gated communities or expensive highrise condominiums); they can pick their own associates (mostly people like themselves or employees they select and control); and they can choose which schools their children attend (often exclusive private schools).

TABLE 4.7 **Regression Predicting Number of Immigration Statements**

	B (SE)	t-Value	Pr(>|t|)
(Intercept)	−1.5993 (0.4570)	−3.50	0.0007
Wealth	0.0280 (0.0127)**	2.22	0.0291
Consumer Facing	−0.4163 (0.2836)	−1.47	0.1454
Heir	0.45167 (0.3123)	1.45	0.1514
Log(Visibility)	0.2407 (0.0712)***	3.38	0.0010
Tech	0.8389 (0.3907)**	2.15	0.0344

**p < .05.
***p < .01.
Note: Residual standard error: 1.242 on 94 DF; multiple R-squared: 0.3876;
adjusted R-squared: 0.3551; F-statistic: 11.9 on 5 and 94 DF; p-value: 6.231e–09.

Perhaps most importantly, billionaires tend to differ sharply from other Americans in their economic concerns and economic interests. Nearly all billionaires are primarily *employers*, not wage workers or salaried employees. None have any serious reason to fear that economic competition from immigrants will undercut their incomes or wealth. Indeed, for many billionaires, high levels of immigration by low-wage immigrants can markedly reduce the labor costs incurred by their businesses. This is especially true of billionaires who own high-tech computer or software firms, which benefit greatly from highly skilled but relatively low-salary workers from India and elsewhere. (Research has indicated that such immigration on special H-1B visas puts substantial downward pressure on computer science job salaries in the United States, while increasing profits for the tech companies.[41]) Similarly, however, high levels of immigration by *lower-skilled* workers tend to increase the profits of wealthy Americans who employ less skilled, low-wage immigrant workers in lower-tech manufacturing, retail, or agricultural businesses.[42]

Thus, few billionaires have reasons to oppose immigration, and many have good economic reasons to support it. That is presumably why we found so many of our billionaires (fifteen of them) speaking out in favor of immigration—especially *high-skilled* immigration—and none at all opposed. Also the reason we found so many (eleven) billionaires taking policy-specific actions in favor of immigration, while no billionaires at all took action against it. (Recall tables 4.1 and 4.3.)

We were able to test the proposition about economic motives more directly through the regression analysis presented in table 4.7. This regression includes a "tech" variable based on whether or not a billionaire's chief business involves the technology sector—where high-skilled immigrants, such as English-speaking engineers from India, are in particularly high demand. The tech variable had a substantial, statistically significant coefficient, indicating that billionaires with high-tech businesses do indeed tend to make statements about immigration—all of which favor immigration of high-skilled workers, and about half of which favor *only* high-skilled immigration. This pattern generally aligns with the findings of David Broockman, Gregory Ferenstein, and Neil Malhotra's study of wealthy elites in the technology industry: that tech entrepreneurs are much more "liberal" on immigration than the general public.[43]

In table 4.7 one can also see the familiar finding that higher visibility leads to more public statements. The most prominent, most visible billionaires tended to speak out more often (always favorably) about immigration. Taking account of billionaires' visibility, the extent of their wealth had a modest but significantly positive impact as well. Perhaps this is because the wealthiest billionaires have the fewest reasons for cultural anxiety about immigration (they live the most sheltered lives[44]) and the biggest economic stakes in high levels of immigration (owning more businesses, they tend to profit more from low-wage labor). We did not find any definite effect of owning consumer-facing businesses, though the coefficient was moderately large and in the expected direction; nor any effect of being an heir (a nonsignificant coefficient with the wrong sign).

It appears likely that the pro-immigration preferences of billionaires— and/or the preferences of affluent or elite Americans more generally[45]— have had an important impact on public policy. How else can we explain the fact that public officials, Republican and Democratic alike, for decades defied the wishes of most Americans and embraced high levels of legal immigration?[46] Relatively open immigration policies, together with policies favoring free trade without much help for those negatively affected by it (another issue on which there have been large gaps between masses and elites), played a big part in fueling recent right-wing populist revolts, from Brexit and anti-immigrant nationalist movements in Europe to the election of Donald Trump in the United States.[47]

It has been suggested that the political behavior of wealthy Americans on immigration, trade, social spending, and certain other issues may have been "greedy and short-sighted."[48] Billionaires' and multimillionaires' insistence on pursuing very unpopular economic policies does appear to have contributed to major tensions—revealed, taken advantage of, and exacerbated by Trump—among various factions of Republican donors, activists, and voters, and between orthodox GOP policies and the American public as a whole.

We see our findings about immigration policy as adding up to a picture of semistealthy politics by billionaires. On immigration, as in the cases of tax and Social Security policies, billionaires have been very active politically in ways that have probably had substantial effects on policy making. As in those cases, the wealthiest billionaires appear to be highly unified in their preferences (not one made a statement or took a policy-specific action aimed at *decreasing* levels of immigration), so that billionaires as a group may have had maximum influence on policy. On immigration policies—as on tax and Social Security policies—billionaires nearly all appear to favor policies that are opposed to the views of most ordinary Americans. And on immigration as well as on taxes and Social Security, most billionaires have been extremely quiet in public about their views and actions.

Yet certain features of stealth politics are not present. The contrast between private actions and public positions is less extreme; the (limited) public face of billionaires' views is less misleading; and there is little or no evidence of inconsistency between individual billionaires' rhetoric and their actions. On immigration policy, billionaires' politics seem to fall somewhere between the stealthiness they pursue on purely economic policies and their mere quietness on purely social policies. With respect to immigration, billionaires tend to be *semistealthy.*

How should we react to this? On the more purely social policies (abortion, same-sex marriage), is unstealthy quietness perfectly OK? We do not believe so.

The Problem with Quiet Politics by Billionaires

Our data make clear that the wealthiest one hundred US billionaires tend to be highly active politically. Most give substantial amounts of money to political causes, chiefly to Republicans and conservative groups. Remarkably, more than one-third of the billionaires we have studied held political fund-raisers or bundled others' contributions.

Billionaires' financial contributions to parties and candidates and their bundling probably have had significant effects on public policy decisions. For example, the Republican candidates that billionaires have supported have nearly all opposed abortion under almost any circumstances. Nearly all Republican officials, during the period we studied, opposed legalizing same-sex marriage or in any way accepting homosexual behavior. [49] And nearly all favored high levels of immigration, especially high-skilled immigration.

To be sure, the orthodox Republican positions on abortion and same-sex marriage went against many billionaires' own preferences, but most billionaires appear to have put a higher priority on economics. Most of them decided to back Republican politicians anyhow. A few billionaires may have tried to funnel their support selectively to candidates—especially Republicans, when they could be found—who took more liberal or libertarian positions on abortion and gay rights.[50] But the money donated by billionaires as a group has almost certainly tended to push actual US policies in a restrictive ("conservative") direction on abortion and same-sex marriage, while going in a socially "liberal" (though economically conservative) direction favorable to immigration.

A fair number of the wealthiest billionaires have also taken direct, policy-focused political actions on one or more of the three social issues we studied, by making financial contributions to, leading, or belonging to policy-oriented organizations that seek to affect government policies on those issues. In nearly every case, the billionaires' direct actions tended to influence policy making in directions favorable to abortion rights, to legalizing same-sex marriage, and to maintaining or increasing high levels of immigration.

At the same time, a large majority of the wealthiest billionaires have, over a long period of time, maintained complete public silence about those issues. Our rigorous web searches, covering a roughly ten-year period, found *no statements whatsoever* about the specifics of any of the three types of social policies by seventy-one of the one hundred billionaires. Only one billionaire—Michael Bloomberg, a political candidate and mayor of New York—spoke out frequently concerning all three issues. Only an additional eight billionaires (most of them enjoying above-average wealth and visibility) made more than one or two statements about any of those issues over the ten-year period.

There can be little doubt that the billionaires' silence is deliberate. Billionaires are of great interest to millions of Americans. Any time they wish to speak out on public policy they can easily find a TV channel, a journalist, or a blogger to publicize their views. They certainly had plenty of time to speak out, during a ten-year period when the issues of abortion, same-sex marriage, and immigration were stirring fierce debate and prompting pundits, politicians, and others to fill the media with countless pronouncements about them. Yet the wealthiest one hundred US billionaires hardly participated in these debates at all.

The billionaires' general silence on these important social issues does not exactly match the stealthy behavior that we found in the realms of tax and Social Security policies. In those areas (especially Social Security benefits and estate taxes), public statements by a handful of the very wealthiest billionaires tended to create the impression that wealthy Americans hold moderate, even liberal views on economic issues, while in fact most billionaires quietly favor—and in many cases spend a great deal of money and effort to enact—highly unpopular policies like cutting guaranteed Social Security benefits.

In the realm of social issues the pattern is different. The billionaires have been quiet, but—with the partial exception of immigration issues— they have not been stealthy. They have had less reason to pursue stealth politics, because they are less out of harmony with average Americans on these issues (again except for immigration, particularly low-skilled immigration) than they are on taxation or Social Security policies.

Still, even absent full-scale stealth politics, we do not see this story as entirely a happy one. Billionaires' silence on social issues—or on any other major issues of public policy—deprives public deliberation of voices that might be helpful to everyone's thinking, the voices of highly intelligent, knowledgeable people who may have important things to say. Public discourse may be poorer without them.

More worrisome is the issue of *accountability*. If—as seems highly likely—billionaires in fact exert outsized influence in the making of public policy, a minimal condition for democratic accountability would seem to be that their views and actions should be open to public scrutiny. Do they have sound, public-regarding reasons for the policies they seek? Or are their actions based on misunderstandings (lack of touch with ordinary peoples' lives, for example), or upon narrow self-interest? It is hard for average citizens to examine, to criticize, or—if necessary—to try to counteract billionaires' political actions, if those actions have low visibility and if the billionaires do not speak out in public to justify them.

Anyone who—like ourselves—believes that the essence of democracy is political equality, and who favors an equal voice for each citizen in the making of public policy, is bound to be troubled by the accumulating evidence of "unequal democracy," in which the voices of affluent or wealthy Americans tend to be amplified.[51] But even those who stop short of advocating full majoritarian democracy would do well to think through the implications of a system in which money-based political influence is not accompanied by open discussion and accountability.

CHAPTER FIVE

Reshaping State and Local Politics

National politics gets most of the buzz, but state and local politics matter too. In our federal system, state governors, state legislatures, and county or municipal governments have primary responsibility for education—elementary, secondary, and college; for medical care; for streets, highways, police, and fire protection; and for much more. They even decide who gets to vote in federal as well as state elections; whether voting is made hard or easy; whether congressional district boundaries are drawn to be competitive or are gerrymandered for partisan advantage. The roughly $2.5 *trillion* that states, counties, towns, and cities spend every year amounts to nearly two-thirds as much as what the national government spends in total—on everything from Social Security and Medicare to national defense.[1]

Many billionaires play an active—though usually very quiet—part in funding candidates' campaigns for state and local offices. Some wealthy donors seek special favors from the states where they live or do business: tax breaks, state contracts, exemptions from regulations. Individually, the cost of each of those special favors may often seem small (if one considers a few million dollars small), but they probably add up across the country to many billions of dollars, dollars that most US taxpayers would not want to give away if they knew about them.

In certain states, including Wisconsin, Kansas, and North Carolina, billionaires' influence has gone much further than that. In those states, billionaires and organizations that they control have helped elect extremely wealthy-friendly governors and so many wealthy-friendly state legislators that the control of state governments has changed drastically, and economics-related public policy has veered in new, extremely conservative directions. It is no exaggeration to say that those billionaires have helped *reshape* state politics.

Often, billionaires' state and local activities are invisible to all but a few attentive observers. Indeed, the very obscurity and invisibility of state politics can be an advantage to wealthy donors and activists. If their efforts successfully escape public attention, they may be able to exert political influence without provoking resentment or opposition.

In this chapter we first take a general look at the state- and local-level political efforts of wealthy contributors, including major efforts to reshape state politics. We then focus on one particular political strategy, the strategy of "boundary control," which some billionaires have used with considerable success. In the boundary-control strategy, federal-level and state-level campaign contributions are coordinated so as to win state-level favors and benefits while warding off federal-level interference.

Billionaires in State and Local Politics

State and local governments are important both because the states enjoy primary (though not always exclusive) jurisdiction over many key areas of public policy, and because they often oversee the implementation of *federal* laws. That means that states (and local governments too) often have substantial discretion about how federal laws will actually work. For example—as the result of a Supreme Court decision[2]—the states get to decide whether or not to use the Affordable Care Act to extend Medicaid eligibility to lower-income Americans who make a little more money than the official poverty line. Beyond medical care, recent years have witnessed substantial policy changes in many states and cities around the country on a diverse range of issues—changes that stand in stark contrast to national-level gridlock.[3] To repeat: state and local politics matter.

Wealthy individuals may actually have more opportunities to have a big impact on political outcomes at lower levels than nationally. Billionaires are even bigger fish than usual in these smaller ponds. And the low visibility of state and local politics means that billionaires' efforts can often go largely undetected and unresisted.

Several political scientists have written about this phenomenon. For example, the localization of politics can serve as one means of what E. E. Schattschneider referred to as restricting the "scope" of political conflict, thereby shutting out much of the population and disproportionately benefiting pressure groups driven by narrow, upper-class interests.[4] Building on Schattschneider's ideas, Grant McConnell warned that a shift in power away from the national government to state governments can increase the power of elites, private organizations, and corporations to win self-interested benefits. As a general matter, McConnell argued that private interests tend to gain more influence as the "size of constituency" involved in governance decreases—as it does when moving from the national government down to lower levels of governance.[5]

One reason why individual billionaires are bigger fish at lower levels is that the total amount of money spent on elections (particularly in the many cases when those elections are not competitive[6]) is significantly less than the amount spent on national elections. So one billionaire's contributions constitute a bigger fraction of the total and can make a very big splash. In Illinois, for example, a 2017 donation of $20,000,000 by billionaire Ken Griffin to support incumbent Governor Bruce Rauner's 2018 reelection campaign was—all by itself—equal to roughly *one-fifth* of the total amount of money previously spent in Illinois by *all candidates* (of both parties) in the most expensive election for governor.[7] (That same donation would have constituted less than 1 percent of the total cost of the 2016 national presidential election.[8])

Such big contributions on the state and local levels probably have an outsized impact on electoral outcomes. They likely "buy" more gratitude and greater loyalty to contributors by the officials they help elect. Billionaires seem to know this—and some of their representatives are shockingly open about it. Andrew Ogles, the Tennessee director of the Koch brothers' Americans for Prosperity group (discussed in depth below), for example, told a *Boston Globe* reporter, "The return on investment in time is much greater at the state than the federal level."[9]

State- and local-level contributors also have an especially good chance of getting something for their money because governments on the state and local levels are frequently controlled by a single dominant party that can actually get things done. As of 2017, seventeen states had lower houses of their legislatures with majority parties that controlled two-thirds or more of the available seats. In even more states, (twenty-four of them) the upper houses were controlled by lopsided majorities.[10] In fact, fully *half* the states—twenty-five of them (if one includes Nebraska[11])—had unified one-party government across both houses of the legislature and the executive.[12] It is difficult to quantify exactly how many of the thousands of local governments around the country are controlled by one party, but given both the increasing partisan homogeneity of cities and our country's history of dominant, one-party political machines, it is unlikely that there is much more partisan diversity in governments on the local than the state level.[13]

In states and cities with strong unified government—unlike the federal government, which has often been paralyzed by divided party government, filibusters, and gridlock[14]—the majority party can often push through just about any policy it wants. As a result, major funders of the dominant party can hope for big returns on their investments.

Wealthy Contributors on the State and Local Levels

Billionaires are heavily involved in both elections and policy-making processes on the state and local levels.

State elections have been flooded with billionaires' money. An analysis by the Center for Public Integrity has identified ten national organizations—comprised of numerous state-level affiliates—that spent more than a million dollars each on state-level elections between 2014 and 2016, with the most prominent groups spending upward of $60 million.[15] These organizations sometimes use complex schemes to shield the identity of their contributors—or simply do not disclose contributors at all. But investigative work has revealed that billionaires are among their biggest investors. The Center for Public Integrity's report indicates, for example, that Sheldon Adelson, Ken Griffin, and the Koch brothers (or Koch Industries) each contributed more than $3 million to the Republican Governors Association over that three-year period. Adelson and the Kochs also contributed millions to the Republican Attorneys General Association. Influential Trump donor Robert Mercer, too, made substantial state-level investments in conservative groups. Billionaires' contributions to the left or center of the political spectrum have generally been fewer and smaller, though Michael Bloomberg has been a top-ten donor to the Democratic Governors Association.

Billionaires have also spent large sums on local races. In Chicago, Ken Griffin—a Republican—gave around $1 million to the 2015 reelection campaign of Mayor Rahm Emanuel, a Democrat.[16] Numerous wealthy Republicans contributed to Emanuel's campaign too. Prominent investor—and extreme fiscal conservative—David Herro kicked in $150,000.[17] Conservative investor Muneer Satter and his wife also made a six-figure contribution.[18] Sam Zell—a conservative billionaire with diversified interests—donated $50,000.[19] In Philadelphia, three libertarian founders of the Susquehanna International Group—a prominent trading and investment firm—contributed a combined $7 million to the mayoral campaign of Democrat Anthony Williams.[20] In Dallas, several billionaires, including

Harlan Crow and Ray Hunt, have created super PACs in order to influence city council races.[21] Billionaires have even spent money on school board elections.[22] Big money has a long reach.

The most important state and local-level political groups have provided more than just money. Some have invested in campaign infrastructure, in ways that parallel or even rival the work of the major political parties. Most prominent among them is Americans for Prosperity (AFP), the central organization in the Koch brothers' network.[23] A team of Harvard-based researchers led by Theda Skocpol found that, as of 2015, AFP had permanent, paid state political directors in thirty-four states. Those directors led a network of about 2.5 million conservative activists who are active in both state and local politics. State directors—many of whom are assisted by paid staffs—raise money, produce political advertisements, lead voter turnout operations, and perform other functions typically associated with political parties.[24]

The billionaire-controlled AFP may be the most important organization in American politics outside the Republican and Democratic parties. Attempts to match or counteract its influence from the left have not been successful so far. Following heavy state-level Democratic Party losses during the Obama presidency, liberal donors—including those involved with George Soros's Democracy Alliance—resolved to invest more in state-level campaign infrastructure,[25] but these efforts did not produce much in the way of immediate results.[26] The stunning Democratic losses of 2016, and alarm at the subsequent Trump presidency, may have mobilized a few centrist and liberal billionaires to do more. So a more robust state-level apparatus for the left may be in the works, though it faces daunting obstacles.[27] The fact is that—at least on economic issues—truly liberal billionaires are very hard to find.

On the right, too, AFP has not gone unchallenged. The politics of billionaires has been shaken up by the election of Donald Trump, who was initially opposed by the Kochs and by most other wealthy Republicans but got crucial support from unorthodox billionaire Robert Mercer and Mercer-funded Steve Bannon.[28] After Trump took office, he gave Bannon a top White House position but was eventually forced to fire him. Bannon returned temporarily to Mercer-funded *Breitbart News* and declared war on "establishment" Republican officials. In 2017 and 2018, Bannon, Mercer, and a few other wealthy Republican donors backed right-wing populist challengers in GOP primaries for the Senate and the House of Representatives, causing considerable turmoil within the party.[29] But the

Kochs' Americans for Prosperity—backed by the much more numerous libertarian and orthodox conservative billionaires—has vast resources to fight back.

Wealthy donor organizations are especially active during election campaigns, but they do not always lie dormant between elections. They often insert themselves into important policy debates through lobbying and grassroots mobilization. AFP and other ideologically conservative groups, for example, were very active during the years immediately after 2010, when state governments were drawing new legislative district boundaries and were deciding whether or not to expand Medicaid as part of the Affordable Care Act.[30] As of early 2017, nineteen states—many of them strongly influenced by AFP—had chosen to turn down free federal dollars and reject Medicaid expansion.[31] AFP and other groups also worked closely with the American Legislative Exchange Council (ALEC) and with ALEC's locally focused subsidiary, the American City County Exchange. ALEC is a conservative policy group that produces "model" state-level legislation and works to get it adopted. Often that legislation benefits business members of ALEC with tax cuts, looser regulations, and right-to-work laws aimed at weakening organized labor. State legislators, who frequently lack the time and resources to learn much about public policies on their own, often rely on ALEC for cues about how to vote.[32] Besides the directly business-friendly measures, ALEC's model bills concern a wide range of other policies including pro-gun stand-your-ground laws and restrictive voter ID requirements that discourage voting by low-income and minority Americans, who generally oppose ALEC's agenda.[33] In many instances, ALEC-drafted bills are pushed into law by AFP and other conservative groups.

Some wealthy donor groups go beyond simply attempting to sway legislators' stands on specific pieces of legislation; they also seek to win over the hearts and minds of important sectors of the population on key political issues. The Koch-led Libre Initiative (aimed at Latino communities) and Generation Opportunity (aimed at millennials), for example, attempt to advance a free-market ideology among groups of Americans who are not usually thought of as receptive to conservative appeals.[34] The conservative State Policy Network (SPN) even created its own "news" service, called "watchdog.org," which is run by the Franklin Center for Government and Public Integrity—an SPN member group. The Franklin Center, funded by contributions from a small number of wealthy individuals who bankroll Donors Trust and the Donors Capital Funds, is designed to appear to be politically neutral and separate from other conservative endeavors. Despite this appearance, the Franklin Center relies on research produced by other conservative SPN entities to develop its news and opinion pieces.[35]

Taken together, billionaires' activities appear to have produced impressive results, helping to win elections and reshape public policy. Electorally, conservative Republicans—who in recent years have had a much more robust state-level infrastructure than Democrats—have thrived in state politics. After the 2016 elections, Republicans controlled a solid thirty-three of fifty state governorships and sixty-nine out of ninety-nine state legislative chambers. They enjoyed unified party control of government in twenty-five states (compared to only seven states for Democrats).[36] This high-water mark capped a series of electoral successes that reflected a long-term strategy, a strategy executed by coordinated conservative activists who were funded by billionaires from across the country.[37]

The Republicans' state-level victories also had implications for future elections on both national and local levels. On the national level, they allowed many of the same activists and investors who contributed to Republicans' electoral successes to play prominent roles in redrawing congressional districts. For example, new, pro-Republican boundaries were drawn by Republican-dominated state legislatures and governors after the 2010 elections and the 2010 Census.[38] On the local level, state-level victories have similarly enabled the Republicans to alter state-level laws that have major impacts on the nature of municipal elections in ways that systematically advantage them.[39]

Republicans' state-level electoral successes have led to policy victories for economic conservatives on a range of issues—particularly cutting government spending, lowering taxes, and weakening labor unions, which are of special interest to wealthy campaign contributors who have invested a lot of money in state politics.[40] Conservative activists—particularly those associated with AFP and the Kochs—have been especially successful at diminishing collective bargaining rights of public-sector workers and in resisting Medicaid expansion as part of Obamacare.[41] Billionaires like John and Laura Arnold, who made billions of dollars in energy trading, have successfully led efforts in several states to chip away at pensions for public-sector workers.[42]

Public-sector pensions have also been a focus in Illinois, where the election as governor of near-billionaire Bruce Rauner (who poured more than $30 million into his own campaign and was aided by generous funding from Ken Griffin and several out-of-state billionaires[43]) led to a long and bitter stalemate with the Democrat-dominated state legislature. Illinois repeatedly failed to enact a state budget, failed to pay employees and contractors on time, and faced downgrades in its bond ratings.[44] As of this writing in late 2017, Rauner is highly unpopular among Illinois voters. But two of the leading Democrats seeking to oppose him in the 2018 gubernatorial election are themselves extremely wealthy. They are J. B. Pritzker (#219 on the 2017 *Forbes* list, worth $3.4 billion) and Chris Kennedy of the famous Kennedy family. The Kennedy family's net worth is still estimated to be in the billions.[45]

A dramatic success for wealthy donors came in Kansas, where Governor Sam Brownback and the Republican-dominated state legislature gutted spending on public education and altered the state's tax system in extremely regressive ways that benefited the wealthy and burdened the poor.[46]

Similarly, in Wisconsin, billionaire-backed Governor Scott Walker (who, as noted in chapter 3, received large contributions from vehemently anti-union billionaire John Menard Jr.) largely dismantled the collective bargaining rights of public-sector workers and signed right-to-work legislation into law to shrink already embattled unions in the private sector.[47]

In North Carolina, the Republican-led state government elected in 2013—which the Kochs and near-billionaire Art Pope played a large role in funding—has made the state's tax code more regressive, cut unemployment benefits, turned down federal dollars to expand Medicaid, and reduced public education financing.[48]

In Michigan, billionaire Betsy DeVos (who later became US Secretary of Education in the Trump administration), along with other members of her family, helped slash financial support for public schools.[49]

In some instances, Republicans' electoral successes on the state level have enabled them to pass laws that have dramatic effects on the *local* level. In Tennessee, for example, an AFP state director worked closely with a Republican state legislator to write and then pass a law expanding the state government's control over transit projects. The explicit purpose of this law was to enable the state to kill an already-approved Nashville mass transit project that would have been highly beneficial to members of Nashville's working class.[50] (AFP took this action despite its supposed dedication to federalism.) Various "preemption" bills that would reduce or eliminate local control (especially urban governments' control) over particular issues were introduced in at least twenty-nine states in 2015. They covered such matters as paid sick days, minimum wages, protections for LGBTQ persons, environmental rules, gun control, and immigration.[51]

We have focused on Republicans, but other conservative successes at the local level appear to have resulted from the actions of Democratic officials who get large contributions from wealthy conservative donors. Such contributions may either influence the positions of the Democratic officials or may help conservative rather than liberal Democrats get elected in the first place. In Chicago, for example, Rahm Emanuel's conservative donors, when asked about their support for a Democrat, point to his stances on education policy.[52] Emanuel has repeatedly sparred with the Chicago Teachers Union,[53] has slashed the city's education budget, and has closed dozens of public schools.[54] Emanuel has also invested public pension funds in hedge funds and other financial vehicles—some of which are connected to his wealthy donors[55]—and privatized various aspects of city infrastructure.[56]

Wealthy conservative contributors have also achieved policy successes by cultivating state-level administrative officials, especially state attorneys general—who are the highest law-enforcement officials in each state. According to a *New York Times* investigative report, Oklahoma Attorney General (later chief of the US Environmental Protection Agency) Scott Pruitt received substantial financial support from oil and gas billionaires, particularly Harold Hamm, who served as chairman of his reelection campaign. Pruitt, in turn, worked in ways that benefited oil and gas interests. For example, Pruitt signed and sent on to federal regulators a letter written by an energy company's lawyers claiming that the feds had overestimated the air pollution associated with oil drilling and discouraging the regulators from intervening in Oklahoma. The *Times* report made clear that the relationship between the state attorney general and wealthy, business-oriented contributors in Oklahoma was not unique to that state, but has also characterized other states, like North Dakota and West Virginia, that have extensive energy resources and Republican attorneys general.[57]

It should be noted that a smaller number of relatively liberal billionaires—despite many election losses—have also scored some state- and local-level policy victories, especially by using state-level referenda to mobilize ordinary voters and establish policies that the state legislatures might not enact. The late insurance billionaire Peter B. Lewis, for example, successfully bankrolled several marijuana legalization referenda. Quite a few billionaires, including Bill Gates and Jeff Bezos, have contributed large sums in support of same-sex marriage.[58] These successes have mostly concerned social issues, on which many billionaires prefer liberal or libertarian policies. Since billionaires (even pro-Democratic billion-aires) tend to be economically conservative, they are much less likely to ride to the rescue of ordinary Americans who want help with jobs, wages, health care, public schools, or retirement pensions.

The Boundary-Control Strategy

Certain billionaires employ strategies at the state level that are more subtle and sophisticated—and often even less visible—than simply supporting like-minded political candidates or organizing referenda on favored poli-cies. One such strategy can be called "boundary control": a coordinated effort to use and preserve one-party dominance of state politics to win spe-cial favors at the state level, while at the national level working to prevent federal regulation or other interference with the spoils.

In this section we lay out a theory of boundary control. We then quanti-tatively test some expectations about what sorts of billionaires tend to en-gage in boundary-control strategies, and we go on to use several system-atically selected cases for qualitative analyses that further test the theory. We find that the regulatory structures of the industries in which billion-aires are active—along with the billionaires' party affiliations—affect the use of this strategy. We also find indications that the boundary-control strategy can produce lucrative results for those who use it.

The Boundary-Control Theory of US Campaign Contributions

Our theory of boundary control is extended from comparative politics scholar Edward Gibson's boundary-control theory of national and subna-tional governments[59] to apply to US electoral and lobbying politics. Spe-cifically, it addresses ways in which US billionaires may coordinate their federal- and state-level political contributions to win direct state-level benefits while warding off federal-level interference.

As applied to US campaign contributions, a boundary-control strategy is necessarily limited to extremely wealthy individuals—or cohesive groups of wealthy individuals with similar financial interests—who are willing to con-tribute millions of dollars to political campaigns in more than one election cycle. Such large investments are likely to reflect optimistic expectations about results: an unusually "high return" on investments, as a members-only ALEC newsletter once boasted.[60] According to the theory, billionaires deploying boundary-control strategies primarily seek financial gains from *state* policies: state tax breaks, subsidies, government contracts, favorable regulations, and so forth.

The boundary-control strategy involves trying to weaken the role of the national government while maintaining and/or increasing the scope and degree of *subnational* jurisdictions—both in general and on particular crucial issues. Boundary-controlling billionaires thus deploy concepts related to "protecting states' rights," "preserving federalism," "ending big government," or "fighting against Washington insiders" to describe their national political goals. Under a boundary-control strategy, the main goal of national-level political contributions is not to benefit directly from the federal government, but rather to limit the extent of the federal government's control over public policy. Boundary control at the federal level, therefore, may involve making significant contributions to a number of candidates who are running for national office (whether from a billionaire's own state or from other states)—particularly candidates who hold or may gain powerful, agenda-setting committee positions. The national part of the strategy may also focus on encouraging legislators to take hard-line positions against federal action and shun compromise, as some billionaire-backed Tea Party members of Congress did during the Obama administration. No problem if that causes gridlock. In fact, that may be the point. Gridlock on the national level can be an effective way to prevent the federal government from increasing the scope of its authority or even from exercising ordinary policy-making powers.[61]

At the state or local level, boundary-controlling contributors attempt to achieve political influence in places where a single dominant party currently controls (or has a good shot at controlling) a state's or a locality's politics. In such places, boundary-controlling donors often make contributions directly to candidates in attempts to "capture" the support of members of the dominant party in order to receive favorable action on issues of importance to them.

The theory suggests that the logic of contributions to *issue-oriented* groups, or to political parties as a whole, is different from the logic of contributing to candidates. Boundary-controlling contributors are more likely to donate to outside "issue" groups or to general party funds on the *national* level than on the subnational level. In order to benefit from policy or patronage at the state or local level, contributors need to purchase the loyalty of individual political officials. On the national level, though, billionaires pursuing boundary control do not need loyalty. All they need

TABLE 5.1 **Boundary-Control Expectations**

	Boundary Control May Be More Likely When . . .
Regulatory Structure	Exposure to regulation is high + regulation is mostly subnational
Market Structure	Barriers to entry are high
	Public costs are geographically concentrated
Party	Contributors are Republicans

is inaction. Their objectives can be met so long as national-level election victors are ideologically dedicated to small government—*regardless of whether those victors are loyal to the contributors.* For example, boundary-controlling billionaires may be willing to run vicious negative advertisements against "big government" opponents, even contrary to the wishes of the small-government candidates that they favor.[62] They care much more about undermining big government than about buying the influence of those who advocate small government.

In recent years, boundary controllers have benefited from the *Citizens United* Supreme Court decision—which held that it is unconstitutional to limit independent political spending by corporations and unions—and from the *McCutcheon* case, which struck down long-standing limits on the total amount of money individuals can donate to campaigns in a single election cycle. Those decisions enhanced the ability of campaign contributors to engage in boundary control by expanding both the methods they can use to make contributions and the amount they can contribute.

Boundary control as a contribution strategy should not be equally attractive to all wealthy individuals. We expect that some are more likely to use it than others, based on their financial interests and certain personal characteristics. Table 5.1 summarizes our expectations about which sorts of billionaires are most likely to use the strategy.

Expectations about Boundary Control

We expect that the most important determinant of the use of boundary control is likely to be the *regulatory structure* that affects industries in which a contributor is active. Boundary control should be most common among billionaires actively involved in industries that are both highly regulated and regulated mostly on the subnational level. People with a big stake in heavily regulated industries have more to gain from political contributions, because the monetary value of controlling government increases as the intensity of regulation increases. Heavy regulation alone, however, is not sufficient to make a boundary-control strategy attractive. If most regulation of an industry occurs on the national level, individuals active in that industry have little incentive to focus on state politics. (Instead they may be forced into the higher-cost and higher-risk national arena.) State- or local-level regulation is key.

A second set of factors that could potentially increase or reduce the attractiveness of boundary control to different billionaires concerns the *market structure* or the *public impact* of industries in which a billionaire is heavily invested. We expect boundary- control strategies to be more common among wealthy individuals who are active in industries with high barriers to entry (that is, industries in which they are protected against competition by other firms). Boundary control should also be common when billionaires' industries impose net costs on the public (that is, when industries produce geographically concentrated public costs like pollution or toxic waste, without creating offsetting public benefits).

High barriers to entry—whether they consist of high capital requirements, limited access to scarce or protected resources, or exclusionary regulations—tend to increase the value of government benefits for a given firm and to reduce "free-rider" problems, in which other firms may benefit from a billionaire's political activities. (Boundary controllers presumably do not want to spend a lot money winning friendly policies and then have their competitors share the benefits.) High barriers to entry reduce the number of firms within an industry and increase the market share of individual firms, thereby decreasing the number of potential free riders.

Social costs created by firms or by public policies related to them— whether financial costs (e.g., when taxpayers lose because firms receive unfair tax breaks or inappropriately generous state or local contracts), or cultural or moral costs (e.g., when gambling is encouraged by governments subsidizing casinos), or environmental costs (e.g., environmental devastation and pollution from coal mines)—should tend to increase the attractiveness of boundary-control strategies. The contribution side of boundary control (giving money to state and local politicians) provides a way to overcome resistance from officials when voters do not want to waste tax dollars or bear the burden of social or environmental damage without substantial offsetting benefits.

We expect, however, that public costs and market structure will have smaller effects than *regulatory structure*: possibly no detectable effects at all. Wealthy contributors generally have an incentive to use boundary control whenever government regulation of an industry in which they are active is heavy in intensity and primarily located within subnational government— regardless of barriers to entry or net costs to the public. High barriers to entry do tend to make use of the boundary-control strategy more valuable. And net costs to the public do tend to increase the chances that the strategy is needed to overcome public opposition. But even in the absence of those factors, there may well be gains to be had for owners and investors in any industry operating within a primarily subnational regulatory structure. Thus we expect that factors related to regulatory structure will have larger effects than those related to market structure.

Finally, we expect that wealthy Republicans are more likely to engage in boundary control than wealthy Democrats. The boundary-control strategy most naturally fits with support for Republican candidates, whose conservative political ideologies align well with billionaires' self-interested pursuit of small government on the national level.[63] It is probably no coincidence that most of the industries with regulatory and market structures in which boundary control is attractive—including high-polluting industries like energy and chemicals, and labor-intensive and union-averse manufacturing firms—have tended to be aligned with Republicans.[64] Since it would be awkward at best for wealthy Democrats to engage in political strategies that require extensive public and private support for conservative Republicans, billionaires' partisanship should matter.

What the Evidence Says

In order to test our expectations about boundary control, we expanded our data set on the one hundred wealthiest US billionaires to include measures of the regulatory structure and market structure faced by the main industry in which each billionaire was currently active. We coded each billionaire's principal industry on four-point scales indicating the intensity with which it was regulated (from light to very heavy), the sites of its regulation (from almost entirely national to almost entirely subnational), the extent of barriers to entry (from low to very high), and the net costs it imposed on the public in the areas in which it was located.[65] Since the boundary-control theory predicts that the strategy is adopted only when regulation is both heavy and subnational, we combined the intensity scale and the site of regulation scale to form an overall regulation index. We also summed the scores on each variable for each industry, in order to develop a total industry score for each industry.[66]

Sixteen of our one hundred billionaires were taking no active role in business during the period of study. Because the point of the boundary-control strategy is to obtain business-specific financial benefits that are irrelevant to those not active in any business, the inactives were removed from this analysis. Of the remaining eighty-four billionaires, forty-three clearly were active only in a single industry, so we used the industry-wide scores for that industry to code each of them. For the forty-one billionaires who were active in two or more industries, we selected the industry that had the highest total score and coded each individual based on that industry.[67] To ascertain billionaires' party attachments, we used federal campaign contribution data to develop a measure of the party with which each billionaire was most aligned.[68]

We measured billionaires' use or nonuse of boundary control—our chief dependent variable—by examining national- and subnational-level contribution patterns. At the national level, boundary-controlling contributors are (by definition) more likely to donate to outside groups—especially small-government groups—or general party funds than to individual candidates. On the subnational level, they are more likely to make donations directly to candidates who are members of dominant state-level parties than to outside groups or minority-party candidates. At the state or local level, direct contributions to candidates or to individual candidates' PACs are necessary as a means to "buy" their support for state-level policy favors.

We therefore coded billionaires as engaging in boundary-control strategies if they met three criteria. First, they had to be active in a state with a dominant state-level party, which we defined as any state that had had unified government (led by the same party) for six or more of the twelve years from 2000 to 2012.[69] Second, at least two-thirds of a billionaire's national-level contributions (in terms of total dollars) had to go to outside groups associated with small-government causes or to Republican Party general funds. Finally, at least two-thirds of their contributions within a state (again in terms of total dollars) had to go directly to candidates themselves (or to the PACs of those candidates) who are members of the dominant state-level party.[70]

One billionaire had to be dropped from the analysis because he was active in a state in which there was no online campaign finance database that allowed for searches by contributor, leaving eighty-three billionaires to be analyzed. Of those eighty-three billionaires, *eight* (nearly 10 percent of those studied, or 8 percent of our entire set of one hundred billionaires) met the criteria for engaging in boundary-control strategies.[71]

TABLE 5.2 **Firth Logistic Regression Model Predicting Use of Boundary Control**

	B (SE)	p-Value	95% CI	
			Lower	Upper
(Intercept)	−17.105 (5.876)	<0.001	−33.210	−7.439
Regulation Index	2.632 (1.645)**	0.038	0.117	7.593
Barriers to Entry	−1.681 (2.018)	0.369	−7.969	2.829
Concentrated Costs	1.017 (1.677)	0.494	−1.622	10.266
Party	2.627 (1.632)**	0.037	0.128	7.587

**$p < .05$.

Note: Likelihood ratio test = 26.025 on 4 DF; p = .00003; n = 83. Wald test = 11.622 on 4 DF; p = .0204.

All boundary controllers came from Republican-dominated states.[72] Although both groups were highly active politically, boundary controllers contributed much more money to politics than non–boundary controllers—three times as much (an average annual sum of just over $1.5 million, compared with about $415,000). They also contributed more money to state politics than non–boundary controllers, particularly if one excludes ballot initiatives (to which a few individuals with intense preferences on social issues like same-sex marriage have donated vast sums). Excluding ballot initiative contributions, boundary controllers on average made state-level contributions of $109,425, nearly double the average annual amount contributed by others ($68,768). At the state level, in terms of total dollars, a much greater proportion of boundary controllers' contributions (85 percent of them) than non–boundary controllers' contributions (57 percent) went directly to candidates.[73] On the national level, a much greater proportion of boundary controllers' dollars (82 percent) than non–boundary controllers' money (54 percent) went to outside groups or parties. The contrast was even greater (82 percent vs. 37 percent) in terms of the proportion of national level contributions that went to conservative groups or the Republican Party.

Because of the limited number of billionaires studied, the rather few cases of boundary control, and the fact that the independent variables together caused quasi-complete separation in a standard logistic regression model, we estimated the relationship between the variables in the data set using a Firth penalized likelihood logistic regression.[74] The Firth approach helps with the problems of separation and rare outcomes.

The main results of our analysis are presented in table 5.2. The model includes four independent variables: *Regulation*, *Barriers to Entry*, *Net Public*

TABLE 5.3 **Estimated Effects of Changes on Boundary-Control Independent Variables**

| | Average Treatment Effect | Standard Error | 95% BCa CI | |
			Lower	Upper
Regulation Index	0.637	0.195	0.125	0.851
Party	0.123	0.044	0.054	0.233

Note: "Average treatment effect" is the predicted change in probability of the outcome variable (i.e., boundary control) when moving from the minimum observed value on each independent variable to the maximum value. Standard errors were calculated using bootstrapping. Bias-corrected and accelerated (BCa) confidence intervals (Efron 1987) are used to account for potential skewness in the bootstrap distribution.

Costs, and *Party*. The *Regulation* and *Party* coefficients, which are very similar in terms of magnitude, are both statistically significant by the usual criteria. But the coefficients for *Barriers to Entry* and *Net Public Costs* are not statistically distinguishable from zero. So our analysis confirmed two of our expectations (hypotheses 1 and 4 in table 5.1) but did not provide support for two others (hypotheses 2 and 3). We earlier explained some possible reasons for those null findings.

These results show a definite relationship between both regulatory structure and partisanship and the use of boundary control. These results are theoretically intelligible and statistically clear. Thus—while they do not *prove* a causal relationship—the quantitative findings suggest that boundary control is a distinctive strategy of Republican billionaires who do business in highly state-regulated industries.

In order to assess *how big* an impact regulatory structure and billionaires' partisanship have on the likelihood of billionaires pursuing a boundary-control strategy, we estimated average independent treatment effects for each: the predicted change in the probability of using boundary control when moving from the minimum to the maximum observed values on the regulation index variable[75] or from Democrat to Republican in party affiliation. The results are presented in table 5.3.

The estimated effect of an increase in state-level regulation is a very substantial 0.637. That is, moving from the (observed) lower end of the regulatory structure variable to the higher end is estimated to increase the likelihood of the use of boundary control by fully 64 percent. The estimated effect of party (that is, of a billionaire shifting from Democrat to Republican) is a smaller but still meaningful 0.123, signifying a 12 percent increase in the likelihood of using boundary control. Thus a billionaire's Republican Party affiliation is estimated to have a small but significant independent impact on the probability that the billionaire will pursue a boundary-control strategy.

But our estimates indicate that the *regulatory structure* of the billionaire's main business (a large amount of state-level regulation) very strongly tends to lead to efforts at boundary control.

Case Studies to Improve Causal Inference

As almost everyone knows, however, correlation is not causation. In order to make more confident causal inferences about which factors lead to the use of boundary-control strategies, it is important to grapple with certain problems that quantitative analyses of observational data cannot by themselves adequately resolve. These problems include the possibility of omitted confounding variables (factors that, when left out, can distort or "confound" findings) and the possibility of measurement errors in independent variables of interest (which can lead to underestimates of the effects of those variables).

Carefully designed case studies can enrich and deepen quantitative analyses by dealing with these problems, which are inherent in regression-type approaches to observational data.[76] Case studies can also illuminate causal pathways, suggest temporal sequences, and contribute in other ways to the analysis of social and political processes.

To advance our analysis of boundary-control strategies, we selected for a closer look cases that were extreme (either extremely high or extremely low) on key independent variables. Such cases are ideally suited to identify omitted confounding variables, as well as to uncover any measurement error that may exist in independent variables of interest.[77] It also turns out—not by accident—that such case selection often produces case studies that are interesting in themselves, illustrate the workings of the theory, and generate new ideas about causal processes.

Measurement error in this context could consist of simple coding errors. Or it could reflect more profound problems in the way we measured variables of interest. (If, for example, some billionaires were deemed to be engaging in boundary control based on the way we operationalized that concept, but were found through closer examination to take actions that in some way indicated otherwise.) Measurement errors might also be revealed by the discovery of campaign contributions that escaped detection during the creation of the data set and alter our understanding of a billionaire's political strategies.

We identified extreme high and extreme low cases by summing individual billionaires' scores on all the independent variables in the model (that is, all the factors we expected to lead to efforts at boundary control) and locating who had the maximum and minimum total values in our data set. *Harold Simmons* was unique as the extreme high case, most strongly predicted to use boundary control. From among billionaires who tied as the extreme low case (least likely to use boundary control) we randomly selected *George Soros*.[78]

We also selected a billionaire—*Robert Rowling*—who was *typical* (in terms of independent variables) of the eight who used boundary control.[79] Study of a typical case is useful for at least two reasons. First, it helps make an otherwise abstract theory more concrete and real. That is, it illustrates how a theory works. Second, and perhaps more importantly for us, studying one of our typical cases can help identify any *politically important effects* of using a boundary-control strategy. Do boundary controllers actually receive direct benefits on the subnational level as a result of their contributions? Our quantitative model helps predict who does or does not *try to use* boundary control. But we also want to know whether that strategy actually *pays off.* Robert Rowling was randomly selected as a typical case from among the eight billionaires scored as utilizing boundary control.

In each of the three case studies below, we first identify the billionaire's financial interests, discuss them in terms of our independent variables (e.g., the regulatory and market structure of his businesses, and his party affiliation) and then detail his national and subnational-level political activities, especially campaign contributions. We then assess whether or not our qualitative assessment aligns with the findings of the quantitative analysis, by searching for each of the potential sources of measurement error discussed above. Finally, for cases in which boundary control was used, we search for evidence on whether or not that strategy was successful in terms of accruing direct, subnational-level financial benefits for the would-be boundary controllers.

HAROLD SIMMONS.   The late Harold Simmons was selected as the extreme high case on the independent variables. (He scored higher on the sum of the four independent variables than any other billionaire studied.) So we strongly expected that he would engage in efforts at boundary control. And we coded him as having indeed done so.

Simmons—born in Golden, Texas, in 1931, to two school-teacher parents—spent his early childhood without indoor plumbing or electricity. He attended the University of Texas and was employed as a bank examiner along the way to becoming a wealthy industrialist active in metals, chemicals, waste management, and industrial manufacturing. Mainly through his privately held company, Contran, Simmons had by 2013 accumulated a net worth of $10 billion.[80] Simmons's highest-scoring company on the independent variables was his waste management firm, Waste Control Specialists. The waste management industry, which includes the disposal of highly toxic commercial waste, is very heavily regulated, mostly on the state and local levels. The waste management industry also has high barriers to entry and involves high localized public costs (pollution, unattractive sights and smells, and the risk of environmental and public health catastrophe if toxic waste is mishandled) with few compensating local public benefits.[81]

Simmons was a major campaign contributor. His involvement in national politics—he once darkly proclaimed that Barack Obama was a "socialist"—has received a fair amount of attention from both academia and the mass media.[82] Simmons's political involvement on the state level, however, has been less noticed.

On the national level, Simmons advocated for a small federal government and noninterference with the states. He supported conservative Republicans and attacked Democrats. Most notably, in 2004 Simmons contributed a substantial amount to the infamous "Swift Boat Veterans for Truth," a group that then proceeded to run vicious attack ads about the military career of Democratic presidential candidate John Kerry, who had served honorably in Vietnam and received a purple heart. Simmons was also responsible for the Bill Ayers–Barack Obama attack ads of 2008, which attempted to link Obama to domestic terrorism.[83] (Ayers, a rebel in his youth, was by 2008 a peaceable and mild-mannered Chicago-area scholar. Ayers and his acquaintances may have been puzzled by the idea of demonizing Obama for association with Ayers, but the ads made big waves nationally.)

In the 2012 elections Simmons gave just shy of $27 million to conservative super PACs, most of which focused broadly on supporting conservatives in tight races rather than on aligning themselves with individual candidates.[84] Simmons also contributed directly to some candidates or their individual PACs, but these donations paled in comparison to the donations he made to groups with a broader focus. In fact, he did not give more than $10,000 to any single candidate or any single candidate's PAC.[85] By contrast, in the year before the 2012 election Simmons gave a hefty $20.5 million to American Crossroads, former Bush adviser Karl Rove's very conservative political vehicle.[86]

In contrast to his national-level activity, Harold Simmons's *state-level* contributions—just as the boundary-control theory would predict— went directly to individual candidates, almost all of them members of the dominant Texas Republican Party. Between 2000 (the first year included in the campaign finance database maintained by the *Texas Tribune*) and his death in 2013, Simmons contributed more than $11 million—spread across 1,184 donations—to Texas state politics. At least $1.2 million of that money went to Governor Rick Perry. Between 2000 and his death, Simmons was one of the most prolific donors in Texas politics, contributing a total amount of money to various politicians that was second only to that given by the late near-billionaire Bob Perry, who made a fortune in home building and spent vast sums on a wide range of far-right causes.[87]

Thus a close analysis of Simmons's political involvement does not reveal any problems related to measurement error on either the dependent or the independent variables. Our case-study analysis reveals neither coding errors nor any unexpected contributions that alter our understanding of Simmons's approach to politics. Most important, Simmons's contributions fit neatly with the boundary-control theory. He did just what the theory predicts a billionaire in his circumstances would do. Simmons was a paradigmatic boundary controller.

Moreover, Simmons's contributions appear to have paid off. He got a lot of value for his money. Most prominently, Simmons owned a waste management firm, Waste Control Specialists, that for decades had sought—but failed—to get permission to build a low-level radioactive waste facility in Texas.[88] Despite plenty of eagerness among waste facility entrepreneurs, and despite the authority that Congress gave the states to license low-level radioactive waste disposal during the small-government era of the 1980s,[89] few states have leapt at the chance to build these facilities, probably because of the safety concerns and negative public reactions that they generally provoke.[90]

Simmons, however, kept on trying. Finally, in 2003—a year in which Simmons infused more than $200,000 into Texas politics—the Texas legislature opened an unusually brief one-month window in which private companies could apply for permits to dispose of waste.[91] Simmons's firm submitted the only application, and ultimately built the facility. (Other firms may have simply been unable to put together a competitive proposal in such a short period of time. Or they may have figured that the project was a done deal for insider Simmons.)[92]

The opening of a short application window was not the only state or local government favor to Simmons. In 2007, three members of the Texas Commission on Environmental Quality (TCEQ) resigned in frustration with the subsequent licensing process. One of them told a journalist that he felt it was inevitable that Simmons's company would receive a license to build

and operate the facility, regardless of its potential environmental effects—
including the potential for contamination of groundwater due to the site's
particular geological properties.[93] Over the course of 2008 and 2009, Simmons's Waste Control Specialists—which had recently hired TCEQ's former executive director as a lobbyist—finally received the licenses necessary
to build and operate a waste facility in Andrews County.[94]

Moreover, in March 2009, the commissioners of Andrews County hast-
ily added a bond measure to the May 2009 ballot to help Waste Control
Specialists finance construction.[95] The bond measure subsequently passed
by a mere three-vote margin over the protests of numerous community
members (including some who formed a nonprofit in opposition named
"No Bonds for Billionaires").[96] Those who voted in favor of the measure
were apparently enticed by the promise of new jobs; it ultimately provided around 180 jobs for individuals who apparently did not mind (or did
not know about) exposure to radiation.[97] In 2011, the Texas Low-Level
Radioactive Waste Disposal Commission—six of the seven members of
which were appointed by Governor Perry—changed the rules govern-
ing the facility to allow it to accept out-of-state waste.[98] Finally, also in
2011, Simmons was given unusual permission to use stock in one of his
other companies as financial assurance in case his waste management firm
should go bankrupt or a disaster situation should arise.[99]

Simmons, seemingly proud of his political efforts, openly boasted
about the actions taken by state and local officials to bring his waste facility to fruition.[100]

In our quantitative analysis, Simmons was strongly predicted to engage
in boundary control and was scored as having done so. Our more in-depth
look has confirmed that Simmons did indeed pursue a boundary-control
strategy. And he appears to have gained a great deal of benefit from it.

GEORGE SOROS.   The relation of Soros to the boundary-control theory is
the polar opposite to that of Simmons. Soros was randomly selected for
a closer look from among several billionaires who tied with extremely
low scores on the four independent variables that predict the use of the
boundary-control strategy. That is, Soros was strongly predicted *not* to
engage in efforts at boundary control. No billionaire in the quantitative
analysis had a lower combined score than Soros did. No one should have
been less likely to engage in boundary control. And indeed, Soros was
coded as not having done so.

George Soros was born in Hungary, attended college at the London
School of Economics, and later immigrated to the United States. He made

his fortune of $20 billion (as of 2013) in finance. In 1970 he founded Soros Fund Management, the investment and hedge fund firm of which he is currently chairman. Soros made his most famous—and perhaps most lucrative—financial coup in 1992. It involved large-scale "shorting" (borrowing and selling, in expectation of a drop in value[101]) of the British pound. Soros made $1.5 billion off that move alone.[102] The securities and investment industry in which Soros Fund Management has been active is highly regulated, but it is regulated almost entirely on the national level. Additionally, it has low barriers to entry and involves few localized costs. Not a promising combination for boundary control.

The political activities of Soros—who has sometimes been cited as a left-leaning megadonor, as a foil in discussions of the right-leaning Koch brothers—are fairly well known. Soros entered national politics in a big way in the 2004 election cycle, angered by George W. Bush's invasion of Iraq and other foreign policy moves that Soros felt were damaging to US interests and to countries around the world, including countries in his native Eastern Europe. Soros was a founding member of the Democracy Alliance, a network of wealthy pro-Democratic contributors.[103] In recent years Soros has contributed very large sums to numerous political efforts on both the national and state levels. On the national level, Soros has donated many millions of dollars to the Democratic Party and to liberal outside groups—including numerous seven-figure donations to the super PAC Priorities USA. On the state level, less than half of Soros's contributions have gone directly to candidates; most go to outside groups dedicated to specific liberal causes.[104]

Our close analysis of Soros's political involvement revealed no problems related to measurement error in independent or dependent variables. We did not find any coding errors or any previously missed contributions that alter our understanding of his approach to politics. There is no new evidence that Soros has engaged in boundary control. Just as the theory predicted, he has not. In fact, he has essentially done just the opposite: ignoring candidates at the state and local level but supporting some at the national level; seeking no state or local favors that we could detect; and working for a relatively active, rather than inactive, federal government.

ROBERT ROWLING. Rowling was randomly selected among *typical* cases on the independent variables from within the subset of billionaires who were coded as engaging in boundary control.[105]

Rowling—born in Corpus Christi, Texas, in 1953, and currently a resident of Dallas[106]—helped his father create the Tana Oil & Gas company. Rowling's fortune boomed in 1989, when he and his late father sold a large portion of this business to Texaco for approximately $500 million.[107] Rowling used the money from that sale to create TRT Holdings. TRT's primary assets consist of Tana Exploration, Omni Hotels, and Gold's Gym (which has more than 700 locations around the world).[108] Outside (though perhaps not totally outside) the business realm, Rowling has served as a member of the University of Texas Board of Regents and has chaired the University of Texas Investment Management Company. Rowling's highest-scoring company on the independent variables used in our analysis was his energy company, Tana Explorations (owned by TRT Holdings). The energy and natural resources industry is very heavily regulated, mostly on the state and local levels. It has high barriers to entry and involves highly localized public costs that are not entirely offset by local benefits. All these factors predict efforts at boundary control.

Rowling has been a very active campaign contributor. He personally gave $6 million to American Crossroads between 2010 and 2012, and during that same period, TRT Holdings gave Crossroads an additional $4.9 million.[109] Rowling has also made numerous $10,000–$30,000 contributions to the Republican Party on the national level.[110] On the state level, Rowling has donated at least $3 million to candidates and to candidates' personal PACs, including large contributions to Texas Governor Rick Perry.[111] Rowling has also made municipal-level contributions, including several to members of the Dallas city government: $10,000, for example, to its Democratic mayor.[112]

On the national level, Rowling—despite some relatively small party and candidate donations—has given overwhelmingly to outside groups. With only two exceptions back in the 1990s (totaling just $2,000), Rowling's national contributions have gone exclusively to Republicans or to groups aligned with Republicans.[113] On the state and municipal levels, by contrast, Rowling's contributions have mostly gone directly to candidates and their PACs. His state-level contributions have gone almost exclusively to members of the dominant Texas GOP.[114] On the municipal level, however—which in the case of Dallas involves significantly greater party competition than on the Texas state level—Rowling has donated to members of both parties, including the Democratic mayor.[115]

The Rowling case was not selected specifically to search for measurement error, but it is nonetheless worth noting that it does not appear to involve any such errors. Upon closer analysis, Rowling's contribution patterns do—just as our quantitative measures indicated—appear to typify boundary control. No additional information about Rowling contradicts his scores on the independent variables. Our closer look does not reveal any coding errors or any additional contributions that would alter the patterns depicted in the data set.

As in Simmons's case, the evidence suggests that Rowling has received direct state and municipal *benefits* as a result of his campaign contributions. An indication that Rowling's prestigious appointments to the University of Texas boards were the result of his contributions to Governor Perry is that these appointments ended (with Rowling's strongly encouraged resignation) shortly after Rowling had shifted his financial support from Perry to Perry's 2010 gubernatorial election challenger, Kay Bailey Hutchison.[116] And in Dallas, after voters narrowly rejected a ballot initiative that would have prevented public ownership of a convention center hotel, the Dallas City Council (with the support of the mayor, who had received a $10,000 donation from Rowling), approved a $500 million financing package for the construction of a city-owned hotel that would be developed and operated by Omni, one of TRT Holding's prime assets. More recently, the city granted TRT Holdings significant tax incentives to move its headquarters into Dallas.[117]

Boundary Control and Stealth Politics

These case studies—integrated with our quantitative analyses—help confirm the boundary-control theory. We find that a number of the very wealthiest American billionaires—about one-tenth of all the billionaires who were still active in business[118]—have engaged in boundary-control strategies. They have supported and worked through the political party that dominates politics in a particular state or locality where they have extensive business interests (usually but not always the Republican Party), in order to win special governmental favors, while at the same time contributing on the national level to "small government" ideological groups that will help fend off any federal interference with their businesses.

One important factor that leads to use of the boundary-control strategy is a favorable regulatory setting, in which their businesses are more subject to state-level than national-level regulation. Another factor is a billionaire's general alignment with the Republican Party. The striking examples of Harold Simmons and Robert Rowling indicate that the boundary-control strategy can work well for those who pursue it. Billionaires have successfully used it to win expensive favors from state and local governments.

If the boundary-control strategy pays off so well for some of the very wealthiest Americans, there is reason to suspect that a fair number of less exalted billionaires and multimillionaires may also quietly take advantage of it too. Across the United States as a whole, expensive special favors won by the wealthy from state and local governments may well add up to many billions—or tens of billions—of dollars' worth of lost tax revenue, excessively expensive government purchases, harm to citizens' health and welfare, and damage to the environment—all borne by ordinary American citizens and taxpayers.

Taking a broader view, boundary control can be thought of as a special case of *stealth politics*, in which billionaires and other wealthy Americans push for public policies that suit their own financial self-interest but go against the interests and wishes of most Americans—while the billionaires stay as quiet as possible about what they are doing and why. Indeed, the *national-level* "small-government" side of boundary-control strategies closely resembles the stealthy politics concerning taxes and Social Security that we analyzed in chapters 2 and 3. Boundary controllers help advance the national agenda of extreme economic conservatives: low taxes, little federal economic regulation, and severely limited social spending. Much the same thing is true of billionaires' broader (but again often very quiet) efforts to reshape state politics by electing conservative public officials and enacting extremely conservative economic policies.

This chapter points to state- and local-focused dimensions of political action by billionaires: actions aimed at boundary control, and broader strategies designed to reshape state politics. Both those strategies, like more purely national-level stealth politics, are problematic for democracy. Both appear to involve unequal political influence—and certainly involve largely *unaccountable* political action—by billionaires and multimillionaires. No ordinary citizen, acting alone, can hope to match such influence. All Americans taken together may have a hard time controlling it.

CHAPTER SIX

What Is to Be Done about Billionaires?

O ur study of billionaires has definite limitations, some of which are inherent in a phenomenon of great interest to us: billionaires' general silence concerning important issues of public policy. It is impossible to conduct a sample survey of billionaires, or (with rare exceptions) to interview them in depth. No matter how thorough our web scraping, how careful our scrutiny of public records, or how diligent our use of historical research and investigative reports by other scholars and journalists, we cannot hope to learn exactly what is in the hearts and minds of all of America's wealthiest billionaires. Especially frustrating is our (and everybody else's) inability to know many billionaires' precise *policy preferences*. Exactly what billionaires want from government probably matters a great deal, since billionaires have the resources to intervene in a big way (if they wish) in elections and in policy-making processes.

Some hints about the overall thrust of billionaires' policy preferences can be gleaned from their officially reported financial contributions to candidates and parties (mostly to conservative Republicans), or—in a few cases—from their vague ideological utterances.[1] But those are not always reliable indicators. We simply cannot be sure about the policy preferences of the many billionaires who stay totally silent about the specifics of public policy.

Nor—despite a lot of helpful data gleaned from our web scraping and from the FEC and various state and local agencies (augmented by the fruits of others' investigative journalism and archival research)—have we or anyone else been able to discover everything that billionaires *do* to influence politics. Aided by lax legal regulations, many billionaires have been able to keep important political actions secret. In recent years, some key facts about the activities by a few secretive billionaires (the Koch brothers, Sheldon Adelson, Robert Mercer, even John Menard Jr.) have been unearthed through litigation or through diligent work by investigative journalists, historians, and others. Some attempts at stealth politics have even come to be widely known among attentive citizens. But this is true of only a small minority of the wealthiest US billionaires. Many others may well have given large dark-money contributions to political candidates and causes but were not caught at it. They did not have to report their actions to the FEC or anybody else. We cannot know how many billionaires continue to remain in the dark.

We have, however, been able to draw some new inferences about silent billionaires' policy preferences by finding and compiling media-reported (but hitherto little-noticed) evidence of certain kinds of *narrowly focused, policy-oriented actions*. These include founding, joining, leading, or contributing money to political organizations that have clearly defined missions to advance particular kinds of public policy. This evidence indicates that quite a few billionaires undertake carefully targeted, policy-specific actions, alongside their broader and vaguer partisan agendas. Such evidence provides exceptionally reliable indicators of concrete policy preferences. It has allowed us to infer with considerable confidence the policy preferences of a sizable subset of billionaires, including some who have been completely silent in public about policy matters. Using that information in multivariate statistical analyses that include *all* of the one hundred wealthiest billionaires, we have discovered patterns that enable us to draw more general inferences about the policy preferences of America's wealthiest billionaires as a group.

A final limitation: although we have been able to learn some interesting things about the *likely effect* on US public policy of billionaires' enormous financial contributions (particularly through the case studies reported in chapters 3 and 5, and from patterns in federal government policies that suggest billionaires and other wealthy Americans often get their way), we have not attempted to make definitive statements about the precise extent of billionaires' political influence. Lacking data from laboratory experiments (a pipe dream) or credible natural experiments, we are aware of no conclusive way to do so. Instead, we have pointed out reasons to believe that billionaires probably have even more political influence than the "affluent" citizens that recent research has shown are much more influential than average citizens. Fundamentally, we operate on the assumption that billionaires have enough political clout so that it is worthwhile to study the specific policies they seek from government and how they go about trying to get those policies enacted. This assumption does not seem very controversial.

Despite all these limitations, we believe we have been able to come up with some important new findings about America's wealthiest billionaires. Our findings supplement, take into account, and build upon the excellent historical and journalistic studies that have been done concerning a few particular billionaires.

One novel aspect of our approach is that we have undertaken a *systematic* political study of *all* the wealthiest billionaires in the United States.

By systematically analyzing the politics of the one hundred wealthiest Americans—the top one-quarter of the *Forbes* 400-wealthiest list—we have been able to learn a great deal about what sorts of political behavior are typical among billionaires and what sorts are not. We have learned, for example, that the centrist or even liberal political behavior of a few of the wealthiest, most highly visible, and most politically vocal billionaires—Bill Gates, Warren Buffett, Michael Bloomberg, George Soros—is quite atypical of the wealthiest American billionaires as a group. Most billionaires are much more conservative on economic issues, and much quieter in public.

We have also learned something about how billionaires' behavior varies according to particular characteristics of the billionaires themselves or the sources of their wealth: just how wealthy they are; whether they got their money mainly through entrepreneurship or inheritance; and what sorts of industries they are most active in—finance or high-technology, consumer facing or not, concentrated or competitive, regulated mostly at the state level or mostly at the national level. For example, we found that boundary-control strategies are employed more frequently by billionaires who are active in industries that are highly regulated and are mostly regulated at the state rather than national level. The inheritors of large fortunes (who are often publicity-shy) and those who run consumer-facing companies (who are vulnerable to boycotts) show a tendency to say or do rather little politically. High-tech billionaires tend to be especially enthusiastic about the immigration of high-skilled workers.

Importantly, we have learned a great deal about what the wealthiest billionaires as a group *say* (or, more often, *do not say*) in public concerning certain major issues of public policy. Our web searches were very thorough. Separately for each billionaire on each key policy issue, we looked closely at everything the billionaire was reported to have said in public (in the billionaire's own prose, in print or electronic interviews, in casual overheard comments, or in any other way) about the specifics of each policy issue we studied. The period covered by our searches was rather long: roughly ten years. The keywords used in the searches were systematically chosen, numerous, and comprehensive.

Our thorough web searches left us confident that we had found virtually everything of relevance that each billionaire said. That confidence was further increased by the results of selected follow-up case studies. The case studies had several objectives, but one chief aim was to reveal possible measurement errors—especially any failures of our systematic web searches to capture important statements or actions by billionaires that might alter our understanding of their behavior. The case studies did in fact uncover a few additional comments. (We had missed some political comments by Warren Buffett in Berkshire Hathaway annual reports and some comments by the Koch brothers that predated our study's time frame.) But these mostly just repeated or elaborated on statements that we had found earlier.

The case studies also revealed some new and inventive types of political action that were employed by the very quiet billionaires John Menard Jr., Robert Rowling, and Harold Simmons. But—even though we selected the cases for study so as to maximize the chances of finding measurement errors—they revealed no relevant statements by billionaires we had previously thought to be silent. When we judged a billionaire to be silent about a policy issue, we can be confident that the billionaire in fact said nothing in public about it.

Our most important discovery has been that—over a fairly lengthy period of time, concerning the specifics of several very important issues of public policy—most of the wealthiest US billionaires have maintained a complete public silence. That silence constitutes a key element of what we call stealth politics.

Evidence of Stealth Politics

The first building block in our evidence about stealth politics is the fact that most billionaires are *highly active in politics*, in ways likely to have significant influence on which candidates win election to public office and what policies they pursue. Most billionaires contribute substantial sums of money to political parties and candidates (mostly Republicans): in the course of recent years, 92 percent contributed to one party or the other. More than one-third of the wealthiest billionaires actively engaged in political fund-raising, and/or bundled political contributions from others. Many supported policy-oriented causes or organizations in one issue area or another.

The high level of political activity—at least in terms of FEC-reported financial contributions—among billionaires is fairly well known. A second, crucial new building block that we add, however, is our finding that— despite all this activity—most of the wealthiest US billionaires *say little or nothing in public*, over an extended period of time, about the specifics of major policy issues.

This is most striking in the case of issues related to Social Security. Most billionaires said little or nothing about whether to increase or decrease Social Security's retirement and disability benefits; whether to privatize the program or to continue making government-guaranteed payments; whether or not to continue the rather low payroll tax cap, which makes all income above roughly $100,000 completely exempt from the tax; whether or not to raise the retirement age (effectively cutting lifetime benefits), or to reduce annual cost-of-living adjustments (ditto), or to change Social Security in some other way.

These are very important issues of public policy. They directly affect millions of retired or disabled Americans, and they potentially affect many more millions of working people who need to plan for their future retirements. In recent years—including the period covered by our study—issues concerning Social Security have engaged many experts, commentators, public officials, and others in vigorous and contentious public debates. Yet we found, remarkably, that fully *96 percent* of the one hundred wealthiest billionaires said nothing whatsoever, over a roughly ten-year period, about the specifics of Social Security policy.

Similarly, most billionaires said little or nothing about tax policy—about personal income taxes; corporate taxes; capital gains taxes on investments; carbon taxes on pollution; or estate taxes. Nothing about whether the rates on one or another type of tax should be raised or lowered. Nothing about whether taxes should be made more or less progressive (that is, whether or not taxes should fall more heavily on those who enjoy the highest levels of income or wealth). Nothing about whether or how more revenue should be gathered to pay for the many government programs that majorities of Americans want. In fact, 71 percent of the one hundred wealthiest billionaires said nothing whatsoever in public about the specifics of any of the tax-related policies we investigated. Among the relatively few who did speak up, most made only one or two comments over a ten-year period.

A similar silence has characterized most billionaires' handling of the issues of abortion, same-sex marriage, and immigration. Although further evidence indicates that the *motives for* and the *effects of* silence about abortion and same-sex marriage have tended to be somewhat different than on other issues, the fact of silence has not. Fully 92 *percent* of the one hundred wealthiest billionaires said nothing at all in public about the many specific policy issues related to abortion. A similar 85 percent maintained a public silence about same-sex marriage.

Notably, roughly the same proportion—84 percent—of the billionaires said nothing at all in public about issues related to immigration policy. Nothing about whether overall levels of immigration should be raised or lowered; whether special new measures should be taken to stop illegal immigration from Mexico or to bar potential terrorists from the United States; whether high-skilled and low-skilled workers should be treated differently; whether undocumented immigrants currently living in the United States should or should not be offered a path to citizenship; or how to deal with refugees from countries devastated by war. Nothing about any of those matters or about any other concrete aspect of immigration policy. Most of the wealthiest billionaires—in public, at least—were totally silent.

A third building block in our evidence about stealth politics is the fact that in most or all cases, billionaires' silence has almost certainly been a matter of *choice*. It has been *intentional*.

How can we know this? Few billionaires have commented openly about their motives, and we lack psychic insight into exactly what they think. But in this case, the intentionality seems close to self-evident. Billionaires are highly newsworthy. Millions of Americans seem eager to hear about almost anything a billionaire says or does. So journalists and TV interviewers have strong, audience-based incentives to provide megaphones for billionaires to talk about anything they want to say. If billionaires wanted to speak out about public policy, they could easily do so.

Just about any billionaire who wanted to, for example, could easily publish an op-ed about public policy in his or her local newspaper. Or grant the great boon of a policy-oriented interview to a local TV reporter. Or, even more easily, make a policy comment on a blog. Many of the wealthiest billionaires could make the national news just about any day of the week by appearing on a radio or TV talk show, or by giving an interview to a national newspaper or magazine. Moreover, if one of the wealthiest billionaires were somehow denied access to the media, he or she (usually he) could simply *buy* a newspaper company or a TV station to amplify his or her political views. The fact that billionaires have rarely addressed the major issues we studied in any public way clearly indicates that most billionaires simply *do not want* to speak out in public about such issues.

Exactly *why* they have not spoken is a harder question, which once again highlights the limits on what we can learn. The near universality of silence—or of very infrequent and sketchy comments—by billionaires on all the diverse issues we have studied suggests that some of the reasons for that silence probably apply broadly to many topics. The most obvious reason: to say anything specific concerning a political issue about which many people disagree with each other is to risk offending someone. Perhaps many someones. Offended political activists on one side or the other might engage in noisy and unpleasant protests. Protests or boycotts by customers or investors in a billionaire's business might dent the stock price or hurt the firm's bottom line. Why risk it? Why not just keep quiet?

This is the same sort of logic that presumably tends to keep most billionaires quiet about sensitive topics concerning race, religion, lifestyle, or sexual orientation, as well as about politics. But motivations for engaging in stealth politics go well beyond that, as is reflected in certain differences among the policy areas we studied.

A fourth building block in our evidence of stealth politics is that, in certain policy areas, many or most billionaires appear to favor, and to quietly work for, *policies that are opposed by large majorities of Americans.*

Not so much on the issues of abortion or same-sex marriage. In those cases, the libertarian inclinations of many billionaires are not very distant from the evolving public consensus on accepting same-sex relationships and on protecting the right of women—at least under some circumstances—to have abortions.

But there appears to be a particularly big gap between billionaires and the general public on certain other issues, including policies related to *Social Security.* A good many billionaires want to cut guaranteed Social Security benefits. Many favor either outright cuts, or benefit decreases through deferred retirement ages or reduced cost-of-living adjustments, or the abandonment of benefit guarantees altogether—moving to private accounts and leaving retirees at the mercy of stock market fluctuations. Many polls and surveys show that just about any such cut in guaranteed benefits would be anathema to overwhelming majorities of the American public. Yet quite a few billionaires (some of them mobilized by their unusually outspoken fellow billionaire, Pete Peterson) have devoted a great deal of money and energy to a multiyear campaign to cut Social Security. Many billionaires have contributed large sums of money to political parties and candidates (most of them economically conservative Republicans) who—quietly, for the most part—have worked for Social Security cuts or privatization.

Similarly, a significant subset of billionaires—12 percent of them—have supported policy-specific organizations dedicated to entirely abolishing the *estate tax*. There are indications that many other billionaires—whose enormous estates are among the very few subject to the tax, and whose heirs have the most to lose from it—likewise want to abolish the estate tax. But most ordinary Americans, when asked sensibly designed survey questions, say they favor keeping estate tax rates on very large estates at a substantial level.

Again, many billionaires have actively sought substantial or increased levels of *immigration* by highly skilled but low-salaried foreign workers, who can enhance their companies' profits. Hardly any billionaires have shown any sign of opposing the high general levels of immigration that have so upset the millions of ordinary Americans who feel beleaguered by fears of job competition or terrorism and/or by social anxieties. Here, too, the billionaires seem to be seriously out of touch with the American citizenry as a whole.

The fifth and final building block in the structure of evidence about stealth politics involves our statistical analyses of relationships between billionaires' talk and their political actions. To put it simply: silence about public policy tends to be particularly common among billionaires who *disagree with majorities of Americans.*

In several important cases, the billionaires who spoke out in public tended to take policy stands that were very different from the policy-specific actions of most of those who took such actions. On Social Security, for example, most of the few billionaires who spoke out expressed support for current benefit levels. But most of the billionaires who took policy-specific *actions* on Social Security worked to privatize or *cut* benefits.

The eight billionaires who spoke out in public about the estate tax tended (by a small margin) to support it, as a way to provide government revenue and to require economic winners to "give back" some of the riches that their fellow citizens helped them amass. But every one of the dozen billionaires who took policy-specific *actions* concerning the estate tax sought to abolish the tax.

On immigration, there was not such a sharp contrast between talk and action. But if the division of opinion among the subset of billionaires who either talked or took policy-specific actions faithfully represents the division of opinion among the whole group of one hundred billionaires, we can infer that many (roughly half) of them favored maintaining or expanding high levels of immigration generally, while the other half favored only high-skilled immigration. None at all agreed with the majority of the public and favored *decreasing* levels of immigration.

It is hard to avoid the impression that many or most billionaires were silent about the specifics of certain public policies at least in part *because* they disagreed with what most Americans wanted. Open disagreement with majorities of citizens on important political issues might provoke even more protesting and unpleasantness than taking a stand on a contentious issue about which opinion is divided but the average (mean or median) citizen and the billionaires do not stand far apart.

Our multivariate regression analyses added some subtle and elusive— but important—support for this inference. The most sophisticated regression analysis we reported in chapter 2, for example, established the existence of rather different statistical bases for the direction of policy-specific actions about tax policy among billionaires who spoke out, as opposed to those who were entirely silent. In particular, a higher level of a billionaires' *wealth*—which by itself is associated with more liberal or centrist talk and actions about taxes (and also with more speaking out)— led to more pro-tax actions among those who made at least one public comment. But it actually led to more *anti-tax* actions among the silent billionaires. This indicates that silence tended to conceal anti-tax sentiments, especially among the very wealthiest billionaires, who have to fork over the most to Uncle Sam.

We believe that these five types of evidence, taken together, indicate that—on several important issues of public policy—*many or most* billionaires have *actively worked* to enact policies *opposed to the wishes of most Americans*, while *intentionally trying to conceal* their thoughts and actions about those policies by staying silent about them.

Billionaires' Impact on Public Policy

It is not easy to figure out exactly how much influence billionaires have on the making of US government policy.

Since we lack comprehensive data about billionaires' policy preferences, we cannot carry out the sort of influence analysis that can be done with Martin Gilens's data—covering nearly two thousand policy decisions—on the relative influence of "affluent" Americans, average Americans, and major interest groups. That sort of analysis is possible because Gilens gathered extensive data on the policy preferences of the affluent top 20 percent of income earners who show up in national surveys; on the policy preferences of average Americans (from the same surveys); and on the pro- and con-lineups of major interest groups. If we had similar preference data on billionaires, we could investigate how well the billionaires' preferences predict (and, therefore, presumably *affect*) policy decisions, taking into account the preferences and alignments of ordinary citizens and interest groups.[2] But we do not have—and cannot imagine how to gather—such data.

We can, however, draw some inferences about the influence of billionaires on policy from the existing research on affluent Americans and on multimillionaires; from various scholarly and journalistic accounts of policy-making processes; and from some of our own research reported in this book.

Recent work by Gilens and others has made clear that affluent Americans and organized interest groups (especially business groups and corporations) have far more influence on the making of US government policies than average citizens do. In fact, when one statistically takes account of what affluent Americans and organized interest groups want from government, the average American's wishes appear to have virtually *no* influence on policy making at all.[3]

If affluent Americans have a lot more political influence than average Americans, it is not much of a logical leap to infer that *truly wealthy* Americans probably have still more clout. And that the very wealthiest billionaires have the most policy-making power of all. Indeed, it seems possible that most or all of the influence apparently exercised by Gilens's "affluents" is actually exerted by a small subset of wealthy Americans among the affluents: by billionaires and their wealthy allies.[4]

Moreover, the best available evidence on the policy preferences of multimillionaires—the Chicago-area SESA study of a representative sample of the top one or two percent of wealth holders—indicates that wealthy Americans tend to disagree sharply with most Americans about many economic policies. Again, if multimillionaires disagree with average Americans, it is not much of a leap to infer that billionaires may disagree even more markedly.[5]

The SESA study was conducted at a time when the United States was still struggling to recover from the Great Recession of 2008–2009. At that time, most Americans agreed that the most important problem facing the United States concerned jobs and the economy. Oddly, however—despite the slackness of the economy, the absence of inflation, and many Americans' cries for economic help—a plurality of the SESA multimillionaires said that the most important problem was *budget deficits*. Most were averse to extensive government spending on any sort of economic stimulus or social welfare programs.[6]

The SESA survey showed that, while most Americans tilted strongly toward expanding government programs on health care and on Social Security, the multimillionaires tilted toward cutting each of them. Large majorities of Americans favored setting the minimum wage high enough so that no family with a full-time worker would fall below the poverty line, but most multimillionaires disagreed. Majorities of ordinary Americans favored having the government in Washington "see to it" that everyone who wanted to work could find a job; favored increasing the earned income tax credit; said that the federal government should *provide* jobs for everyone able and willing to work who could not find private employment; and said that the government should see that no one is without food, clothing, or shelter. But when asked the same survey questions concerning each of those issues, large majorities of the multimillionaires disagreed with most Americans about every one of them.[7]

Policy disagreements between the SESA multimillionaires and average Americans extended to other areas of economic and social welfare policy as well. Regarding health care and retirement pensions, these included national health insurance financed by tax money, and raising the cap on income subject to the Social Security payroll tax. For education policy, they included spending on public schools, access to college, and investing in retraining programs. For macroeconomic policy, they included *not* cutting spending on Medicare, education, or highways in order to reduce federal budget deficits, and support for economic regulation—especially of "big corporations." For tax policy, they included use of the corporate income tax and estate tax rates on large estates. In every one of these cases, the preferences of multimillionaires were markedly out of tune with the preferences of ordinary Americans.[8]

Again, since most multimillionaires hold even more economically conservative views than affluent Americans do—far more conservative views than those of average Americans—it is not much of a logical leap to infer that *billionaires* probably do too. That possibility tends to be supported by the research reported in this book.

If it is indeed true that most billionaires share or exceed the extreme economic conservatism of the SESA multimillionaires, and that billionaires have even more influence than Gilens's affluents, it seems possible that US billionaires and their allies may bear substantial responsibility for pushing our public policies away from many measures that majorities of Americans want—including policies that would soften some of the sharp edges of economic inequality.

In fact, the political clout of wealthy Americans—wielded against many popular economic-welfare policies—may well have brought us to the unhappy place where we are today—where millions of citizens have suffered great economic stress but the government seems little responsive to their needs and wants—and many Americans are very angry about it.

Economic Inequality and Political Inequality

As we approach the question of what, if anything, to do about billionaires and stealth politics, a bit of historical perspective may be helpful.

It is a fact that the United States today—despite our enormous, unprecedented national riches and our astoundingly high level of economic output—is perpetually embroiled in serious conflict over the question of who gets to enjoy how much of those riches. It is also a fact that in the course of some four decades since the 1970s, most working-class and middle-class Americans have seen their wages stay stagnant. Millions of Americans—particularly in the small towns and cities of Middle America—have faced job losses, wage cuts, home foreclosures, and health-care crises. Their children—if lucky enough to go to college—have been stuck with enormous student loan debts and face uncertain job futures. Yet during these same years the fortunes of the wealthiest Americans have soared. Economic inequality has reached peaks not seen in the United States since the glaringly unequal 1920s or the Gilded Age of the 1890s.[9] This is a great time to be an American billionaire. But to be an ordinary American worker, not so much.[10]

Given this historical context, one might expect that democratic accountability would move the US government toward vigorous action to help our battered fellow citizens. It seems natural to expect that—in times of trouble for millions of their citizens—rich democratic countries would act strongly and quickly to help, and that if governments failed to do so, citizens would punish them at the polls. Some governments in Europe and elsewhere have in fact provided such help, while others have implemented austerity policies that moved in the opposite direction. The record of the United States has been mixed, but arguably has fallen more into the austerity camp. Opinion surveys and observations by journalists and others—not to mention various populistic revolts, including the startlingly successful Trump presidential campaign of 2016[11]—all indicate that millions of Americans want help from economic policies, are angry that they haven't gotten more help, and think their political system and the top elites of both major political parties have let them down.[12]

How can that be?

Although the very phenomenon of stealth politics means that we cannot be sure, the answer to that question may take us back to the political actions of billionaires and other wealthy Americans. It seems possible that wealthy Americans have a great deal of political clout, and that they have—often secretly—wielded that clout for purposes contrary to the wishes of most Americans. If so, that may have contributed to the mess we are in. To the extent that billionaires' wealth and political influence are central to both our political problems and our economic problems, those who want to make progress dealing with either one should consider doing something about billionaires' distinctive political clout.

What to Do

We do not favor drastic or punitive action against billionaires.

After all, some of America's wealthiest billionaires have played central parts in bringing us goods and services that have brightened the lives of millions of Americans: innovative computer hardware (Steve Jobs) and software (Bill Gates); wondrous web-ware, from Facebook (Mark Zuckerberg and Dustin Moskovitz) to a seemingly unlimited stream of clever new services and applications like Uber (Travis Kalanick and Garrett Camp) and Snapchat (Evan Spiegel and Bobby Murphy); the Walmart and Amazon retail revolutions (Sam Walton, Jeff Bezos); life-saving pharmaceutical products (Patrick Soon-Shiong); and many others.

The fact is that American capitalism has brought forth what a visitor from the eighteenth or nineteenth century would surely see as miracles of innovation and mass production. A number of smart, creative, energetic, risk-taking, and (sometimes) self-sacrificing billionaires have played critical roles in bringing about those miracles. Strong material incentives—including opportunities to amass great fortunes—have undoubtedly been helpful in spurring their hard work and risk taking.

In our view, many or most American billionaires deserve substantial economic rewards. The existence of such rewards is probably beneficial for society as a whole. We are not "levelers" who would try to confiscate every bit of billionaires' fortunes. Far less are we revolutionaries, who—at times of extreme economic and political inequality in various places around the world—have been known to yell at the holders of great wealth and power, "Up against the wall!" or "Off with your heads!"

But it is not radical or revolutionary to point out that most billionaires would not slack off—and indeed would still be richly rewarded for their efforts—if they had to pay a little more in taxes. As Warren Buffett has often emphasized (citing his own case), great fortunes are not created by a single human being acting alone. They reflect lucky opportunities and a great deal of cooperation and help from many other people. Indeed, great fortunes are generally built with a lot of assistance from the legal arrangements, the public policies, and the productive resources of entire societies. It makes sense to ask billionaires to *share* some of the wealth that is derived, in good part, from others' labor.

Moreover—and more centrally related to concerns about unequal or unaccountable political power—it does not follow that billionaires or other wealthy Americans should be allowed to spend every penny they would like to spend in order to influence *politics*. Politics is very different from ordinary consumption goods that people should be totally free to buy and sell. Spending on politics, unlike the purchase of a yacht or a mansion, can directly affect the welfare of millions of other citizens. Massive spending on politics may undermine a central tenet of democracy, *political equality,* in which each citizen has as equal a voice as possible in deciding how government policies can best serve all citizens.

If one were to conclude that US billionaires currently have too much political power, it is not difficult to imagine ways in which their power might be counterbalanced or curtailed.

Reformers might begin with—but should avoid the temptation of ending with—direct efforts to reduce the influence of big-money political contributions to campaigns. The contemporary Supreme Court has made it very difficult to impose limits on the amounts of money that individuals or corporations are allowed to contribute. So reformers could think about how they might change some of the Court's rulings—either by crafting persuasive new legal arguments or by working for the appointment of new justices. But even without a change in constitutional doctrine, a great deal could be accomplished by creating an entirely *voluntary* system, in which political candidates were offered substantial amounts of public money to pay their campaign expenses, in return for a pledge to accept no private contributions at all. (Or no private contributions larger than some modest, specified amount.) If the public money were allocated through equal-sized "democracy vouchers" that each citizen could pass on to her or his favored candidates, the political power of large fortunes would be significantly reduced and political equality would be increased.[13] Obviously, other policies might be devised to have a similar effect. The point is that there exists a range of options for increasing the financial voice of nonbillionaire citizens in politics without imposing direct and potentially unconstitutional limits on the political speech or action of billionaires.[14]

In order to fully replace money power with power exercised in equal amounts by each citizen, however, it would probably also be necessary to increase the representativeness of who votes in elections. US elections notoriously overrepresent older, whiter, and (especially) more-affluent and educated people, who tend to have different needs and different policy preferences from the underrepresented young people, minorities, and working-class or poor people.[15] Many proposed remedies are familiar: automatic, universal voter registration; election-day holidays; easily accessible polling places; and plenty of voting machines (with paper trails to make sure that vote tallies are accurate).

Further measures to empower ordinary voters and reduce any disproportionate power exercised by billionaires might include shifting primary elections away from obscure times that reduce turnout (low turnout helps donors and activists with extreme views to dominate the outcomes) and/or reducing the number of one-party districts so that the donors and activists cannot so easily get unpopular nominees elected.

A really thoroughgoing effort to erase money power and create equal representation, however, would probably also have to deal with certain structural features of our political system that (so long as private money plays any part in American politics) tend to bias outcomes in ways that benefit the wealthy.[16] Those features include the undemocratic apportionment of the US Senate (two senators for each state, no matter how sparsely populated), which allows floods of outside money to tip the election of senators in small states. Also the rules and procedures (especially the "hold" and the filibuster) that empower a single senator—conceivably working on behalf of just one very wealthy constituent[17]—to block actions favored by large majorities of Americans. And one-party domination of the House of Representatives, so that the minority party—even if it represents a very large minority of Americans—can be altogether ignored.[18] It might also be necessary to tackle the dependence of our political parties on private money and ideologically extreme activists—which can make entire parties unrepresentative even of their own voters. To deal with some of these matters would require major political efforts—perhaps a social movement.[19]

It is not the purpose of this book, however, to engage in a full discussion of far-reaching democratic political reforms. Instead, we want to focus on narrower and easier-to-achieve reforms concerning the *political accountability* of billionaires, a matter which is directly related to our empirical findings. Even if the money-drenched US political system were to continue in pretty much its current form, we believe that democracy could be significantly enhanced, and the making of public policy improved, by making it harder for billionaires to take their political actions in secret.

Get the Stealthiness out of Politics

In principle, at least, it should be relatively easy—without infringing seriously on billionaires' freedoms—to bring many currently stealthy political actions by billionaires into the sunlight for all to see and debate.

Rights to free speech—including *anonymous* speech—must be taken seriously. Back in the days of legally enforced racial segregation in the South, the Supreme Court ruled that it would violate the US Constitution for the state of Alabama to force the NAACP to reveal its membership list.[20] Anonymity is especially important for embattled minorities like civil rights workers in the old South, whose well-being (and even lives) were often at risk. Billionaires are less likely to be vulnerable to violent repression if they express unpopular views or join unpopular organizations. Still, billionaires' rights should be protected, too.

We believe, however, that spending large sums of money to influence politics is significantly different from simply voicing political views or joining a political group. Being able to speak and associate freely is the lifeblood of democracy. Pouring money into politics, on the other hand, has the potential to crowd out other people's speech and association rights, while also (if it affects policy making) perhaps negatively affecting the well-being of millions of people. Even today's Supreme Court, which has tended to conflate money with speech,[21] has not indicated that regulations requiring the *disclosure* of financial contributions—as opposed to legal limitations on their size—would violate the First Amendment.

One idea would be to require that any political activity involving more than a certain amount of money (perhaps $1,000, maybe $10,000) must be reported to the FEC or to some other official body, and that that information must be made easily accessible to the public.

We would not expect ordinary citizens to spend hours poring over FEC records. But if the information were compiled in a well-organized electronic database, we could count on specialists like those at the Center for Responsive Politics or the Center for Public Integrity to issue clear, pithy reports that would alert the citizenry to what is going on. Full disclosure would likely lead to compelling sound bites on TV and the web that could reach nearly all citizens, even those least attuned to politics.

We believe that disclosure requirements should definitely apply to any large financial contribution to—or money spent on behalf of—a political party or a candidate for public office. It should include money that is claimed to be "independent" of the favored campaign. No more dark money in elections.

It is harder to be sure what to do about big financial contributions to political causes or organizations not directly involved in elections. What—if anything—should be done about large sums of money spent on the unregistered lobbying of public officials? Or big money that funds think tanks? Or money spent to own or subsidize media outlets, which may or may not spread slanted "news" and commentary? Such activities, too, are often unaccountable to the citizenry as a whole. They, too, probably contribute to political inequality, by disproportionately affecting public policy and shaping public discourse. They may possibly produce harmful public policies or lead citizens astray in their political thinking. Some critics may argue that these forms of political spending, too, should be subjected to disclosure requirements.

But such activities are arguably less clearly entangled with a broad public interest in disclosure. They may come closer to the sorts of political expression that deserve strict legal protection. We leave it to experts and the citizenry to sort through the legal, moral, and technical considerations involved in deciding precisely how broad or narrow disclosure requirements should be.

When it comes to political parties, candidates, and elections, however, we believe that the case for disclosure is compelling.

Full disclosure would clearly increase the political accountability of billionaires. Voters would get a much better chance to find out what the billionaires are doing, and a better shot (if troubled by their actions) at organizing against them. Politically engaged billionaires might feel pressed to explain themselves: to start speaking out about what kinds of public policies they have been working for and why.

It is even possible that full disclosure of billionaires' political activities might have some effect on the broader issues of political inequality and the political power of wealth. If their actions were made publicly visible, some billionaires' fears of angry reactions from their customers or investors might deter them from working to enact policies opposed by large majorities of Americans. Full disclosure might make wealthy people at least think twice before working to cut Social Security benefits, to dismantle Americans' health insurance coverage, to cut taxes on the highest incomes, or to impose governmental austerity on millions of unhappy citizens.

Even if disclosure did not greatly change billionaires' political aims or efforts, however, it would probably increase their propensity to argue their case publicly—a meaningful gain for democracy in its own right. And disclosure would give ordinary citizens a much better chance to hold billionaires accountable for their political actions.

Appendixes

	2013 Position	2013 Wealth (in $Billions)	2016 Position	2016 Wealth (in $Billions)	Change/ Notes
Bill Gates	I	72	I	81	—
Warren Buffett	2	58.5	3	65.5	−1
Larry Ellison	3	41	5	49.3	−2
Charles Koch	4	36	7	42	−3
David Koch	4	36	7	42	−3
Christy Walton	6	35.4	87	5.6	Previous wealth miscalculated, based on incorrect assumption that late husband left her his entire estate
Jim Walton	7	33.8	11	35.6	−4
Alice Walton	8	33.5	13	35.4	−5
S. Robson Walton	9	33.3	12	35.5	−3
Michael Bloomberg	10	31	6	45	+4
Sheldon Adelson	11	28.5	14	31.8	−3
Jeff Bezos	12	27.2	2	67	+10
Larry Page	13	24.9	9	38.5	+4
Sergey Brin	14	24.4	10	37.5	+4
Forrest Mars Jr.	15	20.5	N/A	N/A	Passed away in July 2016
Jacqueline Mars	15	20.5	16	27	−1
John Mars	15	20.5	16	27	−1
Carl Icahn	18	20.3	26	15.7	−8
George Soros	19	20	19	24.9	—
Mark Zuckerberg	20	19	4	55.5	+16
Steve Ballmer	21	18	15	27.5	+6
Leonard Blavatnik	22	17.8	22	18.2	—
Abigail Johnson	23	17.2	29	13.2	−6
Phil Knight	24	16.3	18	25.5	+6
Michael Dell	25	15.9	20	20	+5

continues

	2013 Position	2013 Wealth (in $Billions)	2016 Position	2016 Wealth (in $Billions)	Change/ Notes
Paul Allen	26	15.8	21	18.9	+5
Ronald Perelman	27	14	33	12.2	−6
Donald Bren	27	14	27	15.2	—
Anne Cox Chambers	29	13.5	N/A	N/A	Distributed her stake in family business to her children
Rupert Murdoch	30	13.4	38	11.1	−8
Ray Dalio	31	12.9	25	15.9	+6
Charles Ergen	32	12.5	28	14.7	+4
Harold Hamm	33	12.4	30	13.1	+3
James Simons	34	12	24	16.5	+10
Laurene Powell Jobs	35	11.7	23	17.7	+12
Jack Taylor	36	10.4	N/A	N/A	Passed away in July 2016
John Paulson	36	10.4	52	8.6	−16
Philip Anschutz	38	10.3	39	10.8	−1
Richard Kinder	39	10.2	69	7	−30
Harold Simmons	40	10	N/A	N/A	Passed away in December 2013
George Kaiser	40	10	61	7.2	−21
Andrew Beal	42	9.8	49	8.9	−7
Steve Cohen	43	9.4	31	13	+12
Edward Johnson III	44	9.3	68	7.1	−24
Patrick Soon-Shiong	45	9	47	9.2	−2
Samuel Newhouse Jr.	46	8.9	42	10.5	+4
Charles Butt	47	8.5	N/A	N/A	Distributed ownership in business throughout family
Pierre Omidyar	47	8.5	54	8.1	−7
Eric Schmidt	49	8.3	36	11.3	+13
Elaine Marshall	49	8.3	N/A	N/A	Reason for drop from list is unclear
Hank & Doug Meijer	49	8.3	70	6.9	−21
Donald Newhouse	52	8.2	42	10.5	+10
David Tepper	53	7.9	35	11.4	+18
Stephen Schwarzman	54	7.7	45	10.3	+9
Ralph Lauren	54	7.7	83	5.9	−29
Leonard Lauder	56	7.6	48	9	+8
John Menard Jr.	57	7.5	46	9.4	+11
James Goodnight	58	7.2	51	8.7	+7
Eli Broad	59	6.9	58	7.4	+1
Richard DeVos	60	6.8	88	5.4	−28

	2013 Position	2013 Wealth (in $Billions)	2016 Position	2016 Wealth (in $Billions)	Change/ Notes
Jim Kennedy	61	6.7	39	10.8	+22
Blair Parry-Okeden	61	6.7	39	10.8	+22
John Malone	61	6.7	61	7.2	—
Elon Musk	61	6.7	34	11.6	+27
Herbert Kohler Jr.	65	6.4	52	8.6	+13
Thomas Peterffy	65	6.4	32	12.6	+33
David Duffield	65	6.4	73	6.7	–8
S. Truett Cathy	68	6	N/A	N/A	Passed away in September 2014
David Geffen	68	6	73	6.7	–5
Micky Arison	70	5.9	61	7.2	+9
Sumner Redstone	71	5.8	117	4.7	–46
Dennis Washington	71	5.8	83	5.9	–12
Leslie Wexner	73	5.7	70	6.9	+3
Richard LeFrak	74	5.6	73	6.7	+1
Ray Lee Hunt	74	5.6	111	4.8	–37
Charles Johnson	74	5.6	105	5	–31
Dannine Avara	77	5.5	94	5.3	–17
Scott Duncan	77	5.5	94	5.3	–17
Milane Frantz	77	5.5	94	5.3	–17
Randa Williams	77	5.5	94	5.3	–17
Rupert Johnson Jr.	77	5.5	131	4.3	–54
Jeffrey Hildebrand	77	5.5	134	4.1	–57
Ira Rennert	77	5.5	148	3.9	–71
Stanley Kroenke	84	5.3	58	7.4	+26
Dustin Moskovitz	85	5.2	44	10.4	+41
Leon Black	85	5.2	105	5	–20
Gayle Cook	85	5.2	N/A	N/A	Passed fortune to son
Charles Schwab	88	5.1	76	6.6	+12
Patrick McGovern	88	5.1	N/A	N/A	Passed away in March 2014
Jin Sook & Do Won Chang	90	5	222	3	–132
Thomas Frist Jr.	90	5	55	7.9	+35
David Green	90	5	81	6.1	+9
Robert Rowling	93	4.9	82	6	+11
Stephen Ross	94	4.8	58	7.4	+36
Bruce Kovner	95	4.7	90	5.3	+5
Ann Walton Kroenke	95	4.7	80	6.2	+15
Henry Kravis	95	4.7	124	4.5	–29
Gordon Moore	98	4.6	56	7.6	+42
Daniel Ziff	98	4.6	111	4.8	–12
Dirk Ziff	98	4.6	111	4.8	–12

Taxation		Social Security
tax policy	tax burden	Social Security payroll tax
double taxation	tax revenue expansion	Social Security payroll tax
capital gains tax	tax revenue enhancement	income cap
grand bargain	Laffer Curve	Social Security retirement
comprehensive tax reform	Earned Income Tax Credit	pension
estate tax	EITC	Social Security privatization
death tax	redistribution	Social Security stock market
corporate tax rates	Robin Hood tax	investment
business taxes	financial transaction tax	Social Security reform
tax credits/deductions/	carbon tax	Social Security benefit reductions
charitable deduction	Buffett Rule	Social Security retirement age
tax extenders	flat tax	Social Security third rail
tax enforcement		Social Security means testing

APPENDIX 3 **Position Taking among *Forbes* Top 100 on Economic Issues**

	Net Worth in $Billions (as of Sept. 2013)	Taxation			Social Security	
		Statements	Index Score	Direction	Statements	Direction
Bill Gates	72	14	5	More	0	
Warren Buffett	58.5	19	4	More	7	More
Larry Ellison	41	0	0		0	
Charles Koch	36	0	0		0	
David Koch	36	1	−1	Less	0	
Christy Walton	35.4	0	0		0	
Jim Walton	33.8	0	0		0	
Alice Walton	33.5	0	0		0	
S. Robson Walton	33.3	0	0		0	
Michael Bloomberg	31	23	1	More	4	Less
Sheldon Adelson	28.5	1	−1	Less	0	
Jeff Bezos	27.2	0	0		0	
Larry Page	24.9	0	0		0	
Sergey Brin	24.4	1	1	More	0	
Forrest Mars Jr.	20.5	0	0		0	
Jacqueline Mars	20.5	0	0		0	
John Mars	20.5	0	0		0	
Carl Icahn	20.3	1	1	More	0	
George Soros	20	9	5	More	1	More
Mark Zuckerberg	19	1	1	More	0	
Steve Ballmer	18	2	−1	Less	0	
Leonard Blavatnik	17.8	0	0		0	
Abigail Johnson	17.2	0	0		0	
Phil Knight	16.3	2	−2	Less	0	
Michael Dell	15.9	0	0		0	

	Net Worth in $Billions (as of Sept. 2013)	Taxation			Social Security	
		Statements	Index Score	Direction	Statements	Direction
Paul Allen	15.8	0	0		0	
Ronald Perelman	14	2	0		0	
Donald Bren	14	0	0		0	
Anne Cox Chambers	13.5	0	0		0	
Rupert Murdoch	13.4	3	−2	Less	0	
Ray Dalio	12.9	1	1	More	0	
Charles Ergen	12.5	0	0		0	
Harold Hamm	12.4	3	−1	Less	0	
James Simons	12	1	1	More	0	
Laurene Powell Jobs	11.7	0	0		0	
Jack Taylor	10.4	0	0		0	
John Paulson	10.4	0	0		0	
Philip Anschutz	10.3	0	0		0	
Richard Kinder	10.2	0	0		0	
Harold Simmons	10	2	−2	Less	0	
George Kaiser	10	4	3	More	0	
Andrew Beal	9.8	0	0		0	
Steve Cohen	9.4	0	0		0	
Edward Johnson III	9.3	0	0		0	
Patrick Soon-Shiong	9	0	0		0	
Samuel Newhouse Jr.	8.9	0	0		0	
Charles Butt	8.5	0	0		0	
Pierre Omidyar	8.5	0	0		0	
Eric Schmidt	8.3	4	1	More	0	
Elaine Marshall	8.3	0	0		0	
Hank & Doug Meijer	8.3	0	0		0	
Donald Newhouse	8.2	0	0		0	
David Tepper	7.9	0	0		0	
Stephen Schwarzman	7.7	5	−2	Less	0	
Ralph Lauren	7.7	0	0		0	
Leonard Lauder	7.6	0	0		0	
John Menard Jr.	7.5	0	0		0	
James Goodnight	7.2	0	0		0	
Eli Broad	6.9	2	0		0	
Richard DeVos	6.8	0	0		0	
Jim Kennedy	6.7	0	0		0	
Blair Parry-Okeden	6.7	0	0		0	
John Malone	6.7	5	−2	Less	1	No stance
Elon Musk	6.7	1	1	More	0	
Herbert Kohler Jr.	6.4	0	0		0	

continues

	Net Worth in $Billions (as of Sept. 2013)	Taxation			Social Security	
		Statements	Index Score	Direction	Statements	Direction
Thomas Peterffy	6.4	1	−1	Less	0	
David Duffield	6.4	0	0		0	
S. Truett Cathy	6	0	0		0	
David Geffen	6	3	0		0	
Micky Arison	5.9	0	0		0	
Sumner Redstone	5.8	0	0		0	
Dennis Washington	5.8	0	0		0	
Leslie Wexner	5.7	0	0		0	
Richard LeFrak	5.6	2	0		0	
Ray Lee Hunt	5.6	0	0		0	
Charles Johnson	5.6	0	0		0	
Dannine Avara	5.5	0	0		0	
Scott Duncan	5.5	0	0		0	
Milane Frantz	5.5	0	0		0	
Randa Williams	5.5	0	0		0	
Rupert Johnson Jr.	5.5	0	0		0	
Jeffrey Hildebrand	5.5	0	0		0	
Ira Rennert	5.5	0	0		0	
Stanley Kroenke	5.3	0	0		0	
Dustin Moskovitz	5.2	0	0		0	
Leon Black	5.2	1	1	More	0	
Gayle Cook	5.2	0	0		0	
Charles Schwab	5.1	0	0		0	
Patrick McGovern	5.1	0	0		0	
Jin Sook & Do Won Chang	5	0	0		0	
Thomas Frist Jr.	5	0	0		0	
David Green	5	0	0		0	
Robert Rowling	4.9	0	0		0	
Stephen Ross	4.8	1	−1	Less	0	
Bruce Kovner	4.7	0	0		0	
Ann Walton Kroenke	4.7	0	0		0	
Henry Kravis	4.7	2	−1	Less	0	
Gordon Moore	4.6	0	0		0	
Daniel Ziff	4.6	0	0		0	
Dirk Ziff	4.6	0	0		0	

Note: Tax index score aggregates statements made about the five tax policy issues in our dataset, based on direction. A positive point is given for each issue on which a subject advocates higher taxes, and a negative point is given for each issue on which a subject advocates lower taxes. The maximum score is 5 and the minimum is −5.

APPENDIX 4 **Position Taking among *Forbes* Top 100 on Social Issues**

	Worth in $Billions (as of September 2013)	Immigration			Abortion			Same-Sex Marriage		
		No. of Statements	Statements' Direction	Actions' Direction	No. of Statements	Statements' Direction	Actions' Direction	No. of Statements	Statements' Direction	Actions' Direction
Bill Gates	72	6	SWO + Path	Increase	0			0		Support
Warren Buffett	58.5	4	SWO + Path		0		PC	2	Support	
Larry Ellison	41	1	SWO		0			0		
Charles Koch	36	0			0		PL	0		
David Koch	36	0			1	PC	PL	3	Support	
Christy Walton	35.4	0			0			0		
Jim Walton	33.8	0			0			0		
Alice Walton	33.5	0			0			0		
S. Robson Walton	33.3	0			0			0		
Michael Bloomberg	31	9	Increase	Increase	3	PC	PC	11	Support	Support
Sheldon Adelson	28.5	4	Increase		2	PC		0		
Jeff Bezos	27.2	0			0			1	Support	Support
Larry Page	24.9	0			0			0		Support
Sergey Brin	24.4	0			0			1	Support	Support
Forrest Mars Jr.	20.5	0			0			0		
Jacqueline Mars	20.5	0			0			0		
John Mars	20.5	0			0			0		
Carl Icahn	20.3	0			0		PC	0		
George Soros	20	0		Increase	0			0		
Mark Zuckerberg	19	6	Increase	Increase	0			2	Support	Support
Steve Ballmer	18	5	SWO	Increase	0			0		Support
Leonard Blavatnik	17.8	0			0			0		
Abigail Johnson	17.2	0			0			0		
Phil Knight	16.3	0			0			0		Support

continues

APPENDIX 4 *(continued)*

	Worth in $Billions (as of September 2013)	Immigration			Abortion			Same-Sex Marriage		
		No. of Statements	Statements' Direction	Actions' Direction	No. of Statements	Statements' Direction	Actions' Direction	No. of Statements	Statements' Direction	Actions' Direction
Michael Dell	15.9	0		Increase	0			0		
Paul Allen	15.8	0			0			0		
Ronald Perelman	14	0			0			1	Support	
Donald Bren	14	0			0			0		
Anne Cox Chambers	13.5	0			0			0		
Rupert Murdoch	13.4	5	Increase		1	State Issue		1	Oppose	
Ray Dalio	12.9	0			0			0		
Charles Ergen	12.5	0			0			0		
Harold Hamm	12.4	0			0			0		
James Simons	12	0			0			0		
Laurene Powell Jobs	11.7	4	Increase	Increase	0			0		Support
Jack Taylor	10.4	0			0			0		
John Paulson	10.4	0			0			0		
Philip Anschutz	10.3	0			0			0		Oppose
Richard Kinder	10.2	0			0			0		
Harold Simmons	10	0			1	PC	PL	0		
George Kaiser	10	0			0			0		
Andrew Beal	9.8	0			0			0		
Steve Cohen	9.4	0			0			2	Support	Support
Edward Johnson III	9.3	0			0			0		
Patrick Soon-Shiong	9	0			0			0		
Samuel Newhouse Jr.	8.9	0			0			0		
Charles Butt	8.5	0		Increase	0			0		
Pierre Omidyar	8.5	0		Increase	0			2	Support	
Eric Schmidt	8.3	1	SWO	Increase	0			1	Support	
Elaine Marshall	8.3	0			0			0		

	Rating		SWO / Increase	Increase		PC	PL / PC		Support / Oppose	Support / Oppose
Hank & Doug Meijer	8.3	0			0			0		
Donald Newhouse	8.2	0			0			0		
David Tepper	7.9	0	SWO		0			1	Support	Support
Stephen Schwarzman	7.7	1			0			0		
Ralph Lauren	7.7	0	SWO		0			1	Support	Support
Leonard Lauder	7.6	1			0			0		
John Menard Jr.	7.5	0			0			0		
James Goodnight	7.2	2	Increase		0			0		
Eli Broad	6.9	0			0			0		
Richard DeVos	6.8	0			0		PL	1	Oppose	Oppose
Jim Kennedy	6.7	0			0			0		
Blair Parry-Okeden	6.7	0			0			0		
John Malone	6.7	0			0			0		
Elon Musk	6.7	2	SWO	Increase	0			0		
Herbert Kohler Jr.	6.4	0			0			0		
Thomas Peterffy	6.4	0			1	PC		0		
David Duffield	6.4	0			0			0		
S. Truett Cathy	6	0			0			0		
David Geffen	6	0			1	PC	PC	1	Support	Oppose
Micky Arison	5.9	0			0			0		
Sumner Redstone	5.8	0			0			0		
Dennis Washington	5.8	0			0			0		
Leslie Wexner	5.7	0		Increase	0			0		
Richard LeFrak	5.6	0			0			0		
Ray Lee Hunt	5.6	0			0			0		
Charles Johnson	5.6	0			0			0		
Dannine Avara	5.5	0			0			0		
Scott Duncan	5.5	0			0			0		
Milane Frantz	5.5	0			0			0		
Randa Williams	5.5	0			0			0		
Rupert Johnson Jr.	5.5	0			0			0		

continues

APPENDIX 4 (*continued*)

	Worth in $Billions (as of September 2013)	Immigration			Abortion			Same-Sex Marriage		
		No. of Statements	Statements' Direction	Actions' Direction	No. of Statements	Statements' Direction	Actions' Direction	No. of Statements	Statements' Direction	Actions' Direction
Jeffrey Hildebrand	5.5	0			0			0		
Ira Rennert	5.5	0			0			0		
Stanley Kroenke	5.3	0			0			0		
Dustin Moskovitz	5.2	0			0			0		
Leon Black	5.2	0			0			0		
Gayle Cook	5.2	0			0			0		
Charles Schwab	5.1	0			0			0		
Patrick McGovern	5.1	0			0			0		
Jin Sook & Do Won Chang	5	0			0			0		
Thomas Frist Jr.	5	0			0			0		
David Green	5	0			1	PL		0		Oppose
Robert Rowling	4.9	1	SWO		0			0		
Stephen Ross	4.8	1	Increase		0			0		
Bruce Kovner	4.7	0			0			0		
Ann Walton Kroenke	4.7	0			0			0		
Henry Kravis	4.7	0			0			0		Support
Gordon Moore	4.6	0			0			0		
Daniel Ziff	4.6	0			0			0		
Dirk Ziff	4.6	0			0			0		

Note: "SWO + Path" indicates support for increased immigration among skilled workers plus a path to citizenship for current undocumented immigrants. "SWO" indicates support for increased immigration among skilled workers only. "PL" indicates a pro-life position, and "PC" indicates a pro-choice position.

Immigration	Abortion	Same-Sex Marriage
immigration reform	abortion	same sex marriage
illegal immigration	family planning	gay marriage
guest worker program	pro-life	homosexual marriage
immigration enforcement	pro-choice	redefining marriage
undocumented immigrants	partial birth abortion	marriage equality
paths to citizenship	sanctity of life	traditional marriage
immigration amnesty	right to life	sanctity of marriage
border protection	reproductive rights	civil union
deportation	abortion rights	domestic partnership
work visas	anti-abortion	freedom to marry
comprehensive immigration	parental consent for abortion	defense of marriage
reform	abortion exceptions	
naturalization		
illegal aliens		
secure our borders		
dream act		

Notes

Introduction

1. See Porter 2017, as well as Nitti 2017.

2. See Alvaredo et al. 2017, Piketty 2014, and Wolff 2002. Kelly (forthcoming) argues that economic inequality and political inequality tend to mutually reinforce and increase each other.

3. *Forbes* 2017b, 86–90.

4. *Forbes* 2016a (global), 128–37; 2016b (US), 140–52. Bloomberg's calculations, which are updated at the end of each trading day, are similar (*Bloomberg* 2017). For IMF data on countries' GDP, see http://statisticstimes.com/economy /countries-by-projected-gdp.php.

5. See chap. 2 below.

6. Vogel 2015.

7. Balcerzak 2017.

8. Bonica et al. 2013.

9. The evidence on these points is strongest concerning *multimillionaires*: Page, Bartels, and Seawright 2013. On billionaires, see chaps. 2 and 5 below.

10. Bartels 2016; Gilens 2012; Gilens and Page 2014; Page and Gilens 2017, chap. 4.

11. As of 2016 (the most recent year covered by the Survey of Consumer Finances at the time of writing), each of the least wealthy members of the top one percent of US wealth holders held around $10 million in net worth, less than *one one-hundredth* of the fortune of the least wealthy billionaires (DQYDJ 2017; see also Hines 2014; Coy 2014).

12. The Survey of Economically Successful Americans (SESA) examined the political attitudes and behavior of a small (n = 102) but representative sample of Chicago-area multimillionaires in the top one or two percent of US wealth holders. See Page, Bartels, and Seawright 2013; Cook, Page, and Moskowitz 2014.

13. West 2014.

14. It is difficult to obtain exact figures regarding the net worth of Olin (who died in 1982) or the Bradley brothers (who died in 1942 and 1965), but all three owned large corporations and were among America's wealthiest individuals.

15. Mayer 2016. See also Mayer (2004, 2017).

16. Skocpol and Hertel-Fernandez, forthcoming; Skocpol and Hertel-Fernandez 2016; Sclar et al. 2016.

17. MacLean 2017.

18. As remarked by Cathy Haggerty, a NORC expert on interviewing the wealthy. On this and other obstacles to conducting interviews with wealthy Americans, see Page, Bartels, and Seawright 2011.

19. Even the highly respected, Federal Reserve-sponsored Survey of Consumer Finances—which oversamples wealthy Americans and has a great deal of clout for getting respondents to cooperate—does not attempt to include the *Forbes* 400 in its sampling (Bricker et al. 2015).

20. See Bonica 2014 and, for an application of his methodology that discusses billionaires, Bonica et al. 2013.

21. The policy stands of party leaders and elected officials tend to be forced into a single dimension by our two-party system.

22. Billionaires' contributions to specific policy-oriented groups provide the best single indicator that we have been able to find for the policy preferences of the many billionaires who have expressed no preferences in public. And billionaire-wide statistical patterns involving those contributions can help us infer the policy preferences of a broader set of billionaires. Still, only a minority of billionaires have made such contributions. Neither we nor anyone else we know of has been able to produce reliable estimates of the policy preferences of *all* individual billionaires.

23. Although the Koch brothers have been highly active in politics for decades, we show in chap. 2 that for most of that period, they were almost totally silent in public about specific matters of public policy. Until recently, very few Americans had heard of them.

Chapter One: Who the Billionaires Are

1. *Forbes* 2013 (US), 18.

2. *Forbes* 2013 (US), 124; Becraft 2014, 49–74. On Gates's biography, see Becraft 2014.

3. *Forbes* 2013 (US), 125. For an excellent biography of Buffett, see Schroeder 2009.

4. Wilson 1997, 43–67.

5. PwC 2016.

6. *Forbes* 2013 (US), 125.

7. Temple 2008; Kerstetter 2008; Mader 2008. On Ellison and Oracle generally, see Wilson 1997.

8. *Forbes* 2013 (US), 125; Schulman 2014; Mayer 2016.

9. *Forbes* 2013 (US), 126; Walton and Huey 1992.

10. *Forbes* 2013 (US), 126.

11. *Forbes* 2013 (US), 128, 137.

12. *Forbes* 2013 (US), 138, 140, 142.

13. *Forbes* 2013 (US), 144–64.

14. *Forbes* 2013 (US), 172.

15. O'Brien 2015.

16. *Forbes* 2017a (global), 38, 82–3, 142; *Forbes* 2017b (US), 124. A "definitive" account of Trump's assets and liabilities as of 2016, including a close look at his major real estate properties, is given in *Forbes* 2016a (global), 80–90. On Trump's financial history, see Johnson 2016.

17. *Forbes* 2013 (US), 125, 128, 137; *Forbes* 2016a (global), 129, 132, 133.

18. Five billionaires in our 2013 group (Forrest Mars Jr., Jack Taylor, Harold Simmons, S. Truett Cathy, and Patrick McGovern) had passed away by 2016. Three (Anne Cox Chambers, Charles Butt, and Gayle Cook) were still alive but dropped off the *Forbes* list because they passed their wealth to heirs. One (Elaine Marshall) dropped off the *Forbes* list for unclear reasons. Eleven billionaires fell out of the top 100 but remained on the *Forbes* 400 list, all but one staying in the top 150. One additional billionaire—Samuel "Si" Newhouse Jr.—was included in the 2016 *Forbes* rankings but passed away in 2017.

19. All figures as of mid-2017.

20. US Census Bureau, n.d.

21. On the lives of America's wealthy, see Frank 2007; Freeland 2012.

22. *Forbes* 2013 (US), 124–37.

23. *Forbes* 2016a (global), 40, 129, 140, 142.

24. *Forbes* 2017a (global), 32.

25. *Forbes* 2013 (US), 34.

26. *Forbes* 2016a (global), 188.

27. *Forbes* 2016a (global), 152, 179.

28. *Forbes* 2016a (global), 143, 147, 148, 162, 163, 172, 174, 178, 182.

29. *Forbes* 2016a (global), 56–70.

30. *Forbes* 2016a (global), 133, 137, 138, 140, 142.

31. *Forbes* 2016a (global), 66.

32. *Forbes* 2017a (global), 138–39.

33. See Piketty 2014, chaps. 3–4.

34. *Forbes* 2017a (global), 138; Fontevecchia 2014.

35. Piketty 2014, chaps. 10–11.

36. Gladwell 2008, 55–68.

37. *Forbes* 2017a (global), 138.

38. Bivens 2013.

39. Friedman 2007.

40. Taub 2017; 2016; 2015; 2014; 2013: *Institutional Investor's Alpha* "Hedge Fund Rich List."

41. *Forbes* 2016a (global), 128, 129, 137; Mallaby 2010.

42. *Forbes* 2016a (global), 138, 140.

43. *Forbes* 2016a (global), 142.

44. Setting aside unscrupulous caregivers to the elderly, or relatives who feign friendliness to—but privately loathe—rich, crotchety Aunt Jane, it would be fanciful to suppose that the amounts of money "earned" through inheritance are set by competitive markets.

45. The idea that entrepreneurs can be incentivized to work harder by the prospect of passing riches on to their children does not rest on any solid evidence we know of. If true, that would be a rather expensive and inefficient incentive.

46. Friedman 1962, 161–66.

47. Here we disagree with Milton Friedman, who apparently assumed that considerations of economic efficiency make payment in accordance with the market value of marginal product "necessary" (1962, 166). Later in *Capitalism and Freedom*, however, Friedman advocated a "negative income tax" to alleviate poverty (1962, chap. 12). And he said nothing in favor of inheritance.

Chapter Two: Stealth Politics on Taxes and Social Security

1. Useful accounts of techniques by which wealthy individuals may be able to influence politics include Domhoff (2014); Ferguson (1995); Hacker and Pierson (2010); and Winters (2011).

2. We decided on a search window of ten years—ending in 2015, our final year of data collection—because the digitization and web-based indexing of media contents appears to be consistently comprehensive starting in about 2005 but is more fragmentary before that. A ten-year period seems long enough to give billionaires abundant time to speak out if they want to, yet short enough that most individuals' positions on major issues would not be expected to change substantially during the period. (In fact, they very rarely did so.) Our searches produced some relevant public statements made before our official starting date, but very few that were not later reaffirmed and included in our data set.

3. Congressional Budget Office 2017. According to the same CBO data, tax revenue in 2016 amounted to about $3.27 trillion, resulting in a deficit of about $587 billion.

4. Of all the OECD countries with lower taxes than the US, Japan and Israel are roughly comparable to our country in terms of GDP. The other OECD countries with lower taxes have per-capita GDPs that are half that of the US or lower: Spain, Slovenia, Portugal, Greece, Korea, Czech Republic, Estonia, Slovak Republic, Hungary, Poland, Latvia, Turkey, Chile, and Mexico. For these countries, the

economic trade-offs related to tax rates are quite different than for the US and other more comparable countries.

5. Organisation for Economic Co-operation and Development 2017. As of the most recent year with data for all OECD countries (2014), the US ranked nineteenth out of thirty-five countries in tax revenue per capita—including state and local as well as federal taxes. The US per-person tax revenue of $14,115 was close to the OECD median of $14,327 but further below the OECD average of $14,916. The difference of $801 per capita, multiplied by the US population, is quite substantial. Raising US per-person tax rates to match the OECD average would have generated about $255 billion in additional revenue in 2014, more than half of the federal deficit in that year. If tax rates had been raised to match those of Finland (the seventh-highest-taxed OECD country, at $21,856 per person), that would have generated $2 trillion in new revenue, completely eliminating budget deficits and opening the way for substantial new policy initiatives.

6. See Hacker and Pierson 2010, especially chap. 2; and Piketty and Saez 2007.

7. Internal Revenue Service 2017.

8. Huang and Cho 2017.

9. Tax Policy Center 2016.

10. Thomson Reuters 2016: Payroll taxes for Social Security—which in 2016 applied only to the first $118,500 of a person's income—are more regressive than Medicare taxes, which are not subject to income caps. However, Social Security makes up most of the total payroll taxes—12.4 percent up to the cap, as opposed to only 2.9 percent to Medicare.

11. The 15.3 percent payroll tax rate combines Social Security and Medicare taxes. It combines the "employee's" and the "employer's" contributions, as most economists say should be done—since the tax "on employers" lowers employees' wages.

12. Thomson Reuters 2016.

13. Page and Jacobs 2009, chap. 4.

14. Our calculation assumes that the billionaire gets at least $118,500 in wages and salaries. Most billionaires' incomes actually derive largely from capital gains, dividends, and interest—all of which are entirely outside the purview of the payroll taxes.

15. Congressional Budget Office 2017.

16. Social Security Administration 2017a.

17. Social Security Administration 2016.

18. Romig and Sherman 2016; Engelhardt and Gruber 2004; Social Security Administration 2017b; Blank 1997; Jencks 2015.

19. Cook and Moskowitz 2014; Gallup, n.d.

20. Bartels 2008, 2016; Gilens 2005, 2012; Gilens and Page 2014; Jacobs and Page 2005; Page and Gilens 2017.

21. Gilens 2009, 2012. Gilens speaks of preferences "at the 90th income percentile." This is the same thing as the median preferences of the top 20 percent of income earners. Soroka and Wlezien 2008 point out that outsized influence by the affluent may be less worrisome if their policy preferences agree with those of ordinary voters, but Gilens 2009 shows that on many important issues this is not the case.

22. Page, Bartels, and Seawright 2013. On the top 4 percent or so, see Page and Hennessy 2010.

23. In 2013, the year of the *Forbes* list used for our research on billionaires, approximately $7.8 million was needed to fall within the top 1 percent of US wealth holders (Hines 2014).

24. For some time, a mere $1.0 billion has not been sufficient to make the *Forbes* 400 list. In October 2013, when a minimum of $1.3 billion was required, sixty-one billionaires fell below the cutoff point. *Forbes* graciously printed their names in a sort of consolation coda to the real list. *Forbes* 2013 (US), 265, 272–75.

25. Zhao, Seibert, and Lumpkin 2010.

26. Bezos purchased the *Post* in 2013 for $250 million (Farhi 2013). Bezos's net worth that year was just over $27 billion.

27. Verba, Schlozman, and Brady 1995; Schlozman, Verba, and Brady 2012; Cook, Page, and Moskowitz 2014.

28. *Forbes* 2013 (US). Daniel, Dirk, and Robert Ziff were—along with Gordon Moore—tied at #98 on the 2013 list. We observed our n = 100 cutoff point by arbitrarily excluding Robert, whose political behavior appears to be virtually identical to that of his brothers. Otherwise we would have ended up with a set of 101 billionaires, the last of whom would effectively duplicate two individuals already included in the analysis.

29. GDP data from International Monetary Fund 2013.

30. See Page, Bartels, and Seawright 2011.

31. Bricker et al. 2014, 38.

32. But see Bonica 2014; Bonica et al. 2013.

33. Since questions about several of these topics were asked on the SESA survey and have also been included in national polls of the general public, policy-related statements and actions by billionaires can be compared with the views of the top 1 percent or so of wealth holders and with the opinions of average citizens.

34. Sartori 2009.

35. Because Google searches are not case sensitive, proper nouns like Social Security and Earned Income Tax Credit were typically not capitalized in our searches. Proper nouns were capitalized in LexisNexis searches and when quotation marks were used in Google searches.

36. Yoon et al. 2007.

37. Quotation marks, which instruct search engines to look for *exact* matches to the words or phrases included within them, were generally not used. In most cases, experimental searches that included quotation marks produced very similar

results to those that did not. But the use of quotation marks sometimes leads to the exclusion of relevant texts. For example, a search for "comprehensive tax reform" would fail to locate texts using the phrase "comprehensive corporate tax reform." Quotation marks were occasionally used, however, when the initial results from a particular search were unusually noisy. For example, quotation marks were placed around "tax revenue expansion," after initial searches without quotation marks mostly returned results pertaining to the expansion of business revenue.

38. For example, the third result produced by a search for "Charles Koch on 'capital gains tax'" was a link to a blog and media aggregation website, Crooks and Liars, that specializes in heavily pro-Democratic "progressive news and media criticism." While this source perhaps has its own value, most of its content is clearly less informative for the present research than, for example, transcripts of MSNBC interviews or profiles in major newspapers.

39. Koch 2016.

40. Statements and narrow policy positions released by organizations led by billionaires in our sample were collected and coded as statements, whereas donations to policy-specific groups are considered policy-specific actions.

41. The authors (chiefly Lacombe) personally conducted all of the searches on tax policy and Social Security, which required approximately 400 hours of work.

42. Searches had to cover a number of years in order to avoid missing relevant statements. We watched carefully for any *changes* in individuals' stands but did not detect any in these policy areas.

43. The only others who came close were Stephen Schwarzman and John Malone, with five tax policy comments each, and George Kaiser and Eric Schmidt, with four each. Three others made three each.

44. For example, John Malone on Social Security: "You know, in my dream of dreams, we would take Social Security and Medicare and make them the legitimate retirement and insurance programs run actuarially that they should be, take them out of politics and not confuse welfare with insurance or retirement savings. That would be a wonderful transition. But the question is, you know, is there the political will to go in that direction and you know, I'm skeptical that there is."

45. As noted above, John Malone showed up in our search as mentioning Social Security once, but without clear expand/contract policy content—though it might be reasonable to interpret his references to actuarial soundness and "welfare" as signaling a preference for a nonredistributive system with defined contributions rather than defined benefits, as in privatization proposals.

46. Altman and Kingson (2015, chap. 9) describe "the billionaires' war against Social Security."

47. Gallup n.d. and Newport and Saad 2005. As discussed earlier, Americans strongly and clearly oppose cuts to Social Security. Public support for or opposition to privatization is less clear; a bare question tends to elicit support, but support declines substantially to less than the majority level when additional information

about privatization (e.g., abolition of guaranteed payments, subjection to stock market fluctuations) is given to respondents.

48. Page, Bartels, and Seawright 2013; Page and Gilens 2017, chap. 4.

49. These numbers do not add up to 26 (the number of individuals taking at least one stand on taxes) because two billionaires—Michael Bloomberg and Ronald Perelman—favored more revenue from some types of taxes but less from others.

50. Sensitivity analysis was carried out with different specifications, including ordinary least squares regression with a logged dependent variable, a logistic regression in which the dependent variable was transformed to capture whether or not a billionaire spoke at all, and a zero-inflated model. The substantive results proved not to be sensitive to these specification changes.

51. Our "heir" measure might more accurately be described as "nonentrepreneur." Rather than attempting to untangle the complicated issues of exactly how much each billionaire got from parents by gift or inheritance, and at what stage of life, we simply coded as an heir anyone who did not participate in starting his or her own business.

52. A dichotomous consumer-exposure variable was measured by identifying whether or not the primary business through which a billionaire acquired his or her wealth marketed products directly to public consumers.

53. Two cases had relatively large Cook's distance values, indicating some influence on the final regression results: Warren Buffett, with a Cook's distance of 0.81; and Bill Gates, with a Cook's distance of 0.23. Estimating the regression while excluding these two cases does not change the substantive patterns discussed above, although the magnitude of the estimated wealth effect drops by about half.

54. The adjusted R-squared for the full regression in table 2.1 was 0.2984; the R-squared for a bivariate regression including only level of wealth was 0.2722.

55. We simply added up a billionaire's scores on each of our five specific tax subissues, with +1 for favoring more taxes and –1 for favoring less, so that the final scale can vary from –5 (favoring lower taxes of all five types) to +5 (favoring more revenue from all five).

56. In this case, the three highly pro-tax cases, as a group, may have played an important part in the regression results, although none of them had a particularly notable Cook's distance—that is, none was individually very influential.

57. Verba, Schlozman, and Brady 1995.

58. Overby 2007: Even back in 2004, a bundler had to raise $200,000 to qualify as one of George W. Bush's "Rangers." In 2008, when Barack Obama and John McCain voluntarily listed their bundlers, they numbered only 558 and 536, respectively. Center for Responsive Politics 2009.

59. Cook, Page, and Moskowitz 2014, 389–90.

60. This last figure is probably understated, due to unreported dark-money contributions.

61. Smith et al. 2009.

62. Our calculations of billionaires' contributions use data from the National Institute on Money in State Politics' online database, which compiles federal, state, and local campaign finance data. Their database includes federal data beginning in 2010 and state data beginning in 2000 (with the exception of ballot initiative data, which begins in 2003). Our figures utilize federal data from 2010–12 and state data from 2001–12. Average annual contributions were calculated by adding together average annual amounts contributed to national and state politics. Although some small gaps may exist in the data, we believe we have captured nearly all—if not all—of the contributions made to federal and state-level candidates and parties, state ballot initiatives, and outside groups, by the billionaires under study for the years covered by the data. Care was taken to capture variants of billionaires' names. Any gaps (with the exception of dark money) in the data most likely involve small contributions that would amount to rounding errors in our overall calculations.

63. The figures in this paragraph include candidate, party, ballot initiative, and outside group contributions. Not all ballot initiative contributions could be coded in partisan and/or ideological terms, which is why the Republican and Democratic figures combined do not equal the total average annual contribution figure.

64. See Page and Jacobs 2009, chap. 4. Poll data on taxes should be interpreted with caution. Survey questions that inquire about "repeal" of the estate tax, for example, tend to elicit replies favoring repeal, but queries about the preferred *rate* of taxation on large ($100 million) estates yield median responses well above zero. See Bartels 2016, chap. 6; Page and Jacobs 2009, 92.

65. This analysis uses a linear probability model rather than a logit or probit model. The linear probability model usually produces similar estimates of marginal effects as maximum-likelihood models, but requires somewhat fewer assumptions or (often arbitrary) modeling decisions (Angrist and Pischke 2009, 102–7). No results in this chapter are noticeably changed by using a logit or probit model in place of the linear probability model.

66. Knowles 2015; Voorhees 2015; Gold 2014; *Washington Post* 2014; Center for Responsive Politics 2014; MacColl 2010.

67. Bertoni 2012.

68. Mayer 2016, 57–59 and chaps. 6–14. In gripping detail, Jane Mayer chronicles the Koch brothers' subsequent quiet but increasingly active and important roles in funding and shaping conservative Republican politics. See also Nancy MacLean's (2017) eye-opening archival research on the Kochs' long-term funding of the libertarian intellectual network centered at George Mason University. On the contemporary Koch funding network, see Skocpol and Hertel-Fernandez, forthcoming. For three decades or more, the Koch brothers succeeded in staying below the radar of the general public and most political observers.

69. Buffett 2011.

70. Fox Business Channel 2011.

71. Bloomberg 2008; see also *Talk of the Nation* 2012. It is not surprising that Bloomberg, a former political candidate and mayor of New York, has taken a number of specific policy stands. But many of those stands have concerned issues unrelated to city government, on which neither election campaigns nor his role as mayor required him to speak out.

72. *Citizens United v. FEC* (2010) did not substantially change the legal status of dark money (Bump 2015). Dark money existed prior to that decision and is allowed by the IRS for 501(c)(4) "social welfare" groups and 501(c)(6) "business leagues" (Prokop 2015). However, the use of dark money has increased markedly since *Citizens United*, suggesting that the Supreme Court's generally favorable outlook on "money as speech" may have encouraged the use of dark money. Earlier Supreme Court decisions, from *Buckley v. Valeo* (1976) onward, have severely limited the regulation of political money.

73. Sargent 2015, Lichtblau 2015.

74. West 2014, 11–15.

75. A few prominent donors like the Kochs and Adelson have been spotlighted by investigative journalists and scholars looking into dark money, but other, less scrutinized billionaires may well have been contributing large amounts of dark money without being detected.

76. Gilens 2012; Gilens and Page 2014; Page and Gilens 2017.

77. Perhaps more important than the very occasional, random appearance of a multimillionaire in national samples is the possibility that the policy preferences of the affluent act as statistical *proxies* for the preferences of the truly wealthy, which tend to differ from those of average citizens in similar—but sharper—ways than the preferences of the affluent do.

78. Across Gilens's 1,779 issues, the correlation between the preferences of "economic elites" (affluent Americans) and the alignments of business interest groups was nonsignificant—essentially zero—at –.02. Gilens and Page 2014, 571.

79. Gilens and Page 2014, 575. Page and Gilens 2017, chaps. 4–5.

80. See Altman and Kingson 2015. On Obama: Wallsten, Montgomery, and Wilson 2012. On Clinton: Gilon 2008.

81. Graetz and Shapiro 2005. But see Bartels 2016, chap. 6.

82. Wolters 2017; Huang and Cho 2017.

83. Hacker and Pierson 2010, especially chaps. 5 and 8.

Chapter Three: Four Billionaires Up Close

1. See Collier, Brady, and Seawright 2004; Lieberman 2005; and Seawright 2016.

2. This included using search terms not specific to the policy area of interest, and weeding through the large number of resulting false positives to check whether

relevant material emerged that was missed in the systematic searching. Thus, for example, when conducting the case study of Warren Buffett, we searched using terms like "Buffett AND politics," "Buffett AND government," or "Buffett AND Washington." These terms produce results that overlapped with the data from structured searching, as well as irrelevant articles and web pages about the Buffett Institute for Global Studies at Northwestern University, the political activities of "Margaritaville" singer Jimmy Buffett, and Howard Graham Buffett's foundation dedicated to ending world hunger. The case study process also included reading all Berkshire Hathaway shareholder letters written by Buffett in search of political content, as well as working through websites of collected Buffett quotes (e.g., http://www.suredividend.com/warren-buffett-quotes/ and https://en.wikiquote.org/wiki/Warren_Buffett) and perusing edited volumes of Buffett statements (Lowe 2007; Andrews 2012).

3. Random numbers were generated using data on atmospheric radio noise from random.org.

4. Seawright 2016; and Seawright and Gerring 2008.

5. *Forbes* 2013 (US), 32, 125.

6. *Forbes* 2016b (US), 129. As of early 2017 Buffett had regained his #2 position among the wealthiest Americans, with a fortune of $75.6 billion (*Forbes* 2017a [global], 138). But by October 2017 Bezos had overtaken Buffett again (*Forbes* 2017b [US], 86).

7. Schroeder 2008, 38–43, 61, 79.

8. Schroeder 2008, 88–96, 113–114, 146, 147, 178–180.

9. Schroeder 2008. The "snowball" image came to Buffett as a child when he read *One Thousand Ways to Make $1,000* and learned about compound interest (Schroeder 2009, 59–61).

10. Schroeder 2009, 540, 592, 667; De la Merced 2009.

11. Quick 2016; Cabural 2015.

12. Berkshire Hathaway 1994. This letter discussed the year 1993 but was issued on March 1, 1994.

13. NBC 2007.

14. *CNBC Squawk Box* 2011a.

15. *CNBC Squawk Box* 2011b.

16. National Economic Council 2012.

17. Kavoussi 2012.

18. Berkshire Hathaway 2003.

19. Drawbaugh 2007.

20. White 2005.

21. Isidore and Harlow 2015.

22. Larson 2015.

23. Storch 2003.

24. Lambert 2016.

25. *Forbes* 2013 (US), 148.

26. *Forbes* 2016b (US), 142. Early the following year, *Forbes* (2017a [global], 140) estimated Menard's fortune at $10.2 billion; later in 2017, *Forbes* put it at $9.9 billion (2017b [US], 92).

27. *Forbes* 2013 (US), 148.

28. Van de Kamp Nohl 2007.

29. Murphy 2013.

30. Isikoff 2015.

31. Aronson 2011.

32. Menard's reportable donations have been much smaller than his dark-money contributions, totaling an annual average of around $9,000 (86 percent of which went to Republicans or conservative groups), according to the data we collected from the National Institute on Money in State Politics.

33. Lueders 2015.

34. Lueders 2016.

35. Geoghegan 2004; Lichtenstein 2013.

36. Nolan 2016.

37. *Forbes* 2013 (US), 137. A remarkable biography of Icahn—which includes the intriguing story of how it came to be written—is Stevens 2014 [1993], which takes Icahn through his 1980s–1990s struggle with USX.

38. GuruFocus 2016.

39. Icahn's net worth dropped sharply, from $23.5 billion in February 2015 to $15.7 billion in fall 2016; it recovered only a bit, to $16.6 billion by February 2017 and $16.7 billion by October of that year. *Forbes* 2015 (global), 151; 2016b, 138; *Forbes* 2017a (global),138; *Forbes* 2017b (US), 91.

40. Dodds 2015; Stevens 2014, chap. 9.

41. On one engagement in the USX battle, see http://www.nytimes.com/1990 /05/08/business/icahn-seen-as-loser-in-usx-vote.html.

42. Gupta 2013.

43. Harwell 2016.

44. Gass 2015.

45. Lipton 2017.

46. Keefe 2017.

47. See http://carlicahn.com/. Accessed 14 June 2017.

48. Icahn 2013.

49. Cox 2016.

50. *CNBC Fast Money Halftime Report* 2015.

51. Icahn 2015a.

52. Icahn 2015b.

53. Icahn 2016.

54. As we have noted—and as we pursue further in chap. 4—among US billionaires *social* issues do not fit smoothly with the economic liberal/conservative

dimension either. Many billionaires are libertarians, conservative on economics but liberal on social matters. On social issues, they generally disagree less with average Americans and have less reason to pursue stealthy political strategies.

55. *Forbes* 2013 (US), 125.

56. *Forbes* 2016b (US), 132; *Forbes* 2017b (US), 86–87.

57. Mooney 2015.

58. Leonard 2013.

59. Leonard 2013.

60. See the remarkable research by Nancy MacLean (2017).

61. Sclar et al. 2016. This amount was reduced and redirected mainly to Senate races after Donald Trump was nominated as Republican presidential candidate.

62. Mayer 2016; Skocpol and Hertel-Fernandez 2016 and forthcoming.

63. See Mayer 2010 and 2016; Skocpol and Hertel-Fernandez, forthcoming; *Washington Post* 2014.

64. In New York City, David Koch is chiefly known as a major philanthropist and patron of the arts, a role that tends to smooth his social relations and shield his conservative political activities from criticism in that liberal bastion. See Schulman 2014, chap. 15.

65. Fang 2014.

66. Mayer 2016.

67. Skocpol and Hertel-Fernandez 2016.

68. Mayer 2016, especially chap. 8; Skocpol and Hertel-Fernandez 2016.

69. Mayer 2016, chap. 4.

70. Mayer 2016, 56–58; Schulman 2014, 109–14.

71. Koch 1980.

72. Koch 2016.

73. The only other billionaire we are aware of who resembles Icahn in his unusual mix of policy stands and his energetic backing of Donald Trump is Robert Mercer, who played a key role in installing Steve Bannon as Trump's campaign chairman. Sheldon Adelson also supported Trump in the autumn 2016 campaign, but apparently for different reasons (Mayer 2017; Addady 2016.) See Ferguson, Jorgensen, and Chen 2018.

74. Lee Drutman (2015, 72–79) reports evidence that corporations often (perhaps 40 percent of the time) lobby for narrowly targeted distributive benefits for themselves, but even more often (60 percent of the time) seek industry-wide benefits.

75. See Mayer 2016; Skocpol and Hertel-Fernandez, forthcoming; and Domhoff 2014, chaps. 4–5. Domhoff outlines a comprehensive theory of how wealthy individuals operate through a "policy-planning network" and an "opinion-shaping network," each of which involves foundations, think tanks, universities, policy discussion groups, the media, and other institutions.

76. *Citizens United v. Federal Election Commission* 558 U.S. 310, 2010. *Citizens United*, of course, was only one in a series of Supreme Court decisions that have eviscerated efforts to regulate the role of money in American politics.

77. Downs 1957, 94. Downs left unanswered the question whether—even if he was right—the *extent* of political inequality might be significantly altered through human choices.

Chapter Four: Keeping Quiet on Social Issues

1. See, for example, Chauncey 2004; McVeigh and Diaz 2009.

2. Gerring 1998; Karol 2009; Noel 2013.

3. Jelen and Wilcox 2003, 490–91; Saad 2016.

4. Baunach 2012. For more-recent data—including evidence that in 2013, for the first time, a majority of Americans approved of same-sex marriage—see http://www.pewforum.org/2016/05/12/changing-attitudes-on-gay-marriage/; McCarthy 2016.

5. Dubner 2016. Chick-Fil-A's late founder, S. Truett Cathy, was included among the 100 wealthiest billionaires we studied and was one of only four to take action against same-sex marriage. Cathy passed away shortly after the 2013 *Forbes* list was compiled. His fortune was divided between his two sons: current Chick-Fil-A CEO Dan Cathy, and Dan's brother, Bubba. As of autumn 2017, Dan and Bubba Cathy each had a net worth of $4.6 billion, which tied them at #144 on the *Forbes* 400-wealthiest list (*Forbes* 2017b [US], 106).

6. See Page, Bartels, and Seawright 2011. As we have noted, even the Federal Reserve Board's authoritative Survey of Consumer Finances, which oversamples affluent and wealthy Americans, does not attempt to reach the *Forbes* 400-wealthiest list (Bricker et al. 2014, 38).

7. For our earlier research on taxes and Social Security, we initially did both Google News/general web and LexisNexis Academic searches. As noted in chap. 2, Google and LexisNexis provide somewhat complementary resources. Google produces a very large number of potentially relevant web pages and, helpfully, includes links to videos of interviews with our subjects. Google's search results, however, are sometimes noisy and include numerous websites of dubious authority. LexisNexis produces a smaller number of results and does not include video links, but it draws exclusively from mainstream journalistic and academic sources. After collecting data for approximately one-quarter of our billionaires, we discovered that LexisNexis searches did not uncover any relevant political statements missed by Google searches. After this discovery, we decided to use Google exclusively. We continued to do so on social issues.

8. Quotation marks, which instruct search engines to look for *exact* matches to the words or phrases included within them, were generally not used. In most cases, experimental searches that included quotation marks produced very similar results to those that did not. But the use of quotation marks sometimes leads to the exclusion of relevant texts. For example, a search for "defense of marriage" would fail to locate texts using the phrase "marriage defense." Quotation marks were

occasionally used when the initial results from a particular search were unusually noisy. For example, quotation marks were placed around "Paul Allen," after initial searches without quotation marks mostly returned results pertaining to people named either Paul or Allen, but not to the Paul Allen who cofounded Microsoft.

9. The terms "liberal" and "conservative" in US political discourse are contested, may be in flux, and—when applied simultaneously to both the economic and the social realms—seem to us not to be logically coherent. (Indeed, efforts to compress both into a single dimension have increasingly become a major source of tension within the political parties.) For convenience in analyzing the social issues, however, we refer to positions relatively favorable to abortion, same-sex marriage, and immigration as "liberal" positions.

10. Verba, Schlozman, and Brady 1995.

11. Cook, Page, and Moskowitz 2014, 389.

12. Only 18 percent of Americans reported making campaign contributions in a 2008 general-population survey (Smith et al. 2009.) In the SESA survey of multimillionaires, 60 percent reported contributing an average of $4,633 (Cook, Page, and Moskowitz 2014, 389, 390).

13. See Mayer 2016. For information on our calculations of billionaires' contributions, see note 62 to chap. 2.

14. As noted in chap. 2, our searches had to cover a number of years in order to avoid missing relevant statements. We watched carefully for any *changes* in individuals' stands over the ten-year period but did not detect any in these policy areas.

15. The marriage search terms included "marriage equality," "same-sex marriage," and "gay marriage." Since different actors use different terms to signal their divergent attitudes, it is necessary to consider more than one term on this issue.

16. Given the large number of states that have passed highly restrictive abortion laws, we consider the position that abortion should be a "state issue" to be antiabortion.

17. Newport 2016; Saad 2014.

18. Kramer 2014.

19. Mehta and Mishak 2010.

20. Sarkar 2015.

21. Baker 2010.

22. Lowery 2014.

23. Mundy 2012.

24. Mishra and Ganguli 2009.

25. CBS New York 2012.

26. On social liberalism among the top 4 percent or so of income earners, see Page and Hennessy 2010.

27. See chap. 2, table 2.6.

28. For total statements, visibility b = 0.43, adjusted r-squared = 0.24; for total actions, visibility b = 0.13, adjusted r-squared = 0.30.

29. As noted earlier, our "heir" measure might more accurately be described as "nonentrepreneur." Rather than attempting to untangle the complicated issues of exactly how much each billionaire got from his or her parents by gift or inheritance, and when he or she did so, we simply coded as an heir anyone who did not participate in starting his or her own business.

30. A dichotomous consumer-exposure variable was measured by identifying whether or not the primary business through which a billionaire acquired his or her wealth markets products directly to public consumers.

31. A complex regression analysis involving nine independent variables produced an adjusted r-squared of 0.26, and highly significant coefficients for making at least one relevant statement and for the interactions of statement-making with wealth level, being an heir, and level of visibility. But only eight billionaires actually took actions; most were coded zero as a middle category between pro and con. The independent variables were highly collinear.

32. These results suggest that the *meaning* of wealth effects is different for economic issues (where greater wealth entails increased liberalism) than for social issues (where wealth is mainly relevant as a factor that increases prominence and available resources).

33. Regression analyses that "control" for posttreatment variables, i.e., for variables that are caused by x and influence y, will ordinarily produce biased estimates of the effect of x on y (Rosenbaum 1984). If the posttreatment variable captures the main causal pathway by which x causes y, then the causal inference will be biased toward zero.

34. Brenner 1992.

35. But most Americans do support a pathway to citizenship (contingent on meeting certain requirements) for those already in the US illegally (Jones 2016; Smeltz et al. 2016, 18). See Pew 2015. On attitudes concerning high- vs. low-skilled immigrants, see Hainmueller and Hiscox 2010.

36. Page and Bouton 2006, 41, 50, 185. A hefty 74 percent said "very important" in 1994; majorities continued to do so in four other surveys through 2004.

37. Fully 72 percent of Americans saw large numbers of immigrants as a "critical threat" in economically stressed 1994, but majorities continued to perceive a threat in every survey in which this question was asked until 2012.

38. Sides, Tesler, and Vavreck 2017.

39. See Ferguson and Page 2017.

40. In one analysis of 2002 CCGA data, for example, Americans' judgments about the importance of controlling and reducing illegal immigration were significantly and independently predicted by their assessments of terrorism as a critical threat; by the importance they attributed to the goals of protecting American jobs or reducing the trade deficit; and by their feelings (controlling for those security and economic factors) about Mexico (Page and Bouton 2006, 189).

41. Bound, Khanna, and Morales 2017.

42. The clearest case is probably that of wealthy farmers or owners of agribusinesses, who profit from cheap immigrant farm laborers. But very few if any owners of agricultural businesses have made it into the ranks of the very wealthiest billionaires, so we have not studied them.

43. Broockman, Ferenstein, and Malhotra 2017.

44. Enos (2014) finds that contact with Hispanics can induce a sense of group threat, in turn driving down support for immigration. Therefore, more sheltered lifestyles among the wealthy, with lower levels of intergroup contact, may result in more pro-immigration attitudes. *Change* in contact may be key.

45. In the SESA survey of multimillionaires, only 10 percent of respondents wanted to reduce legal immigration from current levels, whereas a total of 80 percent wanted to increase it (35 percent) or keep it at its current levels (45 percent).

46. CCGA survey data on the immigration views of the American public and foreign policy leaders have regularly found especially large "gaps" between the opinions of the two groups on *economic* policies. The gap on immigration may have reached a peak in the mid-1990s (under a Democratic administration), when 57 percent of the public wanted to decrease levels of legal immigration but only 8 percent of foreign policy leaders agreed (Page and Bouton 2006, 212–13). But large gaps have appeared every time the Chicago Council has looked.

47. Kaufmann 2016; Ferguson and Page 2017; Inglehart and Norris 2016.

48. Page and Gilens 2017, 129–30.

49. Even as late as 2016, the Republican Party Platform continued to oppose same-sex marriage (Naylor 2016).

50. For example, billionaires Paul Singer and Seth Klarman have devoted considerable resources to advocating for stronger LGBT rights (Palmer and Sherman 2014).

51. See Bartels 2016; Page and Gilens 2017.

Chapter Five: Reshaping State and Local Politics

1. US Office of Management and Budget, n.d.; Urban Institute 2017.

2. *National Federation of Independent Business v. Sebelius*, 567 US 1 (2012).

3. Hertel-Fernandez 2016.

4. Schattschneider 1960, chap. 2.

5. McConnell 1967, especially chaps. 4, 6.

6. Klarner 2015.

7. Robbins 2017.

8. Center for Responsive Politics, n.d.

9. Kranish 2015.

10. National Conference of State Legislatures, n.d.

11. Nebraska's unicameral legislature is technically nonpartisan, but Republican-affiliated politicians make up a strong majority of it and are led by Republican

Pete Ricketts, a member of the billionaire Ricketts family. See Stoddard and Nohr 2016.

12. National Conference of State Legislatures, n.d.

13. Kron 2012.

14. See Page and Gilens 2017, chap. 6. At the federal level it is generally easy for wealthy contributors to *stop* new legislation they oppose, but much harder hard to win new legislation they favor.

15. Weir, Zubak-Skees, and Wieder 2017.

16. Blumenthal 2015a.

17. Blumenthal 2015a; Harris 2012.

18. Blumenthal 2015a.

19. Byrne 2014.

20. Blumenthal 2015b.

21. Jeffers 2015; Blumenthal 2015c.

22. Blumenthal 2015c.

23. The Koch network has a complex structure. It includes many organizations under the Americans for Prosperity rubric (see Skocpol and Hertel-Fernandez, forthcoming.)

24. Skocpol and Hertel-Fernandez 2016; Sclar et al. 2016.

25. Gold 2015.

26. Hertel-Fernandez 2016.

27. Debenedetti 2017.

28. For details on Mercer's key role in Trump's campaign and in installing Steve Bannon as head of the campaign, see Ferguson, Jorgensen, and Chen 2017.

29. Vogel and Peters 2017.

30. Skocpol and Hertel-Fernandez 2016; Hertel-Fernandez, Skocpol, and Lynch 2016.

31. Kaiser Commission on Medicaid and the Uninsured 2017.

32. Hertel-Fernandez 2014.

33. Scola 2012; Hertel-Fernandez 2014.

34. Sclar et al. 2014.

35. Mayer 2016, 345, 347–48.

36. Phillips 2016; http://www.ncsl.org/Portals/1/Documents/Elections/Legis _Control_2017_August_4th_10am_26973.pdf.

37. Confessore 2014.

38. Mayer 2016.

39. Fausset 2015.

40. Hertel-Fernandez 2016.

41. Skocpol and Hertel-Fernandez 2016; Hertel-Fernandez, Skocpol, and Lynch 2016.

42. West 2014.

43. Confessore 2015b. On Rauner's income and wealth, see Grimm 2016.

44. Garcia 2017; Rhodes 2017.

45. *Forbes* 2017b (US); Janssen 2017.

46. Ehrenfreund 2015; Smith and Bosman 2017.

47. Samuels 2015; Umhoefer 2016.

48. Mayer 2016, chap. 13.

49. Straus 2016.

50. Kranish 2015.

51. MacLean 2017, 230; Fischer 2016.

52. Blumenthal 2015a.

53. Byrne and Perez 2016.

54. Keefe 2013; Green 2015.

55. Cunningham-Cook and Sirota 2015.

56. Blumenthal 2015a.

57. Lipton 2014.

58. West 2014.

59. Gibson (2013) analyzed how—in federal, democratic political systems—dominant subnational political parties often work on their national levels to keep as many political issues and powers as possible off the national agenda and within their own subnational jurisdictions, while simultaneously working to establish and maintain one-party rule within those regional, provincial, or local jurisdictions. That is, they work to control the subnational level and keep the federal government out—by creating "boundaries" around the areas they rule. Our theory of boundary control as a campaign contribution strategy differs from Gibson's theory in many respects, but it is similar in that a symbiotic relationship between national and subnational politics is used to restrict central authority and gain power and benefits from subnational governments.

60. Mayer 2016, 346.

61. Stolberg and McIntire 2013; Goldfarb 2013.

62. A possible example of this occurred during the 2004 presidential election, when President Bush criticized the "Swift Boat" attack advertisements that denigrated John Kerry's military service. (Of course, we cannot be sure how sincere Bush's criticism was.) The ads were financed by an outside group that drew much of its funding from billionaire Harold Simmons, who is discussed later in this chapter. Milbank 2004; Fitzsimmons 2013.

63. Most of the minority of billionaires who are liberal to moderate favor some sort of vigorous action by the federal government, if only to guarantee federal protection of civil rights and civil liberties that they see as threatened by social conservatives.

64. On industrial sectors and party affiliations, see Ferguson 1995.

65. We examined the costs that firms with numerous locations impose on each location. A billionaire's firms were coded as having high net costs if they imposed such costs on at least one of the places where they were located.

66. A supplementary appendix listing the scores for each industry and the sources used to code them can be obtained by contacting the authors.

67. Selecting an individual billionaire's highest-scoring industry most accurately captures that billionaire's incentive to use the strategy in at least one place.

68. For previously noted reasons, using campaign contributions to infer the *ideological* positions of donors is potentially problematic. But contributions data are useful for constructing a general measure of *partisan alignment* roughly equivalent to party identification (which could be ascertained with complete confidence only through survey data that are not available on billionaires). We created this dichotomous variable by adding together a billionaire's contributions to each party and each party's candidates, and identifying which party received more money.

69. We also tried using a slightly stricter standard—eight or more years of unified government. The number of cases scoring 1 ("boundary controller") on the dependent variable did not change.

70. We used data from the online *Follow the Money* database of the National Institute on Money in State Politics. The database includes federal data beginning in 2010 and state data beginning in 2000 (with the exception of ballot initiative data, which begins in 2003). Our calculations thus utilize federal data from 2010 to 2012 and state data from 2001 to 2012. Although some gaps may exist in the data, we believe we have captured nearly all—if not all—of the contributions made (to federal- and state-level candidates and parties, state ballot initiatives, and outside groups) by the billionaires under study for the years covered by the data. Care was taken to capture various versions of billionaires' names. When possible, this data was combined with data collected by journalists tracing unreported contributions back to certain individuals. Inclusion of this second type of data affected only one case of boundary control: that of David Koch, whose national-level contributions are understated in FEC-reported data.

71. Of the eighty-three billionaires included in this analysis, thirty-two were active in states with dominant parties, twenty-seven met the national-level contribution criterion, thirty-five met the state-level contribution criterion, and twelve met both the national- and state-level criteria.

72. Ten billionaires were active in states that were dominated by Democrats during the period of study, but none of them made contributions that fit the definition of boundary control.

73. Somewhat counterintuitively, a slightly greater proportion of non–boundary controllers' contributions (vs. boundary controllers' contributions) go toward state politics. This is very likely a result of the large size of the national-level contributions made by boundary controllers to outside groups. Within each level, the relative balance of candidate-specific vs. general donations among members of each group aligns with expectations (i.e., a much greater proportion of boundary controllers' national-level dollars relative to non–boundary controllers' go to outside groups and parties, and the opposite is true on the state level).

74. Firth 1993.

75. The *minimum possible* score on the regulation variable is 2, referring to an industry that faces only light, non-industry-specific regulation and has no specific regulations on the state level. The *maximum possible* score is 8, which refers to a highly regulated industry in which all important industry- or firm-specific regulation occurs on the state or local level. The *minimum actually observed* score in our data was 4 and the *maximum actually observed* score was 7.

76. Seawright 2016, chaps. 2–3.

77. Seawright 2016, chap. 4.

78. Random numbers to select among fifteen billionaires who tied as extreme low cases were generated using random.org.

79. Rowling was randomly selected (using random.org) among boundary controllers with the modal score on the summed independent variables.

80. Helman 2013.

81. Langley 2013.

82. Langley 2013.

83. Fitzsimmons 2013.

84. Fitzsimmons 2013.

85. Simmons did contribute to super PACs dedicated to electing presidential candidates Newt Gingrich and Mitt Romney, including $2.8 million to a Romney-specific (though nominally "independent") super PAC, Restore Our Future. But Simmons's contributions to candidate-specific super PACs were still minuscule compared with his contributions to more general causes.

86. Center for Responsive Politics, n.d.

87. *Texas Tribune*, n.d. In addition to Bob Perry, Antonio Sanchez and David Dewhurst also donated more money than Simmons. But both Sanchez (who launched a failed gubernatorial campaign in 2002) and Dewhurst (who became Texas's lieutenant governor) donated exclusively to their own campaigns. Subsequent to our use of the excellent *Texas Tribune* database, it appears to have disappeared from public view.

88. Harkinson 2011.

89. See Ryan, Lee, and Larson 2007.

90. Wald 2014.

91. Allison 2012.

92. Hunter 2006.

93. Harkinson 2011; Allison 2012.

94. Harkinson 2011.

95. Allison 2012; Campbell 2009.

96. Allison 2012; Thurber 2009.

97. Thurber 2009; Waste Control Specialists, n.d.

98. Harkinson 2011.

99. See Wilder 2013. It is more typical for firms to provide financial assurance through assets that are highly stable and very liquid. By providing stock in one of his other firms as collateral, Simmons was able to avoid the liquidation of any of his assets and shift risk away from himself to the state of Texas.

100. Hunter 2006; Wilder 2013.

101. Soros's big short of the pound was widely seen as *precipitating*—if not all by itself *causing*—the sharp drop in the pound's value that enabled Soros to buy pounds cheaply, pay them back to his lenders, and make an enormous profit.

102. Schaefer 2015.

103. Confessore and Preston 2016.

104. National Institute on Money in State Politics, n.d. As we have noted elsewhere, however, there are definite limits to Soros's *economic* liberalism. Soros warmly appreciates the property rights and free markets that made him rich. He has not expressed a great deal of concern about inequality of income or wealth, or much enthusiasm for heavy taxation of the wealthy. See Mayer 2004.

105. The top-scoring industry in which Rowling has been active—energy and natural resources—scored a very high 14 out of a possible 16 on factors predicting efforts at boundary control. This was the modal score among billionaires we scored as boundary controllers.

106. Duszak 2012. See *Forbes* 2014.

107. Robinson-Jacobs 2016.

108. Duszak 2012; Gold's Gym 2012.

109. It is also important to note that Crossroads GPS, a group closely associated with American Crossroads, does not have to disclose its donors. So any contributions Rowling has made to GPS are not included in these totals.

110. Center for Responsive Politics, n.d.

111. *Texas Tribune,* n.d.

112. Waltzman 2012.

113. Center for Responsive Politics, n.d.

114. *Texas Tribune*, n.d.

115. City of Dallas, n.d.

116. Waltzman 2012.

117. Waltzman 2012.

118. That is, eight of the eighty-three billionaires who were active in business, and therefore *might* conceivably have pursued this business-oriented strategy, were in fact boundary controllers. Note, however, that the number of billionaires about whom the theory makes predictions is actually smaller, limited to those from states dominated by one political party.

Chapter Six: What Is to Be Done about Billionaires?

1. Some readers have suggested that that we should "triangulate" in on billionaires' policy preferences by taking into account their financial contributions to candidates and any broad ideological statements they have made. But this enticing idea is an illusion. As we have noted, contributions are a very imperfect guide

to policy preferences. (Inferences from contributions to Republicans would completely distort most billionaires' liberal or libertarian views on social issues, for example, while social- or access-oriented contributions to Democrats would mask their economic conservatism.) Most ideological utterances are too vague to be very useful, but, in any case, they are extremely rare. We have looked hard. In extensive searches, using broad search terms, we found little beyond the phrases that we have quoted from the Koch brothers and Sheldon Adelson. Hardly any other billionaires who have been quiet about policy specifics have spoken about their general political ideologies.

2. See Gilens 2012; Gilens and Page 2014; Page and Gilens 2017. In Gilens's data, the policy preferences of "the average American" refer to the estimated preferences of the *median-income* respondent at the fiftieth percentile of the income distribution. These are nearly identical to the median preferences among survey respondents.

3. See Bartels 2008, chap. 9, 259; Gilens 2012, chaps. 3 and 5; Gilens and Page 2014, 571, 575.

4. In methodological terms, Gilens's measures of the policy preferences of the affluent—which differ from average Americans' preferences in the same directions but to a lesser extent than the preferences of very wealthy Americans do—may serve as *proxies* for the opinions of the truly wealthy.

5. Existing research does not provide enough data points to estimate the full shape of the relationship between individuals' levels of wealth and the extent of their economic conservatism. Data on average Americans, affluent Americans, and the SESA multimillionaires, however, suggests that the relationship is monotonic. The more wealth, the more conservative preferences. Even if there is a diminishing marginal effect of wealth—or, conceivably, a reversal of this trend at the very top—it seems likely that the average US billionaire is much more economically conservative than the average US adult.

6. Page, Bartels, and Seawright 2013, 54.

7. Page, Bartels, and Seawright 2013, 54, 56, 57. See also Page and Gilens 2017, chap. 4.

8. Page, Bartels, and Seawright 2013, 58, 59, 61, 62.

9. See Alvaredo et al., n.d.; Piketty 2014; and the US data at http://wid.world/.

10. See Khoury 2016; Cramer 2016; and Hochschild 2016. Some of these matters are addressed in Page and Gilens 2017, chap.2.

11. Once in office, however, President Trump pursued very conservative, orthodox Republican economic policies that seemed quite at odds with his populistic campaign rhetoric ("Drain the swamp!" "Plenty of jobs!"). At the time we write, one result appears to be electoral trouble for the Republicans and a high level of public resentment and cynicism aimed at both parties.

12. See, for example, Page and Gilens 2017, chap. 3; Cramer 2016; Hochschild 2016.

13. The "democracy voucher" idea comes from Lessig 2011, 266–68 (see the revised version in Lessig 2015, 43–44). It has roots in Hasen's 1996 "coupons for democracy" and in Ackerman and Ayres's 2002 "patriot dollars." For a particularly egalitarian version of democracy vouchers, see Page and Gilens 2017, 191–92.

14. This has been an important theme in legal scholars' proposals for—and critiques of—campaign finance reforms. See Lessig 2011, 364–66; Lessig 2015, chap. 6.

15. See Leighley and Nagler, especially 2013, also 1992a, 1992b, 2007; Schlozman, Verba, and Brady 2012. A number of "equal voice" reforms are discussed in Page and Gilens 2017, chap. 7.

16. On structural reforms, see Page and Gilens 2017, chap. 8. Reich 2015 discusses a number of egalitarian economic reforms that have important political implications.

17. See the discussion of the "get a senator" strategy in West 2014, 11–15.

18. The so-called Hastert rule, which dictates that only bills backed by a "majority of the majority party" will be considered in the House, can mean that bills favored by as many as 74 percent of all House members (an entire 49 percent minority party plus nearly half of a 51 percent majority party) can be blocked by a slight majority of the majority party.

19. See Page and Gilens 2017, chaps. 8–9.

20. *NAACP v. Alabama*, 357 US 449 (1958).

21. See the line of cases from *Buckley v. Valeo*, 424 US 1 (1976), to *Citizens United v. Federal Election Commission*, 558 US 310 (2010), and *McCutcheon v. Federal Election Commission*, 134 S. Ct. 1434 oe 572 U.S. ___, (2014).

References

Ackerman, Bruce, and Ian Ayres. 2002. *Voting with Dollars: A New Paradigm for Campaign Finance*. New Haven: Yale University Press.

Addady, Michal. 2016. "Donald Trump Gains the Support of a Former 'Never Trump' Billionaire." *Fortune*, September 20. http://fortune.com/2016/09/20/donald -trump-donation/.

Allison, Bill. 2012. *Stealthy Wealthy: How Harold Simmons' Political Giving Has Benefited His Business Empire*. Sunlight Foundation online report, March 13. https://sunlightfoundation.com/2012/03/13/simmons/.

Altman, Nancy J., and Eric R. Kingson. 2015. *Social Security Works! Why Social Security Isn't Going Broke and How Expanding It Will Help Us All*. New York: The New Press.

Alvaredo, Facundo, Lucas Chancel, Thomas Piketty, Emmanuel Saez, and Gabriel Zucman. *World Wealth and Income Database, 2017*. http://wid.world/. Accessed October 25, 2017.

Andrews, David. 2012. *The Oracle Speaks: Warren Buffett in His Own Words*. Chicago: Agate.

Angrist, Joshua D., and Jorn-Steffen Pischke. 2009. *Mostly Harmless Econometrics: An Empiricist's Companion*. Princeton, NJ: Princeton University Press.

Aronson, Gavin. 2011. "Exclusive: The Koch Brothers' Million-Dollar Donor Club." *Mother Jones*, September 6. http://www.motherjones.com/mojo/2011/09 /koch-brothers-million-dollar-donor-club.

Baker, Kevin. 2010. "GQ Men of the Year 2010, Leader: Michael Bloomberg." *GQ*, November 18. http://www.gq.com/story/michael-bloomberg-new-york-mayor -men-of-the-year-leader. Accessed June 2, 2017.

Balcerzak, Ashley. 2017. "Richest Billionaires Are Also Top Political Spenders." *OpenSecrets* blog, March 31. https://www.opensecrets.org/news/2017/03/richest -billionaires-are-top-political-spenders/.

Barber, Michael J. 2016a. "Ideological Donors, Contribution Limits, and the Polarization of American Legislatures." *Journal of Politics* 78 (1): 296–310.

Barber, Michael J. 2016b. "Donation Motivations: Testing Theories of Access and Ideology." *Political Research Quarterly* 69 (1): 148–59.

Bartels, Larry M. 2008. *Unequal Democracy: The Political Economy of the New Gilded Age*. Princeton, NJ: Russell Sage Foundation and Princeton University Press.

Bartels, Larry M. 2016. *Unequal Democracy: The Political Economy of the New Gilded Age*. 2nd ed. Princeton, NJ: Russell Sage Foundation and Princeton University Press.

Baunach, Dawn Michelle. 2012. "Changing Same-Sex Marriage Attitudes in America from 1988 through 2010." *Public Opinion Quarterly* 76 (June): 364–78.

Becraft, Michael B. 2014. *Bill Gates: A Biography*. Santa Barbara, CA: Greenwood.

Berkshire Hathaway. 1994. *Annual Report*. http://www.berkshirehathaway.com/letters/1993.html. Accessed June 14, 2017.

Berkshire Hathaway. 2003. *Annual Report*. http://www.berkshirehathaway.com/2003ar/2003ar.pdf. Accessed June 14, 2017.

Bertoni, Steven. 2012. "Billionaire Sheldon Adelson Says He Might Give $100M to Newt Gingrich or Other Republican." *Forbes*, February. https://www.forbes.com/sites/stevenbertoni/2012/02/21/billionaire-sheldon-adelson-says-he-might-give-100m-to-newt-gingrich-or-other-republican/#a28f4fc44003.

Bivens, Josh. 2013. "Using Standard Models to Benchmark the Costs of Globalization for American Workers without a College Degree." Economic Policy Institute Briefing Paper no. 354, March 22.

Blank, Rebecca M. 1997. *It Takes a Nation: A New Agenda for Fighting Poverty*. Princeton, NJ: Princeton University Press.

Bloomberg. 2017. Bloomberg Billionaires Index. https://www.bloomberg.com/billionaires/. Accessed April 25, 2017.

Bloomberg, Michael. 2008. "Michael Bloomberg's Advice to the Next President." *Newsweek*, October 24. http://www.newsweek.com/michael-bloombergs-advice-next-president-92443.

Blumenthal, Paul. 2015a. "Republicans Heap Money on Rahm Emanuel's Re-election Campaign." *Huffington Post*, March 19. https://www.huffingtonpost.com/2015/03/19/rahm-emanuel-republicans_n_6904566.html.

Blumenthal, Paul. 2015b. "3 Libertarians Fuel $7 Million Super PAC in Philadelphia's Mayoral Democratic Primary." *Huffington Post*, May 14. https://www.huffingtonpost.com/2015/05/14/philadelphia-mayor-super-pac_n_7268872.html.

Blumenthal, Paul. 2015c. "Your State and Local Elections are Now a Super PAC Playground." *Huffington Post*, October 31. https://www.huffingtonpost.com/entry/2015-elections-super-pac_us_5633d165e4b0c66bae5c7bbb.

Bonica, Adam. 2013. Database on Ideology, Money in Politics, and Elections: Public version 1.0. https://data.stanford.edu/dime. Stanford, CA: Stanford University Libraries.

Bonica, Adam. 2014. "Mapping the Ideological Marketplace." *American Journal of Political Science* 58 (2): 367–86.

Bonica, Adam, Nolan McCarty, Keith T. Poole, and Howard Rosenthal. 2013. "Why Hasn't Democracy Slowed Rising Inequality?" *Journal of Economic Perspectives* 27 (3): 103–24.

Bound, John, Gaurav Khanna, and Nicolas Morales. 2017. "Understanding the Economic Impact of the H-1B Program on the US." National Bureau of Economic Research Working Paper 23153, February. http://www.nber.org/papers /w23153.pdf.

Brenner, Joel Glenn. 1992. "Planet of the MM's." *Washington Post*, April 12. https:// www.washingtonpost.com/archive/lifestyle/magazine/1992/04/12/planet-of-the -mms/e9daf119-3ec1-4432-91a9-f84979cc98ab/?utm_term=.6706477b9e32.

Bricker, Jesse, Lisa J. Dettling, Alice Henriques, Joanne W. Hsu, Kevin B. Moore, John Sabelhaus, Jeffrey Thompson, and Richard A. Windle. 2014. "Changes in US Family Finances from 2010 to 2013: Evidence from the Survey of Consumer Finances." *Federal Reserve Bulletin* 100 (4).

Bricker, Jesse, Alice M. Henriques, Jake A. Krimmel, and John E. Sabelhaus. 2015. "Measuring Income and Wealth at the Top Using Administrative and Survey Data," Finance and Economics Discussion Series 2015–030. Washington: Board of Governors of the Federal Reserve System.

Broockman, David E., Gregory Ferenstein, and Neil Malhotra. 2017. "Wealthy Elites' Policy Preferences and Economic Inequality: The Case of Technology Entrepreneurs." Working paper.

Buckley v. Valeo, 424 US 1, 1976.

Buffett, Warren. 2011. "Stop Coddling the Super-Rich." *New York Times*, August 15, A21.

Bump, Philip. 2015. "How Citizens United Is—and Isn't—to Blame for the Dark Money President Obama Hates So Much." *Washington Post*, January 21. https:// www.washingtonpost.com/news/the-fix/wp/2015/01/21/how-citizens-united-is -and-isnt-to-blame-for-the-dark-money-president-obama-hates-so-much/?utm _term=.5a84cecfa5c3.

Byrne, John. 2014. "Pro-Emanuel PAC Raises Another $1 Million." *Chicago Tribune*, October 1. http://www.chicagotribune.com/news/ct-rahm-emanuel-pac-met -20141001-story.html.

Byrne, John, and Juan Perez Jr. 2016. "Emanuel: If Teachers Strike, They Chose Disrupting Children's Education Over Pay Raises." *Chicago Tribune*, September 29. http://www.chicagotribune.com/news/local/politics/ct-chicago-schools -teachers-emanuel-0930-20160929-story.html.

Cabural, Marie. 2015. "Berkshire Hathaway Becomes Majority Owner of H. J. Heinz Company." *ValueWalk*, June 18. http://www.valuewalk.com/2015/06/berk shire-hathaway-becomes-majority-owner-of-h-j-heinz-company/. Accessed June 14, 2017.

Callahan, David. 2017. *The Givers: Wealth, Power, and Philanthropy in a New Gilded Age.* New York: Knopf.

Campbell, Ruth. 2009. "Andrews County Sets Bond Election to Finance Waste
    Control Specialists' Project." *Midland Reporter-Telegram*, March 23.
CBS New York. 2012. "Obama Administration Makes Dramatic Shift in Illegal Im-
    migrant Deportation Policy." June 15. http://newyork.cbslocal.com/2012/06/15
    /bloomberg-praises-obama-administration-for-sparing-some-from-deporta
    tion/. Accessed June 2, 2017.
Center for Responsive Politics. n.d. *OpenSecrets* database. https://www.opensecrets
    .org/donor-lookup.
Center for Responsive Politics. 2009. "Barack Obama 2008 Bundlers." https://www
    .opensecrets.org/pres08/bundlers.php?id=n00009638.
Center for Responsive Politics. 2014. "Adelson, Sheldon G. & Miriam O.: Donor De-
    tail." https://www.opensecrets.org/outsidespending/donor_detail.php?cycle=2012
    &id=U0000000310&type=I&super=N&name=Adelson%2C+Sheldon+G.+%2
    6+Miriam+O.
Chauncey, George. 2004. *Why Marriage: The History Shaping Today's Debate Over
    Gay Equality*. New York: Basic Books.
Chin, Fiona. 2015. *"View from the Top: Stratification Ideologies of the Wealthy."*
    PhD diss. in progress, Department of Sociology, Northwestern University.
Citizens United v. Federal Election Commission, 558 US 310 (2010).
City of Dallas. n.d. Campaign Finance Electronic Filing System. http://campfin
    .dallascityhall.com/.
CNBC Fast Money Halftime Report. 2015. Episode dated Sep. 30, 2015. http://video
    .cnbc.com/gallery/?video=3000427512&play=1.
CNBC Squawk Box. 2011a. Episode dated July 7, 2011.
CNBC Squawk Box. 2011b. Episode dated Nov. 14, 2011.
Collier, David, Henry E. Brady, and Jason Seawright. 2004. "Sources of Leverage
    in Causal Inference." In *Rethinking Social Inquiry: Diverse Tools, Shared Stan-
    dards, edited by Henry E. Brady and David Collier,* chapter 13. Lanham, MD:
    Rowman and Littlefield.
Confessore, Nicholas. 2015a. "Koch Brothers' Budget of $889 Million for 2016
    Is on Par With Both Parties' Spending." *New York Times*, January 26. https://
    www.nytimes.com/2015/01/27/us/politics/kochs-plan-to-spend-900-million-on
    -2016-campaign.html.
Confessore, Nicholas. 2015b. "A Wealthy Governor and His Friends Are Remaking
    Illinois." *New York Times*, November 29. https://www.nytimes.com/2015/11/30
    /us/politics/illinois-campaign-money-bruce-rauner.html. Accessed June 6, 2017.
Confessore, Nicholas, and Julia Preston. 2016. "Soros and Other Liberal Donors
    to Fund Bid to Spur Latino Votes." *New York Times*, March 10.
Congressional Budget Office. 2017. "Historical Budget Data" (supplemental ma-
    terial for *The Budget and Economic Outlook: 2017 to 2027*, January 24). http://
    www.cbo.gov/publication/52370.
Cook, Fay Lomax, and Rachel L. Moskowitz. 2014. "The Great Divide: Elite and
    Mass Opinions about Social Security." In *The New Politics of Old Age Policy*.

3rd ed., edited by Robert Hudson, 69–98. Baltimore: Johns Hopkins University Press.

Cook, Fay Lomax, Benjamin I. Page, and Rachel L. Moskowitz. 2014. "Political Engagement by Wealthy Americans." *Political Science Quarterly* 129 (3): 381–98.

Cox, Jeff. 2016. "Carl Icahn: Here's Why I'm Supporting Trump for President." CNBC, September 13. http://www.cnbc.com/2016/09/13/carl-icahn-heres-why -im-supporting-trump-for-president.html.

Coy, Peter. 2014. "The Richest Rich Are in a Class by Themselves." *Bloomberg Business*, April 3.

Cramer, Katherine J. 2016. *The Politics of Resentment: Rural Consciousness in Wisconsin and the Rise of Scott Walker*. Chicago: University of Chicago Press.

Cunningham-Cook, Matthew, and David Sirota. 2015. "Chicago Teacher Pension Money Invested with Rahm Emanuel's Friends and Donors." *International Business Times*, March 11. http://www.ibtimes.com/chicago-teacher-pension-money -invested-rahm-emanuels-friends-donors-1843104.

De la Merced, Michael J. 2009. "Berkshire Bets on U.S. With a Railroad Purchase." *New York Times*, November 3.

Debenedetti, Gabriel. 2017. "Democrats Launch Super PAC to Win Back Statehouses." *Politico*, September 6. https://www.politico.com/story/2017/09/06/demo crats-launch-super-pac-to-win-back-statehouses-242330.

Dodds, Colin. 2015. "Carl Icahn Biography." *Investopedia*, August 31. http://www .investopedia.com/university/carl-icahn-biography/.

Domhoff, G. William. 2014. *Who Rules America: The Triumph of the Corporate Rich*. 7th ed. New York: McGraw-Hill.

Downs, Anthony. 1957. *An Economic Theory of Democracy*. New York: Harper & Row.

DQYDJ. 2017. "United States Net Worth Brackets, Percentiles, and Top One Percent in 2017." DQYDJ (blog), October 23. https://dqydj.com/net-worth-brack ets-wealth-brackets-one-percent/. Accessed October 25, 2017.

Drawbaugh, Kevin. 2007. "Buffett Backs Estate Tax, Decries Wealth Gap." *Reuters*, November 14. https://www.reuters.com/article/us-buffett-congress/buffett -backs-estate-tax-decries-wealth-gap-idUSN1442383020071114.

Drutman, Lee. 2015. *The Business of America Is Lobbying: How Corporations Become Politicized and Politics Becomes More Corporate*. New York: Oxford University Press.

Dubner, Stephen J. 2016. "Do Boycotts Work?" *Freakonomics* podcast, January 21. http://freakonomics.com/podcast/do-boycotts-work-a-new-freakonomics-radio -podcast/.

Duszak, Alexandra. 2012. *Donor Profile: Robert Rowling—Quick Stats on the Biggest Financial Backers of Election 2012. Center for Public Integrity online report*, August 22. http://www.publicintegrity.org/2012/08/22/10741/donor-pro file-robert-rowling.

Efron, Bradley. 1987. "Better Bootstrap Confidence Intervals." *Journal of the American Statistical Association* 82 (March): 171–85.

Ehrenfreund, Max. 2015. "How Kansas Keeps Making Life Harder for the Poor." *Washington Post Wonkblog*, June 12. https://www.washingtonpost.com/news /wonk/wp/2015/06/12/kansas-is-about-to-raise-taxes-on-the-poor-again/?utm _term=.c141ec897ce8.

Engelhardt, Gary V., and Jonathan Gruber. 2004. "Social Security and the Evolution of Elderly Poverty." National Bureau of Economic Research Working Paper No. 10466, May. http://www.nber.org/papers/w10466.pdf.

Enos, Ryan D. 2014. "Causal Effect of Intergroup Contact on Exclusionary Attitudes." *Proceedings of the National Academy of Sciences* 111 (10): 3699–704.

Fang, Lee. 2014. "The Koch Brothers Spent Twice as Much on the 2012 Election as the Top Ten Unions Combined." *The Nation*, March 7. https://www.thenation .com/article/koch-brothers-spent-twice-much-2012-election-top-ten-unions -combined/.

Farhi, Paul. 2013. "*Washington Post* Closes Sale to Amazon Founder Jeff Bezos." *Washington Post*, October 1. https://www.washingtonpost.com/business/econ omy/washington-post-closes-sale-to-amazon-founder-jeff-bezos/2013/10/01 /fca3b16a-2acf-11e3-97a3-ff2758228523_story.html.

Fausset, Richard. 2015. "With State Control, North Carolina Republicans Pursue Smaller Prizes." *New York Times*, April 6. https://www.nytimes.com/2015/04 /07/us/with-state-control-north-carolina-republicans-pursue-smaller-prizes .html.

Ferguson, Thomas. 1995. *Golden Rule: The Investment Theory of Party Competition and the Logic of Money-Driven Political Systems*. Chicago: University of Chicago Press.

Ferguson, Thomas, Paul Jorgensen, and Jie Chen. 2018. "Industrial Structure and Party Competition in an Age of Hunger Games: Donald Trump and the 2016 Presidential Election." Institute for New Economic Thinking Working Paper no. 60, February.

Ferguson, Thomas, and Benjamin I. Page. 2017. "The Hinge of Fate? Economic and Social Populism in the 2016 Presidential Election: A Preliminary Exploration." Paper delivered at the conference of the Institute for New Economic Thinking, Edinburgh, UK, October 20–23.

Ferguson, Thomas, and Joel Rogers. 1986. *Right Turn: The Decline of the Democrats and the Future of American Politics*. New York: Hill and Wang.

Firth, David. 1993. "Bias Reduction of Maximum Likelihood Estimates." *Biometrika* 80 (1): 27–38.

Fischer, Brendan. 2016. "Corporate Interests Take Aim at Local Democracy." *PR Watch*, February 3. https://www.prwatch.org/news/2016/02/13029/2016-ALEC-lo cal-control.

Fitzsimmons, Emma. 2013. "Harold Simmons Dies at 82; Backed Swift Boat Ads." *New York Times*, December 29, A20.

Fontevecchia, Agustino. 2014. "The New Forbes 400 Self-Made Score: From Silver Spooners to Bootstrappers." *Forbes*, October 2. https://www.forbes.com/sites

/afontevecchia/2014/10/02/the-new-forbes-400-self-made-score-from-silver
-spooners-to-boostrappers/#77596fe52aff.

Forbes. 2013. "Special Edition: The *Forbes* 400, the Richest People in America."
Vol. 192, no. 5, October 7.

Forbes. 2014. "Robert Rowling Profile." October. http://www.forbes.com/profile
/robert-rowling/.

Forbes. 2015. "Special Issue: Meet the Richest People on the Planet." Vol. 195,
no. 4, March 25.

Forbes. 2016a. "Special Issue: Billionaires, The Richest People on the Planet."
Vol. 197, no. 4, March 21.

Forbes. 2016b. "Special Issue: The *Forbes* 400, The Richest People in America."
Vol. 198, no. 5, October 25.

Forbes. 2017a. "Special Issue: Billionaires." Vol. 199, no. 3. March 28.

Forbes. 2017b. "Special Issue: The 400 Richest People in America." Vol. 200, no. 5,
November 14. https://www.forbes.com/forbes-400/list/#version:static.

Fox Business Channel. 2011. "Buffett and Gates on the Estate Tax." May 7. http://
video.foxbusiness.com/v/3887799/buffett-and-bill-gates-on-the-estate-tax/?play
list_id=#sp=show-clips.

Frank, Robert. 2007. *Richistan: A Journey Through the American Wealth Boom
and the Lives of the New Rich*. New York: Three Rivers.

Freeland, Chrystia. 2012. *Plutocrats: The Rise of the New Global Super-Rich and
the Fall of Everyone Else*. New York: Penguin.

Friedman, Milton, with the assistance of Rose D. Friedman. 1962. *Capitalism and
Freedom*. Chicago: University of Chicago Press.

Friedman, Thomas L. 2007. *The World Is Flat: A Brief History of the Twenty-First
Century*. New York: Picador.

Gallup. n.d. "In Depth Topics A to Z: Social Security." http://www.gallup.com
/poll/1693/social-security.aspx. Accessed May 17, 2017.

Garcia, Monique. 2017. "Credit Agency Warns of 'Long-Term Damage' in Illinois
If No Budget Deal by May 31." *Chicago Tribune*, March 30. http://www.chicago
tribune.com/news/local/politics/ct-illinois-budget-moodys-rauner-met-0331
-20170330-story.html.

Gass, Nick. 2015. "Billionaire Carl Icahn Launches $150 Million Super PAC."
Politico, October 21. http://www.politico.com/story/2015/10/billionaire-carl-icahn
-launches-super-pac-215005.

Geoghegan, Thomas. 2004. *Which Side Are You On? Trying to Be for Labor When
It's Flat on Its Back*. Rev. ed. New York: The New Press.

Gerring, John. 1998. *Party Ideologies in America, 1828–1996*. Cambridge, UK:
Cambridge University Press.

Gibson, Edward. 2013. *Boundary Control: Subnational Authoritarianism in Federal Democracies*. Cambridge, UK: Cambridge University Press.

Gilens, Martin. 2005. "Inequality and Democratic Responsiveness." *Public Opinion
Quarterly* 69 (5): 778–96.

Gilens, Martin. 2009. "Preference Gaps and Inequality in Representation." *PS: Political Science & Politics* 42 (2): 335–41.

Gilens, Martin. 2012 *Affluence and Influence: Economic Inequality and Political Power in America.* Princeton, NJ: Russell Sage Foundation and Princeton University Press.

Gilens, Martin, and Benjamin I. Page. 2014. "Testing Theories of American Politics: Elites, Interest Groups, and Average Citizens." *Perspectives on Politics* 12 (3): 564–80.

Gilon, Steven. 2008. *The Pact: Bill Clinton, Newt Gingrich, and the Rivalry That Defined a Generation.* Oxford: Oxford University Press.

Gladwell, Malcolm. 2008. *Outliers: The Story of Success.* New York: Little, Brown.

Gold, Matea. 2014. "Koch-Backed Political Coalition, Built to Shield Donors, Raised $400 Million in 2012 Elections." *Washington Post,* January 5. https://www.washingtonpost.com/politics/koch-backed-political-network-built-to-shield-donors-raised-400-million-in-2012-elections/2014/01/05/9e7cfd9a-719b-11e3-9389-09ef9944065e_story.html?utm_term=.5181ace51f63.

Gold, Matea. 2015. "Wealthy Donors on Left Launch New Plan to Wrest Back Control in the States." *Washington Post,* April 12. https://www.washingtonpost.com/politics/wealthy-donors-on-left-launch-new-plan-to-wrest-back-control-in-the-states/2015/04/12/ccd2f5ee-dfd3-11e4-a1b8-2ed88bc190d2_story.html?utm_term=.60bccdd00ac1.

Goldfarb, Zachary. 2013. "Years-Long Effort to Cut Spending Laid Groundwork for Funding Showdown." *Washington Post,* October 3, A12.

Gold's Gym. 2012. "Gold's Gym International Acquires 11 Spectrum Athletic Club Locations in San Antonio." Press release, February 14. http://www.goldsgym.com/press_release/golds-gym-international-acquires-11-spectrum-athletic-club-locations-in-san-antonio/.

Graetz, Michael J., and Ian Shapiro. 2005. *Death by a Thousand Cuts: The Fight over Taxing Inherited Wealth.* Princeton, NJ: Princeton University Press.

Green, Emma. 2015. "Rahm Emanuel: 'I Am Not an Education Reformer.'" *Atlantic,* July 3. https://www.theatlantic.com/education/archive/2015/07/rahm-emanuel-chicago-education-reform/397673/.

Grimm, Andy. 2016. "Bruce Rauner Made $176 Million, Paid $50 Million in Taxes in 2015." *Chicago Sun-Times,* November 11. http://chicago.suntimes.com/news/bruce-rauner-made-176-million-paid-50-million-in-taxes-in-2015/.

Gupta, Poornima. 2013. "Icahn Sues Dell in Latest Attempt to Foil Buyout." *Reuters,* August 1. http://www.reuters.com/article/us-dell-icahn-idUSBRE970125 20130802?feedType=RSS&feedName=topNews&dlvrit=992637.

GuruFocus. 2016. "With Big Losses in Energy, Icahn Sells Most of Stake in Transocean." *Forbes,* September 30. https://www.forbes.com/sites/gurufocus/2016/09/30/with-big-losses-in-energy-icahn-sells-most-of-stake-in-transocean/#68ddc187afe6.

Hacker, Jacob S., and Paul Pierson. 2010. *Winner-Take-All Politics: How Washington Made the Rich Richer—and Turned Its Back on the Middle Class.* New York: Simon & Schuster.

Hainmueller, Jens, and Michael J. Hiscox. 2010. "Attitudes toward Highly Skilled and Low-Skilled Immigration: Evidence from a Survey Experiment." *American Political Science Review* 104 (1): 61–84.

Hall, Andrew B. 2016. "Systemic Effects of Campaign Spending: Evidence From Corporate Campaign Contribution Bans in State Legislatures." *Political Science Research and Methods* 4 (2): 343–59.

Hall, Richard L., and Frank W. Wayman. 1990. "Buying Time: Moneyed Interests and the Mobilization of Bias in Congressional Committees." *American Political Science Review* 84(3): 797–820.

Harkinson, Josh. 2011. "Harold Simmons' Texas-Sized Plan for Nuclear Waste." *Mother Jones*, March 29. http://www.motherjones.com/environment/2011/03/texas-nuclear-waste-dump.

Harris, Melissa. 2012. "Paul Ryan Has Picked Up Cash, Ideas in Chicago." *Chicago Tribune*, August 14. http://articles.chicagotribune.com/2012-08-14/business/ct-biz-0814-confidential-20120814_1_paul-ryan-prosperity-pac-anne-griffin.

Harwell, Drew. 2016. "Inside the Rocky Billionaire Bromance of Donald Trump and Carl Icahn." *Washington Post*, April 30. https://www.washingtonpost.com/politics/carl-icahn-donald-trump-business-rivalry-partnership/2016/04/30/4cc69316-024a-11e6-9d36-33d198ea26c5_story.html?utm_term=.9d7091ac73a5.

Hasen, Richard L. 1996. "Clipping Coupons for Democracy: An Egalitarian/Public Choice Defense of Campaign Finance Vouchers." *California Law Review* 84: 59.

Helman, Christopher. 2013. "Texas Billionaire Harold Simmons Dies; Called Obama 'Most Dangerous Man In America.'" *Forbes*, December 30. https://www.forbes.com/sites/christopherhelman/2013/12/30/texas-billionaire-harold-simmons-dies-called-obama-most-dangerous-man-in-america/#34187075cf3c. Accessed June 7, 2017.

Hertel-Fernandez, Alexander. 2014. "Who Passes Business's 'Model Bills'? Policy Capacity and Corporate Influence in U.S. State Politics." *Perspectives on Politics* 12 (3): 582–602.

Hertel-Fernandez, Alexander. 2016. "Explaining Liberal Policy Woes in the States: The Role of Donors." *PS: Political Science and Politics* 49 (3): 461–65.

Hertel-Fernandez, Alexander, Theda Skocpol, and Daniel Lynch. 2016. "Business Associations, Conservative Networks, and the Ongoing Republican War Over Medicaid Expansion." *Journal of Health Politics, Policy, and Law* 41 (2): 239–86.

Hines, Joseph. 2014. "It Takes Nearly $8 Million to Join the Wealthiest One Percent." *Demos Policyshop*, September 19.

Hochschild, Arlie Russell. 2016. *Strangers in Their Own Land: Anger and Mourning on the American Right.* New York: The New Press.

Huang, Chye-Ching, and Chloe Cho. 2017. *Ten Facts You Should Know About the Federal Estate Tax. Center on Budget and Policy Priorities* research report, May 5.

Hunter, Glenn. 2006. "'I'm Going to Start Thinking Bigger': After Netting $1B Investing with Boone Pickens, Businessman Harold Simmons Says He's Ready to

Begin Making Larger Philanthropic Contributions." *Dallas Business Journal*, August 13.

Icahn, Carl. 2013. "Carl Icahn: Challenging the Imperial Boardroom." *Wall Street Journal*, September 18. http://www.wsj.com/articles/SB10001424127887324665 604579081703521362462.

Icahn, Carl. 2015a. "Letter Discussing Desperately Needed Legislation." *CarlIcahn .com*, October 21. http://carlicahn.com/needed-legislation-letter/.

Icahn, Carl. 2015b. "How to Stop Turning US Corporations into Tax Exiles." *New York Times*, December 14, A23.

Icahn, Carl. 2016. "Carl Icahn Issues Statement in Response to Bernie Sanders Remarks." *CarlIcahn.com*, May 9. http://carlicahn.com/carl-icahn-issues-re-bernie -sanders-remarks/.

Inglehart, Ronald, and Pippa Norris. 2016. "Trump, Brexit, and the Rise of Economic Populism: Economic Have-Nots and Cultural Backlash." HKS Working Paper No. RWP16-026. https://ssrn.com/abstract=2818659.

Internal Revenue Service. 2017. "What's New—Estate and Gift Tax." Updated on January 18. https://www.irs.gov/businesses/small-businesses-self-employed/whats -new-estate-and-gift-tax.

International Monetary Fund. 2013. *World Economic Outlook Database, April 2013*. https://www.imf.org/external/pubs/ft/weo/2013/01/weodata/index.aspx.

Isidore, Chris, and Poppy Harlow. 2015. "Buffett: I Won't Give Millions to Candidates." *CNN Money*, April 2. http://money.cnn.com/2015/04/02/news/compa nies/buffett-hillary-donation/.

Isikoff, Michael. 2015. "Secret $1.5 Million Donation from Wisconsin Billionaire Uncovered in Scott Walker Dark-Money Probe." *Yahoo! Politics*, March 23. https://www.yahoo.com/politics/wisconsin-gov-scott-walker-photo-charlie-114 429739886.html.

Jacobs, Lawrence R., and Benjamin I. Page. 2005. "Who Influences US Foreign Policy?" *American Political Science Review* 99 (1): 107–23.

Janssen, Kim. 2017. "Size of Billionaire-Bashing Chris Kennedy's Fortune a Mystery, Still." *Chicago Tribune*, June 1. http://www.chicagotribune.com/news/chi cagoinc/ct-chris-kennedys-money-0601-chicago-inc-20170601-story.html.

Jeffers, Gromer, Jr. 2015. "In Dallas Council Runoffs, Interests in North Inject Cash to Sway Races in South." *Dallas News*, May. https://www.dallasnews.com /news/local-politics/2015/05/31/in-dallas-council-runoffs-interests-in-north-inject -cash-to-sway-races-in-south.

Jelen, Ted G., and Clyde Wilcox. 2003. "Causes and Consequences of Public Attitudes toward Abortion: A Review and Research Agenda." *Political Research Quarterly* 56 (December): 489–500.

Jencks, Christopher. 2015. "Did We Lose the War on Poverty?—II." *New York Review of Books*, April 23. http://www.nybooks.com/articles/2015/04/23/did-we -lose-war-poverty-ii/.

Johnston, David Cay. 2016. *The Making of Donald Trump*. Brooklyn, NY: Melville House.

Jones, Jeffrey M. 2016. "More Republicans Favor Path to Citizenship Than Wall." Gallup, July 20. http://www.gallup.com/poll/193817/republicans-favor-path-citi zenship-wall.aspx.

Kaiser Commission on Medicaid and the Uninsured. 2017. *Current Status of State Medicaid Expansion Decisions*. KCMU Tracking Reports, January 1. https:// www.kff.org/health-reform/slide/current-status-of-the-medicaid-expansion -decision/. Accessed October 15, 2017.

Karol, David. 2009. *Party Position Change in American Politics: Coalition Manage- ment*. Cambridge, UK: Cambridge University Press.

Kaufmann, Eric. 2016. "Trump and Brexit: Why It's Again NOT the Economy, Stupid." *New Statesman* blog, November 10. http://www.newstatesman.com/politics /economy/2016/11/it-s-not-economy-stupid-busting-myth-how-donald-trump-won.

Kavoussi, Bonnie. 2012. "Warren Buffett: High Corporate Taxes Are an American 'Myth.'" *Huffington Post*, February 27. http://www.huffingtonpost.com/2012/02 /27/warren-buffett-corporate-taxes_n_1304432.html.

Keefe, Alex. 2013. "Emanuel: CPS School Closures 'Not Taken Lightly,' but Must Be Done." *WBEZ News*, March 23. https://www.wbez.org/shows/wbez-news /emanuel-cps-school-closures-not-taken-lightly-but-must-be-done/3deee2ba-9d 89-4702-9727-b5511fae1037.

Keefe, Patrick Radden. 2017. "Carl Icahn's Failed Raid on Washington." *New Yorker*, August 28. https://www.newyorker.com/magazine/2017/08/28/carl-icahns-failed -raid-on-washington.

Kelly, Nathan J. Forthcoming. *America's Inequality Trap: How Economic Inequal- ity Feeds on Itself and Why It Matters*. Chicago: University of Chicago Press.

Kerstetter, Jim. 2008. "Oracle's Larry Ellison Got a $3 Million Tax Break and You Didn't." *CNET*, March 27. https://www.cnet.com/news/oracles-larry-ellison-got-a -3-million-tax-break-and-you-didnt/.

Khoury, Rana. 2016. *As Ohio Goes: Life in the Post-Recession Nation*. Kent, OH: Kent State University Press.

Klarner, Carl. 2015. "Democracy in Decline: The Collapse of the Close Race in State Legislatures." *Ballotpedia* online report, May 6. https://ballotpedia.org /Competitiveness_in_State_Legislative_Elections:_1972-2014.

Knowles, David. 2015. "Koch Brothers Plan to Fund 'Several' GOP 2016 Presiden- tial Hopefuls." *Bloomberg Politics*, May 24. https://www.bloomberg.com/politics /articles/2015-05-24/koch-brothers-plan-to-fund-several-gop-2016-presidential -hopefuls.

Koch, Charles. 2016. "Charles Koch: This Is the One Issue Where Bernie Sanders Is Right." *Washington Post*, February 8. https://www.washingtonpost.com/opinions /charles-koch-this-is-the-one-issue-where-bernie-sanders-is-right/2016/02/18 /cdd2c228-d5c1-11e5-be55-2cc3c1e4b76b_story.html?utm_term=.a885c5a32d46.

Koch, David. 1980. "Free Up the Energy System." Speech at Benson Hotel, Portland, Oregon, May 31. https://www.nytimes.com/interactive/2017/admin/10000 0002885748.embedded.

Kramer, Katie. 2014. "Buffett: I Don't Control Berkshire Subsidiaries' LGBT Policies." CNBC, October 3. http://www.cnbc.com/2014/10/03/buffett-i-dont-control -berkshire-subsidiaries-policies-for-gay-workers.html. Accessed June 2, 2017.

Kranish, Michael. 2015. "A City's Immovable Roadblock." *Boston Globe*, October 10. https://www.bostonglobe.com/news/nation/2015/10/10/nashville-mayor-wanted -bring-two-parts-his-city-together-then-was-crushed-state-legislators/QT91unb8 xk4xPBqkTumgMP/story.html.

Kron, Josh. 2012. "Red State, Blue City: How the Urban-Rural Divide Is Splitting America." *Atlantic*, November 30. https://www.theatlantic.com/politics/archive/2012 /11/red-state-blue-city-how-the-urban-rural-divide-is-splitting-america/265686/.

Lambert, Fred. 2016. "Warren Buffett Explains His Logic for Killing Rooftop Solar in Nevada [Video]." *Electrek*, March 1. https://electrek.co/2016/03/01/warren-buffett -explains-his-logic-for-killing-rooftop-solar-in-nevada-video/. Accessed June 14, 2017.

Langley, Monica. 2013. "Texas Billionaire Doles Out Election's Biggest Checks." *Wall Street Journal*, January 22.

Larson, Leslie. 2015. "Warren Buffett Didn't Realize His Hillary Clinton Contribution Went to a Super PAC." *Business Insider*, April 2. http://www.businessinsider .com/warren-buffett-didnt-realize-his-hillary-clinton-contribution-went-to-a-super -pac-2015-4.

Leighley, Jan E., and Jonathan Nagler. 1992a. "Individual and Systemic Influences on Turnout: Who Votes? 1984." *Journal of Politics* 54 (3): 718–40.

Leighley, Jan E., and Jonathan Nagler. 1992b. "Socioeconomic Class Bias in Turnout, 1964–1988: The Voters Remain the Same." *American Political Science Review* 86 (3): 725–36.

Leighley, Jan E., and Jonathan Nagler. 2007. "Unions, Voter Turnout, and Class Bias in the US Electorate, 1964–2004." *Journal of Politics* 69 (2): 430–41.

Leighley, Jan E., and Jonathan Nagler. 2013. *Who Votes Now? Demographics, Issues, Inequality, and Turnout in the United States*. Princeton, NJ: Princeton University Press.

Leonard, Christopher. 2013. "The New Koch." *Fortune*, December 19. http://fortune .com/2013/12/19/david-charles-koch/.

Lessig, Lawrence. 2011. *Republic, Lost: How Money Corrupts Congress—and a Plan to Stop It*. New York: Hachette.

Lessig, Lawrence. 2015. *Republic, Lost: The Corruption of Equality and the Steps to End It*. Rev. ed. New York: Hachette.

Lichtblau, Eric. 2015. "F. E. C. Can't Curb 2016 Election Abuse, Commission Chief Says." *New York Times*, May 3, A1.

Lichtenstein, Nelson. 2013. *State of the Union: A Century of American Labor*. Rev. and expanded ed. Princeton, NJ: Princeton University Press.

Lieberman, Evan S. 2005. "Nested Analysis as a Mixed-Method Strategy for Comparative Research." *American Political Science Review* 99: 435–52.

Lipton, Eric. 2014. "Energy Firms in Secretive Alliance With Attorneys General." *New York Times*, December 6. https://www.nytimes.com/2014/12/07/us/politics/energy-firms-in-secretive-alliance-with-attorneys-general.html.

Lipton, Eric. 2017. "Icahn Raises Ethics Flags With Dual Roles as Investor and Trump Adviser." *New York Times*, March 27, A1.

Loomis, Carol J. 2013. *Tap Dancing to Work: Warren Buffett on Practically Everything, 1966–2013.* New York: Portfolio/Penguin. A *Fortune* magazine book.

Lowe, Janet. 2007. *Warren Buffett Speaks: Wit and Wisdom from the World's Greatest Investor.* Hoboken, NJ: John Wiley & Sons.

Lowery, Wesley. 2014. "David Koch: 'I'm Basically a Libertarian.'" *Washington Post*, December 14. https://www.washingtonpost.com/news/post-politics/wp/2014/12/14/david-koch-im-basically-a-libertarian. Accessed June 2, 2017.

Lueders, Bill. 2015. "Managers at Menards Stand to Lose Big Money If Unions Form." *The Progressive*, December 8. http://www.progressive.org/news/2015/12/188450/managers-menards-stand-lose-big-money-if-unions-form.

Lueders, Bill. 2016. "Investigation by The Progressive Leads NLRB to Bust Menards for Labor Law Violations." *The Progressive*, March 31. http://www.progressive.org/news/2016/03/188644/investigation-progressive-leads-nlrb-bust-menards-labor-law-violations.

MacColl, Spencer. 2010. "Capital Rivals: Koch Brothers vs. George Soros." *OpenSecrets* blog, September 21. https://www.opensecrets.org/news/2010/09/opensecrets-battle—koch-brothers.html.

MacLean, Nancy. 2017. *Democracy in Chains: The Deep History of the Radical Right's Stealth Plan for America.* New York: Viking.

Mader, Marjorie. 2008. "Ellison Wins 60% Tax Cut on Woodside Estate." *The Almanac,* March 25. https://www.almanacnews.com/news/2008/03/25/ellison-wins-60-tax-cut-on-woodside-estate.

Mallaby, Sebastian. 2010. *More Money Than God: Hedge Funds and the Making of a New Elite.* New York: Penguin Press.

Mayer, Jane. 2004. "The Money Man: Can George Soros's Millions Insure the Defeat of President Bush?" *New Yorker*, October 18. http://www.newyorker.com/magazine/2004/10/18/the-money-man.

Mayer, Jane. 2010. "Covert Operations: The Billionaire Brothers Who Are Waging a War against Obama." *New Yorker*, August 30. http://www.newyorker.com/magazine/2010/08/30/covert-operations.

Mayer, Jane. 2016. *Dark Money: The Hidden History of the Billionaires Behind the Rise of the Radical Right.* New York: Doubleday.

Mayer, Jane. 2017. "The Reclusive Hedge-Fund Tycoon Behind the Trump Presidency." *New Yorker*, March 27. https://www.newyorker.com/magazine/2017/03/27/the-reclusive-hedge-fund-tycoon-behind-the-trump-presidency.

McCarthy, Justin. 2016. "Americans' Support for Gay Marriage Remains High, at 61%." Gallup, May 19. http://www.gallup.com/poll/191645/americans-support-gay -marriage-remains-high.aspx. Accessed June 1, 2017.

McConnell, Grant. 1967. *Private Power & American Democracy*. New York: Knopf.

McVeigh, Rory, and Maria-Elena D. Diaz. 2009. "Voting to Ban Same-Sex Marriage: Interests, Values, and Communities." *American Sociological Review* 74 (6): 891–915.

Mehta, Seema, and Michael Mishak. 2010. "EBay Founder Praises Whitman but Refuses to Endorse Her." *Los Angeles Times*, September 22. http://articles.latimes .com/2010/sep/22/local/la-me-0922-governor-20100922. Accessed June 2, 2017.

Milbank, Dana. 2004. "Bush Campaign Drops Swift Boat Ad Figure." *Washington Post*, August 22, A13.

Mishra, Pankaj, and Bodhisatva Ganguli. 2009. "There's No Recession, It's a Reset for the Economy: Steve Ballmer." *Economic Times*, May 13. http://economictimes .indiatimes.com/opinion/interviews/theres-no-recession-its-a-reset-for-the-eco nomy-steve-ballmer/articleshow/4522602.cms?intenttarget=no. Accessed June 2, 2017.

Mooney, Michael J. 2015. "Inside the Koch Brothers' Industrial Empire." *Popular Mechanics*, October 9. http://www.popularmechanics.com/technology/infrastruc ture/a17558/koch-industries-inside-story/.

Mundy, Alicia. 2012. "Sheldon Adelson: 'I'm Basically a Social Liberal.'" *Wall Street Journal*, December 5. https://blogs.wsj.com/washwire/2012/12/05/sheldon-adel son-im-basically-a-social-liberal. Accessed June 2, 2017.

Murphy, Bruce. 2013. "The Strange Life of John Menard." *Urban Milwaukee*, June 20. http://urbanmilwaukee.com/2013/06/20/murphys-law-the-strange-life-of-john -menard/. Accessed June 14, 2017.

National Conference of State Legislatures. n.d. "2017 State & Legislative Partisan Composition." http://www.ncsl.org/research/about-state-legislatures/partisan-com position.aspx. Accessed 15 October 2017.

National Economic Council. 2012. "The Buffett Rule: A Basic Principle of Tax Fairness." White House report, April. https://obamawhitehouse.archives.gov/sites /default/files/Buffett_Rule_Report_Final.pdf.

National Federation of Independent Business v. Sebelius, 567 US 1 (2012).

National Institute on Money in State Politics. n.d. *Follow the Money* database. https://www.followthemoney.org/. Accessed May 30, 2017.

Naylor, Brian. 2016. "Republican Platform Tilts Right of Trump on LGBT Issues." NPR, July 13. http://www.npr.org/2016/07/13/485899139/republican-platform -tilts-right-of-trump-on-lgbt-issues. Accessed June 1, 2017.

NBC Nightly News. 2007. Episode dated October 30, 2007.

Newport, Frank. 2016. "In US, Support for Decreasing Immigration Holds Steady." *Gallup News Service*, August 24. http://www.gallup.com/poll/194819/support-dec reasing-immigration-holds-steady.aspx. Accessed June 2, 2017.

Newport, Frank, and Lydia Saad. 2005. "Americans Appear Open to Arguments on Privatizing Social Security." *Gallup News Service*, February 7. http://www.gallup .com/poll/14815/americans-appear-open-arguments-privatizing-social-security .aspx.

Nitti, Tony. 2017. "Trump's 'Massive' Middle-Class Tax Cuts Are Tiny Compared to Those Promised to the Rich." *Forbes*, March 1. https://www.forbes.com/sites /anthonynitti/2017/03/01/president-trump-promises-massive-middle-class-tax -cuts-but-will-he-deliver/#1bfcc3136b9e.

Noel, Hans. 2013. *Political Ideologies and Political Parties in America*. Cambridge, UK: Cambridge University Press.

Nolan, Hamilton. 2016. "Documents: How a Major Company Bombards Employees With Right-Wing Propaganda." *Gawker*, June. 13. http://gawker.com /documents-how-a-major-company-bombards-employees-with-1781111355.

O'Brien, Timothy L. 2015. "How Much Is Trump Worth? Depends on How He Feels." *Newsweek*, October 19.

Organisation for Economic Co-operation and Development. 2017. Tax Revenue (Indicator). doi: 10.1787/d98b8cf5-en. https://data.oecd.org/tax/tax-revenue.htm.

Overby, Peter. 2007. "Explainer: What Is a Bundler?" *NPR Politics*. http://www .npr.org/templates/story/story.php?storyId=14434721.

Page, Benjamin I., Larry M. Bartels, and Jason Seawright. 2011. "Interviewing Wealthy Americans." Paper presented at the annual meeting of the Midwest Political Science Association, Chicago, March 30–April 3. Available as WP-11-07, Institute for Policy Research, Northwestern University.

Page, Benjamin I., Larry M. Bartels, and Jason Seawright. 2013. "Democracy and the Policy Preferences of Wealthy Americans." *Perspectives on Politics* 11 (1): 51–73.

Page, Benjamin I., with Marshall M. Bouton. 2006. *The Foreign Policy Disconnect: What Americans Want from Our Leaders but Don't Get*. Chicago: University of Chicago Press.

Page, Benjamin I., and Martin Gilens. 2017. *Democracy in America? What Has Gone Wrong and What We Can Do About It*. Chicago: University of Chicago Press.

Page, Benjamin I., and Cari Lynn Hennessy. 2010. "What Affluent Americans Want from Politics." Paper presented at the annual meeting of the American Political Science Association, Washington, DC, September 2–5. Available as WP-11-08, Institute for Policy Research, Northwestern University.

Page, Benjamin I., and Lawrence R. Jacobs. 2009. *Class War? What Americans Really Think about Economic Inequality*. Chicago: University of Chicago Press.

Page, Benjamin I., and Jason Seawright. 2014. "What Do US Billionaires Want from Government?" Paper presented at the annual meetings of the Midwest Political Science Association, Chicago, April 3–6.

Palmer, Anna, and Jake Sherman. 2014. "Billionaires Push GOP on Gay rights." *Politico*, April 9. http://www.politico.com/story/2014/04/gay-rights-bill-republicans -billionaires-105537. Accessed June 1, 2017.

Pew Research Center. 2015. "Modern Immigration Wave Brings 59 Million to US, Driving Population Growth and Change Through 2065: Views of Immigration's Impact on US Society Mixed." http://www.pewhispanic.org/files/2015/09/2015 -09-28_modern-immigration-wave_REPORT.pdf. Accessed June 1, 2017.

Phillips, Amber. 2016. "These 3 Maps Show Just How Dominant Republicans Are in America after Tuesday." *Washington Post*, November 12. https://www.washing tonpost.com/news/the-fix/wp/2016/11/12/these-3-maps-show-just-how-domi nant-republicans-are-in-america-after-tuesday/?utm_term=.52600f607a78.

Piketty, Thomas. 2014. *Capital in the Twenty-First Century*. Translated by Arthur Goldhammer. Cambridge, MA: Harvard University Press.

Piketty, Thomas, and Emmanuel Saez. 2007. "How Progressive Is the US Federal Income Tax? A Historical and International Perspective." *Journal of Economic Perspectives* 21 (1): 3–24.

Porter, Eduardo. 2017. "'Carnage' Indeed, but Trump's Policies Would Make It Worse." *New York Times*, March 29, B1.

Powell, Lynda W. 2012. *The Influence of Campaign Contributions in State Legislatures: The Effects of Institutions and Politics*. Ann Arbor: University of Michigan Press.

Prokop, Andrew. 2015. "The Citizens United Era of Money in Politics, Explained." *Vox*, July 15. https://www.vox.com/cards/super-pacs-and-dark-money.

PwC. 2016. "PwC Global 100 Software Leaders: Digital Intelligence Conquers the World Below and the Cloud Above." PwC Technology Institute report. http:// www.pwc.com/gx/en/technology/publications/global-software-100-leaders /assets/global-100-software-leaders-2016.pdf.

Quick, Becky. 2016. "Buffett's Berkshire Takes Stakes in Four Major Airlines." CNBC, November 14. http://www.cnbc.com/2016/11/14/buffetts-berkshire-takes -stakes-in-four-major-airlines.html. Accessed June 14, 2016.

Reich, Robert B. 2015. *Saving Capitalism: For the Many, Not the Few*. New York: Knopf.

Rhodes, Dawn. 2017. "Illinois Budget Backlog Is Giving Health Care Providers, Patients a Headache." *Chicago Tribune*, July 27. http://www.chicagotribune.com /news/local/breaking/ct-state-health-insurance-university-employees-20170627 -story.html.

Robbins, Brian. 2017. "2018 Illinois Governor's Race Likely to Be Most expensive in U.S. History." *State Journal-Register*, April 22. http://www.sj-r.com/news /20170422/2018-illinois-governors-race-likely-to-be-most-expensive-in-us-history.

Robinson-Jacobs, Karen. 2016. "In Rare Interview, Omni Owner Bob Rowling Gets Last Laugh 20 Years after Purchase." *Dallas News*, April 19. https://www .dallasnews.com/business/hotels/2016/04/19/omni-owner-thankful-1996-bid-to -diversify-led-to-hotel-purchase. Accessed June 7, 2017.

Romig, Kathleen, and Arloc Sherman. 2016. *Social Security Keeps 22 Million Americans Out of Poverty: A State-By-State Analysis*. Center on Budget and Policy

Priority Policy Futures report, October 25. http://www.cbpp.org/sites/default
/files/atoms/files/10-25-13ss.pdf.

Rosenbaum, Paul R. 1984. "The Consequences of Adjustment for a Concomitant Variable That Has Been Affected by the Treatment." *Journal of the Royal Statistical Society. Series A*.147 (5): 656–66.

Ryan, M. T., M. P. Lee, and H. J. Larson. 2007. "History and Framework of Commercial Low-Level Radioactive Waste Management in the United States." US Nuclear Regulatory Commission's Advisory Committee on Nuclear Waste white paper, August. http://hps.org/govtrelations/documents/nrc_nureg1853.pdf.

Saad, Lydia. 2014. "More in US Would Decrease Immigration than Increase." Gallup, June 27. http://www.gallup.com/poll/171962/decrease-immigration-increase .aspx. Accessed June 2, 2017.

Saad, Lydia. 2016. "Americans' Attitudes Toward Abortion Unchanged." Gallup, May 25. http://www.gallup.com/poll/191834/americans-attitudes-toward-abortion -unchanged.aspx. Accessed June 1, 2017.

Samuels, Robert. 2015. "Walker's Anti-Union Law Has Labor Reeling in Wisconsin." *Washington Post*, February 22. https://www.washingtonpost.com/politics /in-wisconsin-walkers-anti-union-law-has-crippled-labor-movement/2015/02/22 /1eb3ef82-b6f1-11e4-aa05-1ce812b3fdd2_story.html?utm_term=.bab9564745a0. Accessed June 6, 2017.

Sargent, Greg. "Get Ready for a Lot More 'Dark Money' in Politics." *Washington Post*, May 4. https://www.washingtonpost.com/blogs/plum-line/wp/2015/05/04 /get-ready-for-a-lot-more-dark-money-in-politics/?utm_term=.093f6703c9d6.

Sarkar, Monica. 2015. "Gay Pride: How the World Turned into a Rainbow This Weekend." CNN, June 28. http://www.cnn.com/2015/06/28/tech/social-media -gay-pride/. Accessed June 2, 2017.

Sartori, Giovanni. 2009. "The Tower of Babel." In *Concepts and Method in Social Science: The Tradition of Giovanni Sartori*, edited by David Collier and John Gerring. Abingdon, UK: Routledge, 61–96.

Schaefer, Steve. 2015. "Forbes Flashback: How George Soros Broke the British Pound and Why Hedge Funds Probably Can't Crack the Euro." *Forbes*, July 7. https://www.forbes.com/sites/steveschaefer/2015/07/07/forbes-flashback-george -soros-british-pound-euro-ecb/. Accessed June 6, 2017.

Schattschneider, E. E. 1960. *The Semisovereign People: A Realist's View of Democracy in America*. New York: Holt, Rinehart and Winston.

Schlozman, Kay Lehman, Sidney Verba, and Henry E. Brady. 2012. *The Unheavenly Chorus: Unequal Political Voice and the Broken Promise of American Democracy*. Princeton, NJ: Princeton University Press.

Schroeder, Alice. 2008. *The Snowball: Warren Buffett and the Business of Life*. New York: Bantam.

Schulman, Daniel. 2014. *Sons of Wichita: How the Koch Brothers Became America's Most Powerful and Private Dynasty*. New York: Grand Central.

Sclar, Jason, Alexander Hertel-Fernandez, Theda Skocpol, and Vanessa Williamson. 2016. "Donor Consortia on the Left and Right: Comparing the Membership, Activities, and Impact of the Democracy Alliance and the Koch Seminars." Paper presented at the annual meeting of the Midwest Political Science Association, Chicago, April 8.

Scola, Nancy. 2012. "Exposing ALEC: How Conservative-Backed State Laws Are All Connected." *Atlantic*, April 14. https://www.theatlantic.com/politics/archive /2012/04/exposing-alec-how-conservative-backed-state-laws-are-all-connected /255869/.

Seawright, Jason. 2016. *Multi-Method Social Science: Combining Qualitative and Quantitative Tools*. Cambridge, UK: Cambridge University Press.

Seawright, Jason, and John Gerring. 2008. "Case Selection Techniques in Case Study Research: A Menu of Qualitative and Quantitative Options." *Political Research Quarterly* 61 (2): 294–308.

Sides, John, Michael Tesler, and Lynn Vavreck. 2017. "How Trump Lost and Won." *Journal of Democracy* 28 (2): 34–44.

Skocpol, Theda, and Alexander Hertel-Fernandez. 2016. "The Koch Network and Republican Party Extremism." *Perspectives on Politics* 14 (3): 681–99.

Skocpol, Theda, and Alexander Hertel-Fernandez. Forthcoming. *The Koch Effect*. Chicago: University of Chicago Press.

Smeltz, Dina, Ivo Daalder, Karl Friedhoff, and Craig Kafura. 2016. "America in the Age of Uncertainty: American Public Opinion and US Foreign Policy." Chicago Council on Global Affairs 2016 Chicago Council Survey. https://www .thechicagocouncil.org/sites/default/files/ccgasurvey2016_america_age_uncer tainty.pdf.

Smith, Aaron, Kay Lehman Schlozman, Sidney Verba, and Henry Brady. 2009. *The Internet and Civic Engagement*. Pew Internet and American Life Project, September.

Smith, Mitch, and Julie Bosman. 2017. "Kansas Supreme Court Says State Education Spending Is Too Low." *New York Times*, March 2. https://www.nytimes .com/2017/03/02/us/kansas-supreme-court-school-spending.html. Accessed June 6, 2017.

Social Security Administration. 2016. "Fast Facts & Figures About Social Security, 2016." Accessed May 15, 2017. https://www.ssa.gov/policy/docs/chartbooks/fast _facts/2016/fast_facts16.html.

Social Security Administration. 2017a. "Social Security Beneficiary Statistics." https:// www.ssa.gov/oact/STATS/OASDIbenies.html. Accessed May 15, 2017.

Social Security Administration. 2017b. "Historical Background and Development of Social Security." https://www.ssa.gov/history/briefhistory3.html. Accessed May 17, 2017.

Soroka, Stuart N., and Christopher Wlezien. 2008. "On the Limits to Inequality in Representation." *PS: Political Science & Politics* 41 (2): 319–27.

Stevens, Mark. 2014 [1993]. *King Icahn: The Biography of a Renegade Capitalist.* New York: Dutton. Originally pub. Penguin.

Stiglitz, Joseph E. 2012. *The Price of Inequality.* New York: Norton.

Stiglitz, Joseph E. 2015. *The Great Divide: Unequal Societies and What We Can Do About Them.* New York: Norton.

Stoddard, Martha, and Emily Nohr. 2016. "8 of 14 Legislative Candidates Supported by Ricketts Win, Giving the Unicameral a More Conservative Bent." *Omaha World-Herald*, November 9. http://www.omaha.com/news/politics/of-legislative -candidates-supported-by-ricketts-win-giving-the-unicameral/article_d1b991b2 -a642-11e6-a6d5-0b53db88f82c.html.

Stolberg, Cheryl Gay, and Mike McIntire. 2013. "A Federal Budget Crisis Months in the Planning." *New York Times*, October 5. http://www.nytimes.com/2013 /10/06/us/a-federal-budget-crisis-months-in-the-planning.html.

Storch, Charles. 2003. "Feeling the Heat, Warren Buffett Gives in on Giving." *Chicago Tribune*, July 25. http://articles.chicagotribune.com/2003-07-25/features /0307250164_1_pampered-chef-warren-buffett-planned-parenthood. Accessed June 14, 2017.

Straus, Valerie. 2016. "A Sobering Look at What Betsy DeVos Did to Education in Michigan—and What She Might Do as Secretary of Education." *Washington Post*, December 8. https://www.washingtonpost.com/news/answer-sheet/wp/2016 /12/08/a-sobering-look-at-what-betsy-devos-did-to-education-in-michigan-and -what-she-might-do-as-secretary-of-education/?utm_term=.17fcec7a165c.

Talk of the Nation. 2012. "New York City's Mayor Is a Geek at Heart," April 6. http:// www.npr.org/2012/04/06/150123935/new-york-citys-mayor-is-a-geek-at-heart.

Taub, Stephen. 2013. "The Rich List." *Institutional Investor's Alpha*, April 15. http:// www.institutionalinvestorsalpha.com/Article/3190499/The-Rich-List.html.

Taub, Stephen. 2014. "The Rich List: The Highest Earning Hedge Fund Managers of the Past Year." *Institutional Investor's Alpha*, May 6. http://www.institution alinvestorsalpha.com/Article/3337321/The-Rich-List-The-Highest-Earning -Hedge-Fund-Managers-of-the-Past-Year.html.

Taub, Stephen. 2015. "The 2015 Rich List: The Highest Earning Hedge Fund Managers of the Past Year." *Institutional Investor's Alpha*, May 5. http://www .institutionalinvestorsalpha.com/Article/3450284/The-2015-Rich-List-The-Highest -Earning-Hedge-Fund-Managers-of-the-Past-Year.html.

Taub, Stephen. 2016. "The 2016 Rich List of the World's Top-Earning Hedge Fund Managers." *Institutional Investor's Alpha*, May 10. http://www.institutionalin vestorsalpha.com/Article/3552805/The-2016-Rich-List-of-the-Worlds-Top -Earning-Hedge-Fund-Managers.html.

Taub, Stephen. 2017. "The 2017 Rich List of the World's Top-Earning Hedge Fund Managers." *Institutional Investor's Alpha*, May 16. http://www.institutionalin vestorsalpha.com/Article/3716778/The-2017-Rich-List-of-the-Worlds-Top-Earning -Hedge-Fund-Managers.html.

Tax Policy Center. 2017. "Current Law Distribution of Gross Estate and Net Estate Tax by Size of Gross Estate, 2017." Tax Policy Center Model Estimate Table T16-0277, November 30. http://www.taxpolicycenter.org/model-estimates /baseline-estate-tax-tables-nov-2016/t16-0277-current-law-distribution-gross -estate.

Temple, James. 2008. "$3 Million Tax Cut on Larry Ellison's Estate." *SFGate,* March 27. http://www.sfgate.com/realestate/article/3-million-tax-cut-on-Larry -Ellison-s-estate-3290230.php.

Texas Tribune. n.d. "Texas Campaign Finance Database: 2000–2014." http://www .Texastribune.org/library/data/campaign-finance/#individuals.

Thomson Reuters. 2016. "Social Security Wage Base Could Increase to $126,000 for 2017." *Thomson Reuters Tax and Accounting News,* June 24. https://tax.thom sonreuters.com/media-resources/news-media-resources/checkpoint-news /daily-newsstand/social-security-wage-base-could-increase-to-126000-for-2017/.

Thurber, Kathleen. 2009. "Andrews County Citizens Pass WCS Bond by Three Votes." *Midland Reporter-Telegram,* May 9.

Umhoefer, Dave. 2016. "For Unions in Wisconsin, a Fast and Hard Fall Since Act 10." *Milwaukee Journal Sentinel,* October 9. https://projects.jsonline.com /news/2016/11/27/for-unions-in-wisconsin-fast-and-hard-fall-since-act-10.html.

Urban Institute. 2017. *State and Local Finance Initiative.* http://www.urban.org /policy-centers/cross-center-initiatives/state-local-finance-initiative/projects /state-and-local-backgrounders/state-and-local-expenditures. Accessed June 6, 2017.

US Office of Management and Budget. n.d. *Historical Tables.* https://www.white house.gov/omb/budget/Historicals. Accessed June 7, 2017.

Van de Kamp Nohl, Mary. 2007. "Big Money." *Milwaukee Magazine,* April 30. https:// www.milwaukeemag.com/bigmoney-john-menard/. Accessed June 14, 2017.

Verba, Sidney, Kay Lehman Schlozman, and Henry E. Brady. 1995. *Voice and Equality: Civic Voluntarism in American Politics.* Cambridge, MA: Harvard University Press.

Vogel, Kenneth P. 2015. "The Kochs Put a Price on 2016: $889 million." *Politico,* January 26. http://www.politico.com/story/2015/01/koch-2016-spending-goal-11 4604.

Vogel, Kenneth P., and Jeremy W. Peters. 2017. "Alabama Victory Provides Blueprint for New Bannon Alliance." *New York Times,* September 28. https://www.ny times.com/2017/09/28/us/politics/steve-bannon-robert-rebekah-mercer-alliance .html.?_r=0.

Voorhees, Josh. 2015. "Sheldon Adelson Bet Big in 2012 and Lost. Has He Learned From His Mistakes?" *Slate,* April 24. http://www.slate.com/blogs/the_slatest /2015/04/24/sheldon_adelson_2016_casino_mogul_is_expected_to_spend_big_in _gop_primary.html.

Wald, Matthew. 2014. "Texas Company, Alone in US, Cashes in on Nuclear Waste."

New York Times, January 20. http://www.nytimes.com/2014/01/21/business/energy -environment/texas-company-alone-in-us-cashes-in-on-nuclear-waste.html .?_r=0.

Wallsten, Peter, Lori Montgomery, and Scott Wilson. 2012. "Obama's Evolution: Behind the Failed 'Grand Bargain' on the Debt." *Washington Post*, March 17. https://www.washingtonpost.com/politics/obamas-evolution-behind-the-failed -grand-bargain-on-the-debt/2012/03/15/gIQAHyyfJS_story.html.?utm_term =.a77b34438c9f.

Walton, Sam, and John Huey. 1992. *Made in America: My Story*. New York: Doubleday.

Washington Post. 2014. "Inside the $400-Million Political Network Backed by the Kochs." January 5. https://www.washingtonpost.com/politics/inside-the-koch -backed-political-donor-network/2014/01/05/94719296-7661-11e3-b1c5-739e6 3e9c9a7_graphic.html?utm_term=.ef88a9567c4c.

Waste Control Specialists. n.d. "History & Economic Impact of Valhi/WCS in An-drews County." http://www.wcstexas.com/about-wcs/economic-impact/. Accessed October 14, 2017.

Watzman, Nancy. 2012. "Stealthy Wealthy: To Robert Rowling, Political Giving Makes Business Sense." Sunlight Foundation online report, August 8. http:// sunlightfoundation.com/blog/2012/08/08/rowling-version-2/.

Weir, Kytja, Chris Zubak-Skees, and Ben Wieder. 2017. "Meet the 10 Shadowy Groups That Snuck into Your State Races: A Field Guide to the National Power Brokers Trying to Shape Elections." Center for Public Integrity report, Janu-ary 5. https://www.publicintegrity.org/2016/12/08/20511/meet-10-shadowy-groups -snuck-your-state-races.

West, Darrell M. 2014. *Billionaires: Reflections on the Upper Crust*. Washington, DC: Brookings Institution.

White, Ben. 2005. "At Annual Meeting, Buffett Steers Clear of AIG Details." *Washington Post,* May 1, A06.

Wilder, Forrest. 2013. "Problems with a West Texas Radioactive Waste Dump Get Buried." *Texas Observer*, July 3. http://www.texasobserver.org/problems-with-a -west-texas-radioactive-waste-dump-get-buried/.

Wilson, Mike. 1997. *The Difference between God and Larry Ellison: Inside Oracle Corporation*. New York: William Morrow.

Winters, Jeffrey A. 2011. *Oligarchy*. Cambridge, UK: Cambridge University Press.

Winters, Jeffrey A., and Benjamin I. Page. 2009. "Oligarchy in the United States?" *Perspectives on Politics* 7 (4): 731–51.

Wolff, Edward N. 2002. *Top Heavy: The Increasing Inequality of Wealth in America and What Can Be Done About It*. Rev. ed. New York: The New Press.

Wolters, Kluwer. 2017. "Historical Look at Estate and Gift Tax Rates." *2017 Whole Ball of Tax* report. Accessed 17 May 2017. https://www.cchgroup.com/news-and -insights/wbot2017/historical-estate-gift-tax.

Yoon, Sooyeon, Sungmin Lee, Soon-Hyung Yook, and Yup Kim. 2007. "Statistical Properties of Sampled Networks by Random Walks." *Physical Review E* 75: 046114 1–5.

Zhao, Hao, Scott E. Seibert, and G. T. Lumpkin. 2010. "The Relationship of Personality to Entrepreneurial Intentions and Performance: A Meta-Analytic Review." *Journal of Management* 36 (March): 381–404.

Index

References to figures and tables are denoted by an italic "f" or "t," respectively, following the page number.